D1230217

□THE AMERICAN AMUSEMENT PARK INDUSTRY

TWAYNE'S EVOLUTION OF AMERICAN BUSINESS SERIES

Industries Institutions, and Entrepreneurs

Edwin J. Perkins
SERIES EDITOR
UNIVERSITY OF
SOUTHERN CALIFORNIA

OTHER TITLES

The American Automobile Industry
  John B. Rae

DuPont and the International Chemical Industry
  Graham D. Taylor and Patricia E. Sudnik

E. H. Harriman: Master Railroader
  Lloyd J. Mercer

The Credit Card Industry
  Lewis Mandell

American Commercial Banking
  Benjamin J. Klebaner

The United States Tire Industry
  Michael J. French

Riding the Corkscrew looping coaster at Cedar Point park, Sandusky, Ohio. *Courtesy Cedar Point park.*

☐ THE AMERICAN AMUSEMENT PARK INDUSTRY

A History of Technology and Thrills

Judith A. Adams

TWAYNE PUBLISHERS ☐ BOSTON
A Division of G. K. Hall & Co.

The American Amusement Park Industry: A History of Technology and Thrills
Judith A. Adams

Twayne's Evolution of American Business Series:
Industries, Institutions and Entrepreneurs No. 7

Copyright 1991 by G. K. Hall & Co.
All rights reserved.
Published by Twayne Publishers
A division of G. K. Hall & Co.
70 Lincoln Street
Boston, Massachusetts 02111

Copyediting supervised by Barbara Sutton.
Book design and production by Gabrielle B. McDonald.
Typeset in Aldus with Optima display type by Huron Valley Graphics Inc., of Ann
Arbor, Michigan.

10 9 8 7 6 5 4 3 2 1 (hc)
10 9 8 7 6 5 4 3 2 1 (pb)

The paper used in this publication meets the minimum requirements
of American National Standard for Information Sciences—Permanence
of Paper for Printed Library Materials, ANSI Z39.48-1984.⊚™

Printed and bound in the United States of America.

26.55

Library of Congress Cataloging-in-Publication Data

Adams, Judith A.
    The American amusement park industry : a history of technology and
thrills / Judith A. Adams.
        p.   cm. — (Twayne's evolution of American business series ;
no. 7)
    Includes bibliographical references and index.
    ISBN 0-8057-9821-8. — ISBN 0-8057-9822-6 (pbk.)
    1. Amusement parks—United States—History.   2. Amusement parks-
-Economic aspects—United States.   3. Amusement ride industry-
-United States—History.   I. Title.   II. Series.
    GV1853.2.A43   1991
    791'.06'873—dc20   90-20295
                                                                      CIP

65456

In Memory of
My dad, Alvin Adams
and
My friend, Linda Strobel
Always a spirit of fun.

CONTENTS

List of Illustrations   xi

Preface   xiii

Acknowledgments   xv

1   The Origins   1
    *Pleasure Parks and Mechanized
    Amusement Apparatus*

2   The Form Emerges   19
    The World's Columbian Exposition

3   Coney Island and the Enclosed Park   41
    Steeplechase, Luna, and Dreamland

4   From Trolley to Automobile   57
    *Rise and Decline of the Traditional
    Amusement Park, 1900–1950*

5   The Disney Transformation   87
    *Disneyland Park: A Sanitized,
    Electronic Actualization of the
    American Dream*

6   Theme Parks   105
    *Pleasure Zones Where Time and
    Space Are Relative*

7   Walt Disney World Resort   137
    *Pilgrimage Center and "Back to the
    Future" Utopia*

8   Overview and Postscript   162

Contents

Appendix A: Some Parks That
Established the Traditional, Pre-
Disneyland Amusement Park Culture   183

Appendix B: Industry Associations and
Publications   184

Chronology   186

Notes and References   190

Selected Bibliography   204

Index   215

LIST OF
ILLUSTRATIONS

Riding the Corkscrew looping coaster at
    Cedar Point park   frontispiece

Southwark Fair by William Hogarth,
    1733   3

Richard Knudsen's Inclined-Plane
    Railway, 1878   15

L. A. Thompson's Switchback Railway,
    Coney Island, 1884   16

Riders on the Scenic Railway at Coney
    Island, 1886   16

Court of Honor, World's Columbian
    Exposition, 1893   24

View from roof of Manufactures and
    Liberal Arts Building, World's
    Columbian Exposition   26

Ferris wheel, World's Columbian
    Exposition   32

Detail view of Ferris wheel, World's
    Columbian Exposition   33

Destruction of the Ferris wheel by
    dynamite, 1906   35

Steeplechase Park, Coney Island, ca.
    1903   44

Luna Park, Coney Island, ca. 1905   47

Water toboggan, Cedar Point park, 1890   59

Hotel Breakers, Cedar Point park, 1905   79

Aviator Glenn Curtiss at Cedar Point
    park, 1910   80

Scenic Railway, Cedar Point park, ca.
    1920   81

Auction announcement for Crystal
    Beach Amusement Park, 1989   85

Comet roller coaster, Crystal Beach
    Amusement Park   86

The Corkscrew, Cedar Point park   129

The Magnum XL-200, Cedar Point park,
    1989   131

The author at the Keansburg, New
    Jersey, kiddie rides, 1948   226

PREFACE

THE AMERICAN AMUSEMENT PARK HAS evolved from 19th-century sylvan pleasure parks at the end of trolley lines and raucous midways in urban settings to the enclosed, precisely planned and engineered theme parks of the last quarter of the 20th-century. This book traces that development and attempts to place amusement parks within the American experience by studying the social, economic, and cultural factors that have influenced the emergence and the forms of parks over the last century. It also demonstrates and analyzes the effects amusement parks have had on American culture and values over the past century.

Three major themes form the conceptual and structural framework for this volume. First, the World's Columbian Exposition, held in Chicago in 1893, is recognized as a primary influence on the emerging forms of amusement enterprises from the late 19th century to the present. The exposition gave us the midway; the Ferris wheel (the first large-scale harnessing of technology solely for the purpose of fun); the presentation of exotic cultural environments as exhibits; a clearly sectored landscape design; a celebration of American technology and industry in a highly entertaining mode of presentation; the merger of engineering and planning to produce a unified, precisely controlled, and minutely organized environment; and perhaps the exhibition's most important contribution, the actualization of a "Celestial City" serving as a prophetic model for the utopian and spiritual perfection that America has always dreamed is its destiny.

The utopian dream of a "City on a Hill," a future perfect world, is the second formative theme in this study. Ever since the Puritan pilgrims settled in the New World in the seventeenth century, Americans have been convinced of their redemptive role, that is, their ability eventually to transform the City of the World into a Celestial City. Very early in our history, however, the road to perfection veered away from spiritual grace toward technology as savior and utopian engineer. The grand alabaster classical structures of the World's Columbian Exposition presented a hymnbook conception of Heaven on Earth, made possible by the advances in iron and steel technology that formed the hidden framework supporting the splendid mantle of spiritual and aristocratic allegory. The exposition suggested, on artistic and practical levels, that technology joined with a progressive spirit could create a utopian garden city out of the wilderness.

In the succeeding century, Walt Disney would revive the aspiration to create a paradise within the limitations of a protective enclave. Disney and theme park planners after him created ideal visions of history and the future, with an emphasis on technological advances and the achievements of the American corporate system. Most of the theme parks would suddenly appear from the swamplands or other unproductive "wastelands" as miraculous Elysiums of exotic locales, gardens, technological wonders, and thrill rides. Walt Disney World Resort would elevate the concept to that of New World Mecca, a pilgrimage center that has replaced the spiritual shrine as the symbolic glorification of cultural achievement. Instead of sanctification, however, pilgrims seek reaffirmation of the values of corporate culture: progress through technology, control and organization through managerial hierarchy, and consumption. The parks also enshrine myths of American history and elevate cultural heroes to the status of sainthood. In these commercial visions of paradise, decontextualized historical and future worlds inevitably depict technology as the savior. Near the close of the 20th century, our worlds of amusement reflect a society that strives to ignore temporal reality by focusing on and finding refuge in contrived, controlled pleasure enclaves that present glitzy, selective, and wonderful worlds of Mickey Mouse history and technology-inspired dreams of the future.

Finally, *The American Amusement Park Industry* pays careful attention to economic, demographic, technological, and other societal trends that have generated cycles of growth and decline in the industry and have influenced the design of amusement enterprises and the forms of such attractions as roller coasters and simulation "experiences." These trends have shaped an industry that reached a zenith of 2,000 amusement parks in 1920 only to decline to a low of approximately 250 parks in 1940. The appearance of Disneyland Park in 1955 coincided with economic, population, and social conditions that sparked a resurgence of the industry. In the 30 years between 1960 and 1990 the amusement park business has grown from a $100 million industry to an astounding annual $4 billion enterprise.

ACKNOWLEDGMENTS

I AM GRATEFUL FOR THE ASSISTANCE OF many individuals and institutions in the production of this volume. Auburn University Libraries provided not only wide-ranging and extensive collections of materials but also financial grants to support the searching of on-line databases, the securing of materials through interlibrary loan, and photocopying. I want especially to recognize my Auburn colleagues Marcia Boosinger, Kevin Cook, and Harmon Straiton for their research assistance, and Nancy Gibbs, Robert Gibbs, and William Highfill for their support of the project. The State University of New York at Buffalo Libraries, under Director Barbara von Wahlde, generously provided financial assistance for the securing of photographs and illustrations, and the collections provided especially valuable financial data, information on relevant corporations, and government census publications. My SUNY Buffalo colleagues Donald Hartman, Edward Herman, JoAnn O'Rourke, and roller coaster enthusiast Barbara Jagodzinski have provided significant research assistance and support. I want to thank all of my colleagues at both Auburn University and SUNY Buffalo for their unfailing, good-natured enthusiasm for this project. They have kept me on track when the demands seemed insurmountable.

Cedar Point park in Sandusky, Ohio, and its Public Relations Coordinator, Melinda Huntley, have been extraordinarily generous in providing photographs of the park during various eras of its more than century-long existence and in supplying historical and other information about the park. I will retain very fond memories of my visit to Cedar Point.

The Lehigh University Science, Technology, and Society (STS) Program is responsible for generating my interest in both amusement parks and in the relationship between technology and American culture. This project originated in an STS Program lecture I prepared with my colleague Christine Roysdon, "From Coney to Disney: Technology and Thrills," in which we explored the transformation in the use of technologies for amusement. My association and professional collaboration through the years with STS Program colleagues Stephen Cutcliffe, Christine Roysdon, Edward Gallagher, and Steven Goldman have formed the foundation of my concern with inter-disciplinary studies that merge technology, the humanities, and society.

Finally, I express my loving gratitude to my mom, Mary Adams, whose enduring faith in me has given me needed confidence; and I have the memories of my dad, who started it all by taking his little daughter on pleasant summer evenings to the Keansburg, New Jersey, amusement park to be thrilled and entranced by the rides and attractions.

1

The Origins
Pleasure Parks and Mechanized Amusement Apparatus

> He who can look upon a merry-go-round without long-
> ing to ride the wooden horse once more before he dies,
> for all the maturity of his middle age, can hardly be a
> human being.
> —Richard Le Gallienne, "Human Need of Coney Island"

INTEGRAL ELEMENTS OF THE AMERICAN amusement park existed, at least in a germinal form, in the medieval church-sponsored and trade fairs held throughout Europe. Bartholomew Fair in London is representative of these annual events, established for commercial purposes but achieving popularity by provoking uninhibited and bawdy behavior.

As early as the beginning of the 12th century, the monk Rahere, a former jester to Henry I, was granted a charter to build a priory and a hospital on the Smithfield common. Those marshy grounds already possessed an unsavory history as an execution ground for criminals. Sometime after 1133, in an attempt to raise revenue, Rahere inaugurated a 10-day trade fair to be held following Bartholomew's Day on 24 August. The Fair's origins were decidedly commercial, as traders came from all over the country to display and sell their wares. Separate stalls were erected for the exhibiting of cloth, leather, metalware, pewter, livestock, and other commodities. For the first five centuries the commercial emphasis was maintained, but the public was drawn to the fair by the strolling entertainers, the food, and the free-spirited atmosphere.

During the Elizabethan period the fair gradually changed from a trade event into a center of amusement frequented by pleasure-seekers. Ben Jonson's play *Bartholomew Fair*, first performed in 1614, records such distractions as jugglers, puppet shows, genetic "enormityes" and other freaks, fat women, dancers, actors, and so forth. By the reign of Charles II, the fair, extended to three weeks' duration, had become the raucous carnival that survived for the next two centuries. By the 18th century most booths or shows charged a penny for admission and erected a multitude of lamps to lure fairgoers. Recognized early as a provocative form of allurement, lighting became a staple attraction that has maintained its power of enchantment to the present day. The remunerative potential of a booth at Bartholomew Fair is demonstrated by these 1828 receipts:[1]

Wombwell's Menagerie	£1700
Richardson's Show (theatrical)	£1200
Pig-faced Lady	£150
Fat Boy and Girl	£140
Panorama of the Battle of Navarino	£60
Chinese Juggler	£50

Stanzas from a 1729 poem by George Alexander Stevens depict not only the chaos and pleasures of the fair but also the criminal stigma that contributed to its eventual demise a century later:

> There was drolls, hornpipe-dancing, and showing of postures,
> With frying black puddings and opening of Oysters;
> With salt-boxes solos, and gallery folks squalling,
> The tap-house guests roaring and mouth-pieces bawling;
> Pimps, paunbrokers, strollers, fat landladies, sailors,
> Bawds, bailies, jilts, jockeys, thieves, tumblers, and tailors;
> Here's Punch's whole play of the Gunpowder Plot,
> Wild beasts all alive, and peas-pudding all hot;
> Fine sausages fried, and the Black on the wire;
> The whole Court of France, and nice pig at the fire:
> Here's the up-and-downs, Who'll take a seat in the chair?
> Though there's more up-and-downs than at Bartelmy Fair.[2]

Southwark Fair by William Hogarth, 1733. This engraving depicts the typical chaos and raucous behavior at local fairs of the period (note the portable "peep show" in the lower right).

By the middle of the 19th century, 700 years after its inception, the fair was overrun by unruly mobs. Officials severely shortened its length, raised rents for booths, and banned many of the more raucous games and shows in attempts to eliminate the criminal population and the occurrence of riots. The tawdry, criminal elements prevailed, however, and the lord mayor of London opened the last Bartholomew Fair in 1855. The tendency of amusement areas to lure unsavory and criminal populations, established early, would persist as a formative factor in the development of the amusement industry.

□ London's Pleasure Gardens

A trend in outdoor amusement that countered the transitory, chaotic fair emerged in the late 17th and 18th centuries in England and Europe. Beginning as spas or appendages to taverns and inns, "pleasure gardens" appeared as sylvan preserves within the urban landscape. Warwick Wroth's seminal study, *The London Pleasure Gardens of the Eighteenth Century* (1896),[3] provides extensive, detailed descriptions and histories of no less than 65 such establishments. Unlike the brief fairs, the gardens were available to the public throughout the suitable season for outdoor activities.

The heyday of the gardens coincides with the Industrial Revolution in England, and no doubt a desire to preserve idyllic, natural settings amid the smoke, soot, and gray dinginess of the factory environment was a motivating factor for creating and patronizing these gardens. The desired Elysium was not limited to the natural, however, for the pleasure gardens cleverly merged the primitive with the "blessings" of civilization. Common to most of the gardens were intricate landscaping, elaborate and fanciful structures, extensive illumination, concerts and theatrical presentations, balloon ascensions, and fireworks displays.

Paramount among the London pleasure resorts were Vauxhall Gardens and Ranelagh Gardens. Established in 1661 and covering 12 acres in Kensington Lane near Vauxhall Bridge, Vauxhall initially offered free entry, though visitors paid for refreshments. Its walks and arbors, roses, cherries, and nightingales moved many contemporary observers to describe it in Edenic terms. Joseph Addison's famous Sir Roger de Coverley found the "fragrancy of the walks and bowers, . . . the choirs of birds . . . a kind of Mahometan Paradise."[4] In a 1741 poem Farmer Colin rhapsodizes that "No paradise is sweeter, / Not that they Eden call."[5] Many 18th-century literary figures immortalized Vauxhall. Jonathan Swift, Horace Walpole, Samuel Johnson, and James Boswell frequented the gardens, while Henry Fieldings's Amelia and Fanny Burney's Evelina are dazzled by the fashionable patronage, the spectacular illuminations, and the entertainments.

Vauxhall began its long preeminence as a pleasure haunt when Jonathan Tyers obtained its lease in 1728. During Tyers's control the gardens began to display features that not only became characteristic of these urban parks but also survive as central elements of present-day amusement enterprises. Recognizing that competition was demanding more than sylvan surroundings, he inaugurated elaborate entertainments, the building of an exotic, imposing central structure for theatrical and musical presentations, and the addition of thousands of lamps. By 1737 there was an entry fee of one shilling and season "tickets" in the form of silver badges designed by William Hogarth. It is no wonder that the 18th-century public was dazzled by Vauxhall. Living in generally dim, candle-lit urban structures with little opportunity to experience anything beyond ordinary daily concerns, people found the gardens to be full of wonder. Visitors often arrived by boat to pass through a dark, tree-lined passageway from which gardens and ornate structures suddenly erupted in full blaze from thousands of glimmering lamps. The glamour of the lighting and the exotic architecture was heightened by the opportunity of close contact with gorgeously attired members of the titled class.

Despite its favor with the aristocrats, Vauxhall was not exclusive. The upper classes found it amusing to mingle with the merchant and working classes. A listing of the prices for food and drink in the year 1762 indicates that an outing in Vauxhall was relatively costly:[6]

Burgundy, a bottle	6 shillings
Champagne	8 shillings
Claret	5 shillings
Sherry	2 shillings
Cyder	1 shilling
Beer, a quart mug	4 pence
Chicken	2 shillings, 6 pence
Ham	1 shilling
Beef	1 shilling
Salad	6 pence
Tart	1 shilling
Custard	4 shillings
Cheese cake	4 shillings

Nevertheless, by the late 18th century Vauxhall was plagued by rowdy elements; rakes, drunks, thieves, and young hooligans instigated fights, broke lamps, and terrorized young ladies throughout the grounds. By the turn of the century the clientele was decidedly more bourgeois, and the entertainments were accordingly altered. The fashionable haunt became a popular playground. Elaborate fireworks displays were added in 1798, a tightrope walker accompanied by bursting rockets thrilled onlookers, balloon ascents became commonplace, a dramatic representation of the Battle of Waterloo conducted by 1,000 horse and foot soldiers occasioned much notoriety in 1827, and the number of lamps grew to an advertised 60,000 in 1849. After Vauxhall passed from the Tyers family in 1821, however, a gradual decline was evident. The admission price was raised to four shillings in 1826, but a one-shilling night on 2 August, 1833 drew 27,000 visitors. Despite galas of monstrous size, Vauxhall suffered from the lower monetary resources of its clientele, changes in ownership, and competition. In 1859 the closing of Vauxhall was announced by a final, sentimental fireworks display, "Farewell for Ever."

Ranelagh Gardens, which opened in 1742, is notable for its method of financing. The funds to build the famous rotunda and to develop the grounds were furnished by several shareholders who among them held 36 shares of £1,000 each. The exquisite rotunda, built by William Jones, architect to the East India Company, was 555 feet in circumference, with an entrance flanked by four Doric columns and an exterior arcade encircling the building. The interior boasted a circle of 52 boxes, each of which could accommodate six to eight people sampling insipid refreshments of tea, coffee, and buttered bread. Above the boxes was a gallery with a like number of cubicles. In the center, a construction of elaborate pillars and arches supported the building and served as a fireplace, allowing patronage of the rotunda in cooler weather. Crystal chandeliers lit the entire painted and gilded interior, and a painted rainbow encircled the ceiling. The upper classes paid half a crown to frequent this glorious pleasure dome and promenade their fine fashions before society.

Ranelagh's fame was based on its entertainments. Elaborate masquerades and evening concerts were the primary events. On 29 June, 1764 an eight-year-old Wolfgang Amadeus Mozart performed several of his own compositions on the harpsichord and organ. George Frideric Handel composed music for the fireworks. Late in the 18th century ornately embellished exhibitions set an enduring precedent for amusement park spectacle. An example is the "Mt. Etna" exhibition, a special structure from which smoke poured forth, a crater vomited flames, and lava rolled down until a final violent eruption caused an immense explosion. Despite such attractions, by the beginning of the 19th century the exotic buildings, the elegant tea, and the social promenade had lost their appeal, and Ranelagh closed in 1803.[7]

A smaller but quite distinct London resort was Jenny's Whim, which, significantly, was developed by a fireworks engineer and theatrical machinist. It boasted primitive moving mechanical monsters, devices that reappear in contemporary form most notably in the Disney parks. Huge fish and mermaids rose to the surface of ponds when unsuspecting feet activated hidden triggers. Jenny's Whim also pioneered the display of distortion mirrors to frighten and amuse visitors. London society took to patronizing the park on weekdays to avoid mingling with the working classes. Charging sixpence, the resort was popular in the second half of the 18th century, but was reduced to a mere public house by 1804.

☐ The Prater in Vienna

One of the most celebrated amusement parks in all of Europe is the Prater, a vast expanse of woods and entertainment areas encompassing 2,000 acres in Vienna. With truly democratic motives, Joseph II opened his former hunting grounds as a park for the Viennese people in 1766. He had it carefully landscaped, including the transplanting of fully grown trees so that visitors could immediately enjoy the shade and foliage. Soon after the park opened, the king allowed the erection of booths and tents for entertainment and refreshment in an area that became known as the *Wurstelprater* (literally, the "Sausage Prater"). Primitive rides included hand-driven carousels, large swings with decorated chairs, and small up-and-downs, which would later develop into the Ferris wheel. The *Watschenmann* was a stuffed, life-size dummy that when punched registered the power of the blow.

Joseph II envisioned the Prater as a natural area where all classes could enjoy a respite from the steadily intensifying urban environment and participate in the pervasive musical culture of the city, led in turn by Mozart and Schubert but extending well beyond the era of the Strausses. The immersion of all social groups in Vienna's music was undoubtedly a determining factor in the enduring strength of this city's unique culture; even today a visitor can hear the lilt of Strauss and spontaneously join the dancing in many parks and cafés on pleasant afternoons and evenings. In a 1911 photographic study of the Prater, Felix Salten conveys the social and ethnic mingling that has endured through the centuries in the park. New arrivals still in ethnic garb mix with working folk and military officers, burghers with their steins of beer, flirting dancers, and country folk awed by the spectacle.[8]

Unlike the precisely planned theme parks of contemporary America, the *Wurstelprater* began and remains an unstructured hodgepodge. Many of the concession booths originally awarded to individuals remained in the control of the same families nearly to the present day. Besides food, there were also rides, puppet and marionette shows, and theatrical presentations. Beginning in the late 18th century, fireworks extravaganzas became a notable feature of the Prater. A pyrotechnic genius, Johann Stuwer, produced displays of pictorial fantasy structured on large wooden frames with accompanying rockets. Inspired by the democratic spirit of Joseph's reign to allow as many people as possible to enjoy his blazing displays, Stuwer set up his productions not only in the Prater but also on city walls and Mariahilfe mountain.[9]

The role of the Prater in introducing the railroad in Austria demonstrates how an amusement area can adjust and acclimate the public to new technologies. When Franz von Gerstner built the first railroad in Austria in 1823, he faced a populace that had little faith in such an invention and scoffed at its potential for practical utility. But when he shrewdly placed his experimental railroad in and near the Prater, the citizens, viewing it as another of the park's thrilling attractions, found it an exhilarating way to travel around the park. Although families at first disembarked gasping and astonished by the speed, the metal monster quickly lost its aura of danger and became a familiar vehicle of fun from which passengers emerged feeling like explorers and innovators.[10]

Like the English fairs and gardens, the Prater was a convenient location for unsavory and criminal activities. Smugglers and prostitutes found the park conducive to their business, and moral city fathers complained that the pleasures of the park promoted truancy among workers and students. But unlike many other parks that succumbed to the criminal or rowdy elements, the Prater has endured to the present day through city control and a local commitment to a balance of natural green space and popular amusements.[11]

A ride on the 200-feet-high Ferris wheel, modeled after the 1893 Chicago original and erected in the Prater by Britisher W. B. Basset in 1896 as a monument to progress, is a special experience for the student of the history of popular amusements. Each of the 36 cars of the *Riesenrad*, resembling cable cars, holds from 15 to 20 people; as a rider circles the wheel at a snail's pace of two-and-a-half feet per second, the artistry and the endurance of the steel and wires can be experienced with wonder and delight. The rider contemplates the thrill 19th- and early 20-century riders must have felt as they were transported so high, often for the first time in their lives, and were suddenly able to survey their entire world at one glance. Partly because of its slow pace, in such contrast to the whizzing rush of modern amusements, the rider can reflect on the history of the apparatus, familiar to moviegoers as a prominent setting in Orson Welles's *The Third Man*. Its steadfast survival, despite severe damage from fire and bombs during World War II and constant structural decay, is the result of both the loving dedication of engineer F. Beck, who cared for it for 40 years, and of the Viennese commitment to preserve it as a symbol not of "progress" but of the human spirit of a city.

☐ The Beginnings of Mechanized Thrill Machines

Just as the giant *Riesenrad* is the focal point of the Prater, mechanized thrill machines are the essential and central components that transform a sylvan retreat or a picnic grove into an amusement park. A look at the origins and early histories of the most enduring of the mechanical rides, namely the carousel and the roller coaster, will begin to reveal why these devices hold such a powerful grasp on the human psyche. They are icons, immediately recognizable images of fun, thrills, and escape from work and routine. Their allure is an intriguing composite of speed, danger, beauty, participation in new technologies, and illusion.

☐ **The Carousel**   In *A Pictorial History of the Carousel*, Frederick Fried provides an effectively illustrated chronicle of the carousel from its European beginnings to the American merry-go-round.[12] The word *carousel*, ironically, originates from a serious war game engaged in by horsemen in 12th-century Arabia and Turkey. Mounted participants threw small clay balls filled with scented water; a lingering odor tagged those who failed to catch the missiles. Spanish and Italian crusaders brought the game back to Europe, naming it *garosello* or *carosella*. By the 17th and 18th centuries the French had embellished the game, now called *carrousel*, into an extravagant spectacle of horsemanship and costume. Louis XIV staged the most famous *carrousel* on 5 and 6 June 1662 to impress his mistress, Louise de La Vallière. It took place in a square near the Tuileries that is still known as the Place du Carrousel and is graced by the Arc du Carrousel. The lavish costuming and raiment, largely influenced by myth, exotic fantasy, and history, recast the "war" into a daylight masquerade fete.

A ring-spearing tournament became a central aspect of the French *carrousel*. That sport was not new, having been based on the perilous Italian *correre dela quintana*, known in 13th-century England as "tilting at the quintain." An element of the chivalric tradition, it was transformed into a game by eliminating the danger and emphasizing the courtly conventions of costume, romance, and horsemanship. Expertise required the development of equestrian skills, lance handling, and keen hand-eye coordination while riding at a rapid gallop. During the 17th century, young lords desiring to become proficient received training and practice on mechanical devices consisting of a post with arms extending outward like spokes on a wheel and crude wooden horses attached at the end. The young noblemen mounted the horses, which were rotated by servants pushing the arms, and attempted to spear rings with short lances. Because of their entertainment potential, crude carousels were erected at palaces and in parks throughout the 18th century. In time a horse or mule replaced the servant as a power source. By 1832 a system of gears allowed a man at the center to crank a handle to spin the carousel apparatus. But even as late as 1912 the merry-go-round in New York City's Central Park was operated by a mule trudging round and round underneath the floor.

The invention of the steam engine provided the momentum for the commercial manufacture of carousels. The earliest factories appeared in England and Germany. From the beginning, the lavish, exotic trappings of the French *carrousel* remained an essential element of the design not only of the carved animals but also of the carousel structure itself. Frederick Savage, a machinist working in King's Lynn, England, around 1870, is credited with mounting a steam engine to the center truck of his carousel; he also designed and patented the first overhead cranking device, allowing the up-and-down galloping motion of the animals. The steam engine's power allowed Savage to embellish his "roundabouts" with heavy, elaborately decorated horses and other animals as well as massive carvings on the outer rim. Savage's factory was so successful, manufacturing hundreds of roundabouts, swings, and other mechanical amusements which eventually found their way throughout England and Europe, that it generated an industry not only in Britain but in Germany and eventually America. At the beginning of the 20th century Hugo Haase, a leading railroad contractor in Germany, also ran a thriving business manufacturing amusement devices. Having introduced the elaborate enclosure structure for the carousel, he built his most ornate framework in 1911, the facade for the El Dorado carousel at Coney Island's Steeplechase Park.

The first American patent to improve the carousel was granted in 1850 to Eliphalet S. Scripture of Green Point, New York, for an overhead suspension system that raised and lowered the front part of the horse while the hind quarters remained fixed.[13] In 1867 Gustav A. Dentzel, an immigrant from Germany, redesigned his cabinetmaking shop in Philadelphia to accommodate the manufacture of carousels. His early devices were the first in America to be operated by steam engine. By 1885 the Dentzel carousels, with the artistry of carver Salvatore Cernigliaro, boasted lions, giraffes, camels, dragons, and other mythical beasts as well as horses. But carousel manufacturers soon learned that neither unusual, exotic figures nor more ordinary farmyard animals were popular with riders. The noble horse with flowing mane and galloping motion has always been the unquestioned favorite, maintaining its supremacy over assorted rapidly disappearing creatures. Gustav's son, William, took over the business after his father's death in 1909, but the Great Depression brought a sudden end to carousel manufacture for the Dentzel family as well as most other American firms.

By 1899 the carousel industry had sufficient significance in America to warrant the *New York Times Illustrated Magazine*'s sending a reporter to Charles W. F. Dare's New York Carousel Manufacturing Company, located in Brooklyn. The article includes the following financial accounting:

> A carousel costs from $300 to $10,000 according to the decorations and finish. A wooden figure of a prancing horse, with its right foreleg gracefully raised, and its trimming, mane, and saddle carved in the wood, costs from $14 to $35, according to size. . . . A carousel that will seat 60 riders measures 40 feet in diameter and costs $2,200. . . . In one large factory in Brooklyn, twenty-five carvers are kept at work all the year round. . . . Carousel organs cost from $30 to $2000 each according to size, the number of keys, and decorations, and play eight, nine, and ten tunes.[14]

A new type of carousel known as the Tonawanda machine was manufactured in the late 1880s by the Armitage-Herschell Company of North Tonawanda, New York. Designed by Allen Herschell, the carousel ran on a circular track, omitting the need for the central post. Oblong track wheels created a rocking motion. Herschell may have been the first to add a small mechanical organ, which was belted to a track wheel and played music when the ride was in motion. Many of these merry-go-rounds were portable, facilitating travel and thus reaching small villages where inhabitants had not experienced the larger carousels in major cities. The company manufactured and sold 60 machines by 1890, and by the end of the following year, was shipping one riding gallery a day. Herschell and his brother-in-law Edward Spillman bought out the original company and formed the Herschell-Spillman Company, the largest manufacturer of carousels in America. Tonawanda machines are preserved at the Herschell Carrousel Factory Museum on the original site of the factory in North Tonawanda, New York, and at the Henry Ford Museum in Dearborn, Michigan.

Another major firm was the Philadelphia Toboggan Company, established in 1903 by Henry B. Auchy and Chester E. Albright. For 25 years the company built exquisitely decorated carousels for many of the leading amusement parks, such as Elitch Gardens in Denver; Euclid Beach Park in Cleveland; Willow Grove, Pennsylvania; Chestnut Hill in Philadelphia; Summit Beach in Akron; Riverview Park in Chicago; Ocean Park in Los Angeles; Asbury Park, New Jersey; and Luna Park at Coney Island. Some of these carousels are still in operation, most notably at Walt Disney World Resort and Six Flags over Georgia.

Charles Wallace Parker, an amusement device manufacturer in Abilene and Leavenworth, Kansas, is worthy of note because of the ideals he espoused. His public relations man presented Parker in an "aura of saintliness." Like Walt Disney 50 years later, Parker considered it his mission to rescue the amusement business from the hoochie-coochie shows and the snake charmers. His house publication, the *Bedouin*, glorified Parker, his family, the moral superiority of his shows, and his "Perfect Pleasure" carousels, called "carry-us-alls." As with most other manufacturers, Parker's business was another victim of the Great Depression.

The major historian of the amusement industry, William F. Mangels, author of *The Outdoor Amusement Industry from Earliest Times to the Present* (1952), was himself a carousel manufacturer. In 1907 Mangels patented a device that imparted an improved, smooth, galloping motion to the horses and in time became common on all carousels. He and his carver, Marcus Charles Illions, produced finely carved carousels, including the Feltman merry-go-round at Coney Island. This man, who in 1912 also created the first wave machine for the swimming pool at Palisades Park, New Jersey, preserved the heritage of the amusement industry in America by organizing and developing the American Museum of Public Recreation. In 1955 he sold the collections to the Circus Hall of Fame in Sarasota, Florida, now the Ringling Circus Museum.[15]

Far from a thrill machine, the carousel allures with its rococo decorations, including mirrors, lights, gilt, and exquisite carvings, which create an atmosphere of the exotic and grand. The elegant, prancing steeds foster storybook fantasies of chivalrous knights and royal ladies. Its melodious organ music, stately pace, and grand chargers create an atmosphere of innocence, romance, relaxation, and elegance, generally in the midst of a frenetic amusement environment.

☐ **The Roller Coaster**   The seemingly fragile skeletal structure of a giant roller coaster is the immediately recognizable symbol of an amusement park. Since its foundation is firmly anchored in popular recreation, the roller coaster has not received much attention as a cultural symbol. In 1981, however, J. Meredith Neil published a study, "The Roller Coaster: Architectural Symbol and Sign," in the *Journal of*

Popular Culture. He explains that "roller coasters are the only popular rides whose forms are both vertical and gracefully curvilinear. . . . their outlines sweep and dip across the skyline. Ever since William Hogarth in the 18th century praised the serpentine as the optimal line of beauty, the curvilinear has symbolized relaxation and pleasure, while straight lines have sober business-like overtones."[16] Unlike church steeples, which are designed to lift the viewer's eyes and thoughts heavenward, the roller coaster draws the spectator's vision along a soothing, continuous progression of arches and swirls that are noticeably structured on an earthly base. While a mystic may contemplate the glories of the hereafter by focusing on a steeple, the vacationer is thrilled by the pleasures and intense physical sensations immediately available from a mundane, cleverly engineered assemblage of gears, wood (or metal), and speed, which achieves its effect by exploiting the very gravity that confines us to our earthly and human existence.

A popular winter sport in 17th-century Russia provided the beginnings of the roller coaster. In St. Petersburg sledders raced down 70-foot-high inclines whose timber frames had been covered with hard packed snow. Because of the intense speed, a guide escorted each passenger by sitting in the small two-foot-long sled with the passenger in his lap. Passengers wishing to repeat the thrill were forced to lug the sled up the steep steps leading to the embarkation platform.

The first wheeled coaster was built in 1804 in Paris. Named the Russian Mountains after its eastern inspiration, the ride consisted of an artificial hill constructed of timber over which small wheeled carriages ran on a track. The high incline and excessive speed resulted in many accidents. Again passengers faced a tedious climb back up the hill for a second ride. In 1817 a much-improved coaster was constructed in the Parisian Jardin Beaujon. Named the Promenades Aeriennes, it included a guard rail to prevent cars from jumping the tracks if they hit an obstruction. William Mangels explains the coaster's major improvement over previous rides: "The new coaster was double and circular. Two cars started at the same time, one on each side. A carefully designed curve brought them nearly back to the starting point, and a slight effort from the men in charge was sufficient to bring them exactly into position for a new start. The patrons could buy a number of tickets at a time, and without leaving the car give one in at each end of the run. . . . Cars were built for one or two passengers."[17] Despite the issuing of a number of patents for roller coaster mechanisms in France from 1817 to 1826, after that date activity suddenly ceased, and no further advances were made until American inventors recognized the amusement potential of the roller coaster in the last quarter of the century.

The form of early American roller coasters seems to have been inspired by the switchback railway at Mauch Chunk, Pennsylvania. Originally developed to transport coal from the quarry at the top of Mount Pisgah down to the canal at Mauch Chunk, mules rode down in a special car and then hauled the empty cars back up the mountain. By 1844 a return track had been laid and the system was known as the switchback. As the mines spread out over a large area of the mountains, the railroad became less efficient, and it eventually was abandoned as a means of transportation in 1870. The venturesome citizens of Mauch Chunk converted the railroad, running through the rugged and magnificent Pocono scenic region, into a tourist sightseeing vehicle. Cars were hauled to the top of Mt. Pisgah by a steam engine that wound steel cables around a metal drum. A ratchet system between the tracks prevented the cars from slipping backward. Once at the top, cars descended into the valley by gravity. For 5¢ riders not only experienced the panorama from the top of the mountain but also viewed both the open quarry, where the enormous anthracite deposit initiated the beginning of coal mining in America, and the "Amazing Burning Mine," on fire since 1832. As early as 1873 the switchback was carrying 35,000 tourists during the year.[18]

In 1878 Richard Knudsen of Brooklyn patented an amusement coaster he called an "inclined-plane railway."[19] The device consisted of two parallel tracks with undulating hills on which coaster cars holding four passengers each ran by gravity. At the end a lift mechanism raised the cars back to the higher level and into place for another ride. Though Knudsen apparently never transformed his plans into a working coaster, LaMarcus Adna Thompson used Knudsen's system to build his first gravity railway at Coney Island in 1884. Thompson's Switchback Railway, with cars holding 10 passengers each, quickly became popular and highly remunerative. At a nickel a ride, Thompson's receipts exceeded $600 a day, and he recovered his original investment in three weeks. By 1888 he had built nearly 50 coasters in the United States and Europe.

Thompson faced stiff competition at Coney Island from Charles Alcoke, who invented the first oval coaster track to return riders non-stop to the starting position, and from Phillip Hinckle, whose coaster boasted a chain elevator system to convey loaded cars up the first incline. Hinckle's advance was the spark that ignited the development of the giant coasters dominating today's amusement parks. Thompson was quick to respond to the competition, first by incorporating the enhancements of his rivals, then by inventing a safety device: automatic cable grips, fixed under cars, grasped or released the lift cable when cars passed over strategically placed triggers. Thus the grips prevented cars

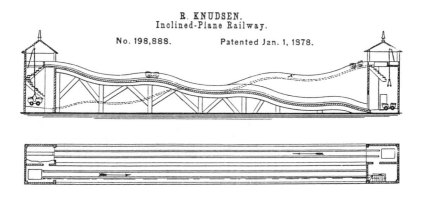

The first patent for an American roller coaster, Richard Knudsen's 1878 plan.

from rolling if an emergency stop was necessary. Thompson also linked two cars together, forming the first roller train and incidentally doubling the capacity of his ride. Between 1884 and 1887 he patented 30 improvements to the gravity ride. He also constructed a tunnel over a portion of the tracks to create a frightening darkness, which was suddenly illuminated by recently invented electric lights to reveal exotic scenes painted on the walls.[20] Walt Disney would exploit this successful darkness/light element in Disneyland's Matterhorn and Walt Disney World's Space Mountain coasters close to a century later.

Thompson recognized and exploited all the ingredients of a successful amusement ride. His coasters combined an appearance of danger with actual safety, thrilled riders with exhilarating speed, and allowed the public to intimately experience the Industrial Revolution's new technologies of gears, steel, and dazzling electric lights. He also paid careful attention to capacity, a factor he quickly learned was critical to a ride's survival. He was also a utopian visionary. Like most of the great amusement entrepreneurs after him, he considered his devices to be socially uplifting as well as entertaining: "Many of the evils of society, much of the vice and crime which we deplore come from the degrading nature of amusements. . . . to substitute something better, something clean and wholesome and persuade men to choose it, is worthy of all endeavor. . . . [we can offer] sunshine that glows bright in the after-

L. A. Thompson's
Switchback Railway,
Coney Island, 1884.

Riders on the Scenic Railway at Coney Island,
1886.

thought and scatters the darkness of the tenement for the price of a nickel or dime."[21]

The continuing demand for steeper dips, faster speed, and increased passenger capacity fostered the development of the immense, high-speed coasters of today. John A. Miller, in the early 1900s, built coasters with ever higher hills, steeper drops, and terrifying speed. Since the speeds necessitated precise safety measures, he invented a set of "undertrack wheels" that prevented the cars from jumping off the tracks while speeding over the tops of hills. Also around this time, the Dayton Fun House and Riding Device Manufacturing Company introduced an automatic lap bar that could be opened only by an attendant with a special key.

The Roaring Twenties, with its drive for reckless excitement, became the Golden Age of the roller coaster. The scream machines built in this decade reflect the culture and collective psyche of the period, when people craved sensual thrills and the automobile gave the privileged a taste for speed. The famous Cyclone at Coney Island, built by Vernon Keenan and Harry Baker in 1927, is a notable example. This stomach-wrenching ride, with an 83-foot drop, includes purposely engineered creaks and grinds to make the rider fear the structure will collapse before the car even reaches the top of the terrifying lift hill. The Cyclone was so successful that it paid off its initial cost of $175,000 in the first year and is still in operation today. By 1929 there were nearly 1,300 large "woodies," as the massive structures were affectionately called, in recreational parks throughout the United States. Many of the rides were designed and built by John Miller, the holder of over 100 patents for coasters and safety devices. He is considered to be the father and "master" of the high-speed coasters. The ultimate "extreme machines" of the period, both built by Harry Traver and Frederick Church, were the Bobs at Riverview Park in Chicago and the Aero-Coaster at Playland Amusement Park in Rye Beach, New York. The Aero-Coaster incorporated an 85-foot lift hill and a whirlpool spiral track that slammed riders against the sides of tilting cars.[22] But the Great Depression and World War II brought a sudden end to roller coasters and amusement parks as well. Money for entertainment purposes was scarce, and the war placed strict rationing on wood and rubber. Most of the scream machines slowly became silent, rotting wooden dinosaurs.

Unlike the traditional carousel, the roller coaster was able to endure, to be reborn in even greater glory in the theme parks developed since the 1970s. A "coaster boom" began with the opening of John Allen's Racer at Kings Island, Cincinnati, in 1972. The megacoaster terror machines built in recent years, such as the Big Bad Wolf and the

Loch Ness Monster at Busch Gardens in Williamsburg, Virginia, and the Magnum XL200 at Cedar Point in Sandusky, Ohio, embrace new technologies of computers, tubular steel, and plastics that demand a multidisciplinary team of engineers for construction and environmental design. More about these recent coasters appears in later chapters, but for now it is intriguing to contemplate why the roller coaster has survived while the carousel has become largely a museum piece. The answer, perhaps, is that the roller coaster is a vigorous reflection of the American spirit. Our dreams have always been focused on the future, with visions driven by speed and the conquest of space. A roller coaster ride leaves one with a sense of pride in mastering a challenge and allows everyone to experience briefly the gravity forces endured by astronauts and jet pilots. Above all, the experience of speed is seemingly uncurbed. J. Meredith Neil finds the coaster's architecture to be an "analog of our national experience." The incomplete coaster structure, with its lack of covering and ornament, reflects the "unfinished landscapes" that Americans have generally inhabited throughout the frontier quest.[23] Even to the city-bred rider then, the coaster skeleton may suggest the pioneer spirit, that is, our willingness to abandon a soundly constructed milieu for the challenge and freedom of the unknown wilderness.

In contrast, the carousel draws the imagination to the chivalric past, which, while romantic, is not part of the American experience. Its simple circular motion is naturally confining, an effect exactly opposite to that generated by the daring leaps and dips of the roller coaster. The carousel is flatly rooted to the earth, while the roller coaster provides its riders with the sensation of being launched into space. In the present world, where bright lights and glitter are often considered visual pollution, the ornate decorations of the carousel are no longer appealing. The starkly bare roller coaster, however, is viewed as clean and unencumbered. For late 20th-century revelers, then, the carousel offers only a rest from the fast pace and a refuge in a remote, decayed past, while the roller coaster can lift our dreams above wordly constraints and launch them toward the future.

2

The Form Emerges
The World's Columbian Exposition

Well, Susan, it paid even if it did take all the burial money.
—midwestern farmer to his wife at the end of their visit to the exposition[1]

THE "WHITE CITY," AS THE WORLD'S CO-lumbian Exposition of 1893 was popularly dubbed, was the plaster actualization of a prophetic New Jerusalem that rose from the swamplands of Chicago in celebration of the 400th anniversary of Columbus's discovery of the New World. Its achievements and its germinal influences made it the "standard by which every subsequent fair would be compared."[2] It also introduced most of the essential elements of American amusement parks from Coney Island to Disney's EPCOT Center. It gave us the midway and the Ferris wheel, but more importantly it created a material Elysium within an enclosed site by means of city planning, architecture, and technology. Its successful merger of entertainment, engineering, and education within a clearly sectored landscape provided a model for Disney and theme park designers. Montgomery Schuyler, the noted architectural critic, found that the profound cultural influence of the World's Columbian Exposition could be summed up by its success in integrating three elements of design: unity, magnitude, and illusion.[3] The brilliance of Schuyler's succinct assessment has become more apparent over the years, as the blend of these three factors has remained the formula for the success of modern amusement enterprises.

The White City, however, had its darker, shadowed side, which remains a significant part of its cultural legacy. The exposition was pointedly elitist in concept and execution, and its presentation of the "City Beautiful" was illusory and temporary. As Frederick Douglass charged, it was indeed a "whited sepulcher" that ignored the realities of urban poverty and the treatment of nonwhite races in America.[4] It presented blacks and American Indians as quasi-ethnological entertainment or as product advertisements, as in the case of Aunt Jemima, who first appeared at the exposition. Although it may have built a utopian city, it was designed to promote responses on emotional and visual levels; it was not a city to be lived in and used. Built as a celebration of capitalist enterprise, the very existence of the grand White City seemed to be a justification for ignoring the horrible effects of capitalism, that is, the growing number of people living in poverty, unemployment, and the spread of slums in urban areas.

☐   The "City on a Hill": The White City and the American Dream

Ever since the voyages of discovery, explorers and colonists had seen America as the locale for the City of God, the site for the Second Coming and the establishment of the millennium. Columbus himself is reported to have claimed that "God made me the messenger of the new heaven and the new earth of which He spoke in the Apocalypse by St. John . . . and He showed me the spot where to find it."[5] Puritan pilgrim colonists were convinced of their holy mission. Even before setting foot on New England soil, John Winthrop affirmed the glory and burden of the enterprise in a sermon to his fellow passengers aboard the ship the *Arabella* in 1630: "We must consider that wee shall be as a Citty upon a Hill, the eies of all people are uppon us."[6] Edward Johnson, in his providentially conceived history *Wonder-Working Providence of Sions Savior in New England* (1654), proclaims, "Know this is the place where the Lord will create a new Heaven, and a new Earth."[7]

Ernest Tuveson, in *Redeemer Nation: The Idea of America's Millennial Role*, explains that the Pilgrims and their followers envisioned a progressive or providential movement in the settlement of New England. In fact, they considered their colonization of the New World as "advancing to the next step beyond the Reformation—the final reign of the spirit of Christ, the amalgamation of the City of the World into the City of God."[8]

The sense of geographic and personal election; the belief in a progressive and redemptive history; a conviction that the limitless frontier wilderness could, through the improvements of civilization, be transformed into a City of God in the New World; and the capitalist dogma that riches could be attained through hard work—these constitute the American dream, a myth that has dominated and shaped our national history and culture. Is it any wonder, then, that the cultural leaders of Chicago should choose to honor the discovery of the New World by building an alabaster prophetic city located in the very midst of the former frontier, which the American spirit and technical know-how had transformed into a concrete metropolis? The White City would be a harbinger of the unity and utopian perfection possible in future American cities, its message intensified by its coexistence with a real city plagued by political corruption, the horrors of the stockyards, a per capita yearly beer consumption of 49 gallons, 7,000 saloons, and 10,000 prostitutes. The White City is poignantly revealing of American values and aspirations and of our propensity to focus on the illusion of the future ideal while ignoring temporal reality. As later chapters make evident, modern theme parks respond to the same American dreams.

The most comprehensive studies of the World's Columbian Exposition, which consider its organization and development, the great fair itself, and its cultural meaning, are David F. Burg's *Chicago's White City of 1893* and Reid Badger's *The Great American Fair: The World's Columbian Exposition and American Culture.*[9]

As visitors entered the gates of the World's Columbian Exposition on opening day, 1 May 1893, they were bedazzled by a gleaming, alabaster Court of Honor composed of immense, ornate, neoclassical structures; vast golden and shimmering white allegorical statuary; and soothing, reflecting canals. To almost everyone it must have been an actualization of the hymnbook image of heaven. The architectural style and the landscape design were largely the work of Daniel H. Burnham, a prominent member of what became known as the Chicago school of architecture, and Frederick Law Olmsted, America's most eminent landscape architect. Burnham and his partner, John W. Root, were responsible for many of the then innovative and celebrated skyscrapers in Chicago. Olmsted designed Central Park in New York City and planned park systems for several other American cities.

The planning and development of the exposition was accomplished by an organization that mirrored the authoritative governing structure of American business corporations. An executive committee, a board of directors, and various chiefs and committees formed the Chicago Company. Burnham, as chief of construction, had the authority to select the architects of the major buildings. Despite the accomplishments and esteem accorded to Chicago's architects in the latter decades of the 19th century, especially for the development of the skyscraper and eclectic architecture, Burnham turned to renowned architects of the eastern establishment. He designated Richard M. Hunt of New York for the Administration Building; McKim, Mead & White of New York for the Agriculture Building; George B. Post of New York for the Manufactures and Liberal Arts Building; Peabody & Stearns of Boston for the Machinery Building; Van Brunt & Howe of Kansas City for the Electricity Building; and Charles B. Atwood of New York for the Arts Building. Under some pressure, he added several Chicago architectural firms: Henry Ives Cobb for the Fisheries Building; Jenney and Mundie for the Horticulture Building; S. S. Beman for the Mines and Mining Building; and the firm of Dankmar Adler and Louis Sullivan for the Transportation Building. Only the designer of the Women's Building was chosen by competition, the winner being the youthful Sophia G. Hayden of Boston.

In January 1891 the architects began a series of meetings that culminated in the presentation of an overall plan and arrangements of buildings on 24 February. A maximum height of 60 feet for building cornices and a classical style, emulating "Baroque Rome," were agreed upon, thus insuring a triumph of unity over diversity and inventiveness. Burnham himself made the decision to paint the Court of Honor uniformly white. The proposal for the Court of Honor itself was drawn from the Cour d'honneur of the Paris World's Fair of 1878 and was probably largely the conception of Olmsted's junior partner, Henry Sargent Codman, who was also responsible for the design of the formal canals and lagoons. Codman's solid academic training, more extensive than that of any of the Chicago architects and even of Olmsted, became a formative factor in the materialization of the White City. Quietly observing throughout the 24 February meeting, America's leading sculptor at the time, Augustus Saint-Gaudens, is reported to have said to Burnham, "Look here, old fellow, do you realize that this is the greatest meeting of artists since the fifteenth century!"[10]

But not all the Chicago architects were united behind Burnham's plans. Most notably, Louis Sullivan, America' most influential architect before Frank Lloyd Wright, was appalled by the rejection of the eminently successful indigenous architecture of Chicago and the preference for archaic, aristocratic, foreign forms alien to the American experience.

In his *Autobiography of an Idea,* written in the early 1920s following a prolonged decline in his career and influence, Sullivan angrily expressed his conviction that the exposition's architecture betrayed the democratic spirit and thwarted the development of new styles:

> Thus architecture died in the land of the free and the home of the brave,—in a land declaring its fervid democracy, its unique daring, enterprise and progress. Thus did the virus of a culture, snobbish and alien to the land, perform its work of disintegration; and thus ever works the pallid academic mind, denying the real, exalting the fictitious and the false, incapable of adjusting itself to the flow of living things, to the reality and the pathos of man's follies. . . . The damage wrought by the World's Fair will last for half a century from its date, if not longer. It has penetrated deep into the constitution of the American mind, effecting there lesions significant of dementia.[11]

Sullivan's Transportation Building, with its natural, earth-tone exterior, was the only major structure that was not classical in design and not painted white. Since it was located outside the Court of Honor, Sullivan was free of the stylistic controls imposed by Burnham. His magnificent, ornate "golden door," the central entrance to the building, generated more concern for its symbolic meaning than for its praised artistic merit. Reid Badger explains that the "gilded gateway" to transportation, with its concentric arches and lavish gold leaf ornamentation, may have signified the Gilded Age itself, wherein the corrupt, powerful robber barons, by developing a railroad system that made millionaires of the powerful few instead of increasing the prosperity of the many, destroyed the golden promise of transportation to provide freedom and liberty as well as access to the unlimited potential of the frontier. It was the discovery of gold in California rather than the pursuit of freedom that spurred the growth of the railroads; Sullivan's gilded archway thus mocked the American potential for "liberty, vitality and imagination" and suggested instead the fortunes and the opulent excess of the railroad tycoons—Vanderbilt, Gould, Hill, Harriman, Carnegie, and Morgan. It is no wonder that Sullivan's golden doorway was referred to as the "Sphinx of the fair."[12]

Sullivan's concerns notwithstanding, the grandeur of the Court of Honor presented a magnificent vista for visitors. While the architecture did imply authority and imperialism, tenets antithetical to democratic principles, it also suggested a certain cultural stature, power, permanence, order, and unity. America in the late 19th century was at a critical juncture where essential values were in conflict: the agrarian

World's Columbian Exposition, 1893: Court of Honor and Daniel Chester French's statue *The Republic*. Photo by Charles Dudley Arnold. *Courtesy Chicago Historical Society, negative # ICHi-02524.*

ideal, the concept of a nation of independent pioneers unfettered by governmental control, and the triumphant conquest of the frontier were all being challenged by industrial capitalism, the recognition that the "limitless" frontier had borders in space and time, the rise of cities, and governmental bureaucracy. The World's Columbian Exposition, with its monumental structures, was contrived to reassure America that its aspirations and toils were "progressive," that its national stature was nearing preeminence, and that the New Jerusalem was well within its grasp. The artist W. Hamilton Gibson gave expression to the feelings of most awed observers when he proclaimed the exposition a realization of the dreams of the sons of Adam for the Heavenly City.[13] On the surface it was successful; doubts appeared only with studious explorations beneath the brilliant facade.

The vastness of the individual structures and the exposition site itself contributed as much to the overall effect as the classical style. Its 686 acres made it more than three times larger than any previous fair. The Manufactures and Liberal Arts Building, 1,687 feet long and 787 feet wide, was the largest enclosed building ever constructed. The Great Basin at the center of the Court of Honor measured 250 by 2,500 feet. At its eastern end was the Peristyle, a series of 48 Corinthian columns (one for each state and territory) with an imposing triumphal arch at the center. On top of the 500-foot-long Peristyle were 85 allegorical figures flanking the *Columbus Quadriga* situated regally atop the arch. This sculpture, by Daniel C. French and E. C. Potter, presented a 14-foot-high explorer in a chariot drawn by four huge horses led by women. Rising within the basin, immediately to the west of the Peristyle, was the imposing statue *The Republic,* also created by Daniel French. The female figure, reaching 100 feet above the water, was clothed in a Grecian-style toga, wore a regal garland in her hair, and held an eagle perched on a globe in one upstretched hand and a staff topped with a liberty cap in the other. The entire effigy (nearly the size of the Statue of Liberty) was encased in gilt. As the crowning feature of the exposition it faced west, its steadfast gaze focused on the promise of the frontier. (Ironically, in his famous paper presented at the exposition, historian Frederick Jackson Turner would pronounce the frontier closed.) At the opposite end of the basin was Frederick MacMonnies's *Columbia Fountain.* The highly allegorical structure portrayed Columbia enthroned high above a triumphal barge rowed by female figures representing the Arts, Science, Industry, Agriculture, and Commerce. Time steered the vessel and Fame set its course.

Surrounding the basin were the main monumental buildings of the exposition. At the western gateway was the Administration Building, with a golden dome rising 277 feet and an entrance portal 50 feet high and 37 feet wide. The Machinery Building, much larger than the Houses of Parliament or the Capitol in Washington, resembled a Renaissance Spanish castle with columns and ornate towers. On the pediment above the columned porch was a relief of Columbia, with a sword in her right hand and a palm in her left, accompanied by Honor, Genius, and Wealth. On a roof just above Columbia were "five heroic female figures" representing Science, Air, Earth, Fire, and Water. The Agriculture Building, 500 by 800 feet, boasted huge Corinthian columns, many rounded arches, and a gilded dome crowned by Saint-Gaudens's *Brazen Diana,* which had been originally created for Madison Square Garden. Across the Great Basin was the Mines and Mining Building, of smaller size but impressive in its early Italian Renaissance design. The Mines Building was unique in its general lack of sculpture, including only an allegorical female figure representing mining and holding a lamp and a

World's Columbian Exposition, 1893: view from the roof of the Manufactures and Liberal Arts Building. Photo by Charles Dudley Arnold. *Courtesy Chicago Historical Society, negative #ICHi-02525.*

pick. The Electricity Building, 690 by 345 feet and devoted entirely to displays of electrical apparatus, was in the Italian Renaissance style with Corinthian and Ionic columns and 40,000 window panes, more than any other building at the exposition. The gigantic Manufactures and Liberal Arts Building completed the Court of Honor. Its comparatively simple exterior served to accentuate its size, with the vaulted roof dwarfing the building's arches and porticos. Remarkable for its construction technology rather than its exterior design, the building contained 44 acres of floor space, and the arched trusses, spanning 386 feet, contained 12 million pounds of steel. The steel arched-frame roof was considered the greatest engineering feat on the grounds.[14]

Beyond the Court of Honor were major buildings, including Transportation, Fisheries, Horticulture, and Art, as well as a multitude of state-sponsored structures. The exposition contained nearly 400 buildings in all. The magnificence of the architecture and its adornment was made possible by the use of a material called "staff," a mixture of powdered gypsum, alumina, glycerine, and dextrine, all mixed with fibers to create a plaster, which formed the exterior facing of all the buildings. Its cheapness and malleability permitted the materialization of splendid architectural visions. Frank Millet, writing about the designers of the exposition, accentuated the contribution of staff: "It permitted them, in fact, to indulge in an architectural spree . . . of a magnitude never before attempted; it made it possible to make a colossal sketch of a group of buildings which no autocrat and no government could ever have carried out in permanent form; it left them free, finally, to reproduce with fidelity and accuracy the best details of ancient architecture, to erect temples, colonnades, towers, and domes of surpassing beauty and of noble proportions."[15] Millet's comments also emphasize the essential drawback of staff—its insubstantiality. Even before the end of the exposition's five-month run, some buildings were showing signs of decay.

Staff serves as a remarkably apropos metaphor for the entire World's Columbian Exposition. With it, a facade of heavenly grandeur was created to cover the skeletal structures of iron and steel. These hidden frameworks were the true advances in architectural construction achieved by the fair, made possible by technology in service to industry. The exposition was erected both financially and structurally on the industrial achievements of America, but it was given a surface glaze of cultural idealism and religious millennial aspirations. The base framework of raw materials stripped from the earth and shaped by the sweat of man was concealed by a celestial mantle of spiritual allegory. By design a fleeting, temporary vision, the splendid White City had no possibility of permanence as an urban environment. Designers, planners, and observers alike could view its utopian potential, but they were under no obligation to extend its imagery beyond the exposition's temporal and physical borders. Perhaps Edward Bellamy, whose seminal science fiction novel *Looking Backward* (1888) depicts a future Boston where universal solidarity replaces capitalist individualism and machine technology creates an efficient, harmonious city, provided the bluntest assessment of the exposition's mode of presentation: "The underlying motive of the whole exhibition, under a sham pretense of patriotism is business, advertising with a view to individual money-making."[16] The very goods on display throughout every building were less important as objects of utility than as manifestations of "progress" and of a prosperous future.

The contradictions embedded in the World's Columbian Exposition elucidate its importance to the development of the amusement park industry. Throughout the 20th century developers of amusement park attractions have designed enclosures progressively more completely segregated from urban environments; the goal is to eliminate the unsavory elements of city life. With ever more massive use of and dependence on sophisticated technologies, they have built utopian enclaves that, because they are unfettered by the practical realities of actual functioning communities, can present landscapes of fantasy, which the public experiences as temporary escapes. Montgomery Schuyler's evaluation of the success of the World's Columbian Exposition, based on its integration of unity, magnitude, and illusion, has been taken to heart by the next century's amusement entrepreneurs. Schuyler explained that unity promotes a sense of confidence and completeness, while magnitude is appropriate because "in this country bigness counts for more than anywhere else." He considered the third element of success, illusion, to be the most dangerous. The "World's Fair buildings have first of all to tell us," he explained, "that they are examples not of work-a-day building, but of holiday building, that the purpose of their erection is festal and temporary."[17] They were created for the purpose of spectacle, not to function in a real city. Reid Badger's final assessment of the White City is equally appropriate to contemporary theme parks and the Disney worlds: "The White City was indeed an illusion, and as an illusion it did not have to conform to the everyday practical realities of American life. . . . It was free, as few events ever are, to reflect the psychological conditions of society—the fears inherent in a confusing period of swiftly accelerating change, and the almost desperate faith in the possibility of the human mind to understand and control the direction of those changes with as little reorientation of basic values as possible."[18]

☐   The Midway

The Paris Exposition of 1889 had demonstrated the lucrative capability of concessions. Revenue from the licensing of individual concession operators on exhibition grounds could clearly make the difference between an overall profit or loss for an exposition. Although the planners and managers of the World's Columbian Exposition intended from the start to include an amusement and concession area, as the grand plans developed, the placing of vulgar amusements in proximity to the serene and aristocratic Court of Honor seemed out of the question. The solution was to segregate the rowdy "entertainment" concessions to an outlying strip, nearly a mile long and 600 feet wide, that linked the exhibition grounds with Washington Park to the west. In an attempt to retain the exposition's educational and cultural aura even in this area, planners placed the concession sector under the Department of Ethnology. Thus the "rare human exotic" freak shows and foreign village reproductions could be promoted as anthropological exhibits.

The Midway Plaisance, as the strip became known, provided the generic name for all succeeding amusement sections of expositions and parks, the *Midway*. Under the direction of Harvard professor F. W. Putnam, the area by 1892 had no firm plans and no promise of forthcoming revenues from concessionaires. Then a 22-year-old entrepreneur without a formal education named Sol Bloom was hired to take charge of the midway. In his 1948 autobiography Bloom said of Putnam: "To have made this unhappy gentleman responsible for the establishment of a successful venture in the field of entertainment was about as intelligent a decision as it would be today to make Albert Einstein manager of the Ringling Brothers and Barnum and Bailey Circus."[19] Bloom would later become prominent in real estate and politics and would help draft the United Nations charter. With Bloom as ringmaster, the Chicago midway arose as an exotic hodgepodge of reproductions of villages from around the world. Arising on the dirt strip were the Streets of Cairo, with picturesque shops, a mosque, camel rides, exotic dancers, and a twice-daily procession performed by many of the exhibit's 160 men, women, and children in native costumes; an Irish village with a recreation of Blarney Castle, complete with a chip of the Blarney Stone to kiss (actually a chunk of Chicago concrete); the German Village, complete with castle and chalet; the Algerian and Tunisian Village with its Bedouin tents, a Moorish café, and dance theater; the Square of Old Vienna, full of eating establishments; the African Dahomey Village; the Javanese South Sea Village, with 300 natives from Java, Borneo, Samoa, Fiji, and other Pacific islands housed in 80 dwellings; and towering over all, the incomparable Ferris wheel.

The village reproduction concept, developed to such detail and with such success by Bloom, would become a staple entertainment venture that masquerades amusement with "educational" pretense. Disney and the developers of theme parks owe a debt of inspiration to Bloom for this concept, the planning foundation of such contemporary parks as Anheuser-Busch's Dark Continent and Old Country parks, the Six Flags parks, the Great America parks, and EPCOT Center.

A contemporary account of the Chicago midway reveals the racial and ethnic prejudice that permeated the exposition. In his massive *History of the World's Fair* (1893), Ben C. Truman, an official of the exposition, assesses the midway as follows:

> Most of the denizens of Midway Plaisance care little for the formalities and niceties of speech. They "size" you up for what

amount of "dust" you may be good for and act accordingly. Here
is a blandly smiling Chinese confidence man who comes out of
his blue and white pagoda and asks you to walk in and have "a
clup of velly nice tlea." Being tired you are likely to accept the
invitation, thinking that you simply accept a gracious offer of
Chinese hospitality. You are treated to a nicely served cup of tea;
you drink it for fear of being thought rude if you should refuse.
Nodding a careless "thank you" to your host in leaving, you are
suddenly taken out of your dream of being entertained by the
shrill demand of "fliftly clents." To expostulate is of no use. You
had drunk the tea, and the bland Ah Sin says that is the "plice for
velly fline tlea." This is only a trifling incident, but serves the
purpose of illustrating the all-absorbing aim of the Midway
Plaisance people—to get all the money they can.[20]

In his 1984 study *All the World's a Fair: Visions of Empire at
American International Expositions, 1876–1916*, Robert W. Rydell
finds that the Chicago midway "provided visitors with ethnological,
scientific sanction for the American view of the nonwhite world as
barbaric and childlike and gave a scientific basis to the racial blueprint
for building a utopia." The actual physical layout of the midway, Rydell
suggests, may have inferred an evolutionary "scale of humanity." Adjacent
to the White City, close behind the Women's Building, were exhibits
of the Teutonic and Celtic races, the German and Irish villages; then
further down the avenue at the center of the midway were the Egyptian,
Muslim, and Asian streets and bazaars. At the farthest extreme from
the White City were the "savage races," the African of Dahomey and
the North American Indian. The "progress" celebrated by the exposition
was not limited to industrial production, technological innovation,
and city development, but also assumed an ascending, progressive movement
in the races of man.[21]

The exposition leaders' white supremacist convictions are even
more overt in the opening speech by the fair's national committee
chairman, J. T. Harris: "It remained for the Saxon race to people this
new land, to redeem it from barbarism, to dedicate its virgin soil to
freedom, and in less than four centuries to make of it the most powerful
and prosperous country on which God's sunshine falls."[22]

Visitors to the midway may or may not have shared the racial
views of the fair's aristocratic planners, but they jammed the midway
boulevard day and night to see the most notorious shows, especially the
various Arab practitioners of the *danse du ventre* or belly dance. The
rhythmic gyrations of Cairo's Little Egypt or the odalisques performing
in the Persian Palace of Eros horrified the women and excited the men to

such an extent that many were reportedly deprived "of a peaceful night's rest for months to come."[23]

☐ The Ferris Wheel

The spectacle of the Court of Honor notwithstanding, the highlight of the exposition for most visitors was a ride on the astounding Ferris wheel. Rising 264 feet above the midway, George Washington Gale Ferris's magnificent engineering feat commanded the exposition by means of both its size and popularity. It is the Ferris wheel that in all likelihood was responsible for the exposition's thin profit margin.[24] Before the wheel's official opening on 21 June 1893, attendance at the exposition had been scanty, but during the rest of the summer crowds dramatically increased. Never before had technology been harnessed so purely for the purpose of creating a pleasure machine. It was the first mechanical amusement device to dominate its landscape and to capture the imagination of a nation. William Dean Howells found it "incomparably vast," but on more sober reflection decided that it was "in the last analysis a money-making contrivance."[25]

As a boy growing up in the mining district of western Nevada, Ferris was fascinated by a huge water wheel that, as it turned slowly, hoisted buckets of water into a trough for mining horses and mules. Years later, the young bridge and tunnel engineer would be stung by Daniel Burnham's remark that American engineers had been unable to come up with anything "novel" and "daring" for the coming exposition. Addressing the challenge, Ferris designed the 264-foot wheel (nearly three times bigger than the largest wheel in history to date, a water wheel on the Isle of Man), actually two concentric wheels from which hung 36 pendulum cars, each able to hold 60 passengers. The axle of the incredible structure was a manufacturing accomplishment without parallel—the largest single piece of steel ever forged to date. Produced by the Bethlehem Iron Company, it was 45 feet 6 inches long, 33 inches in diameter, and weighed over 45 tons. The mammoth towers supporting the axle were 140 feet high and anchored in bedrock well below the quicksand of the Chicago marsh. The entire structure weighed 1,200 tons, had the capacity to carry a total of 2,160 riders, and was powered by two 1,000-horsepower engines.

Since no steel company could handle the job alone, and Ferris's financing was far from secure, he contracted with a dozen companies to produce the bars, trusses, and girders, which were meticulously planned to fit together like giant Tinkertoys when assembled at the site. Despite

World's Columbian Exposition, 1893: the Ferris wheel. *Courtesy Chicago Histori-cal Society, negative #ICHi-02445.*

a freezing winter and a spring of ceaseless rain, the first 2,000 guests enjoyed the wheel's uplifting experience on 21 June. The public thronged the wheel until the close of the exhibition in late October. Howells's assessment proved true: the original construction cost of $350,000 was recovered within weeks, and by the exposition's closing date 1,453,611 customers had ridden the wheel for the exorbitant charge of 50¢ for a 20-minute ride (equal to the exhibition entrance fee, and 10 times the charge for a ride on the merry-go-round). The gross take was $726,805.50.[26] At a time when an entire nation was ambivalent about technological "progress," Ferris showed the world that technology could be used on a grand scale simply for fun.

In addition to its totally visible construction of steel and gears, the Ferris wheel's skeletal structure and vast size generated a visual and psychological appearance of danger, an undeniable aspect of its appeal, just as is the case with modern roller coasters. But safety was a primary concern throughout design and construction. The 1 July 1893 issue of

World's Columbian Exposition, 1893: detail view of the Ferris wheel (note the size of the cars). *Courtesy Chicago Historical Society, negative #ICHi-21713.*

Scientific American went to great lengths to document the safety features of the Wheel: "To avoid accidents from panics and to prevent insane people from jumping out, the windows will be covered with an iron grating. . . . The great wheel is also provided with brakes. . . . If therefore anything should break, and the engine fail to work, the air can be turned into the air brake, and the steel band tightened until not a wheel in the whole machine can turn. . . . a gale of 100 miles an hour would have no effect. . . . if struck by lightning it would absorb and dissipate the thunderbolt so that it would not be felt"[27] The Great Wheel ran for the duration of the exposition without a single accident.

The future of the wheel and its creator would not reflect its success and celebrity during the glorious summer of the White City. After the close of the exposition, the wheel was dismantled and placed in storage. Ferris refused to negotiate with emissaries from Coney Island, Atlantic City, and London for rights to his invention. Finally Ferris obtained a building permit and developed a small park as a site for his wheel in a Chicago neighborhood. Home owners, fearing "undesirable industrialism," were able to force the denial of a liquor license for the park. The venture, eventually including other partners, also suffered from the severe depression plaguing the entire nation. Around the turn of the century, with the park $400,000 in debt, a junk dealer won the wheel in an auction for a bid of $1,800. Ferris himself was spared the misery of witnessing the sale: due to depression and illness brought on by the strain of fighting off bankruptcy, he had been admitted to a hospital in Pittsburgh. He died in November 1896 at only 37 years of age.

The original Ferris wheel would entertain fairgoers one more time at the Louisiana Purchase Exposition in St. Louis in 1904. Transportation and erecting costs of approximately $265,000 kept profits to a minimum. Its owners, rather than dismantle and move it at the close of the exposition, simply abandoned it. Vocal citizens of St. Louis condemned it as a rusting eyesore, and at last on 11 May 1906 the Great Wheel succumbed to a 100-pound dynamite charge. The Chicago *Tribune* reported the melancholy event as follows: "It slowly turned . . . and after tottering a moment like a huge giant in distress, it collapsed, slowly. It did not fall to one side, as the workers planned—it merely crumbled up slowly. Within a few minutes it was a tangled mass of steel and iron forty feet high."[28]

From the point of view of the late 20th century, a photograph of the fallen iron behemoth is an effective depiction of the death of the Industrial Revolution. Its huge axle, a triumph of American industrial ingenuity and skill, is reduced to a rusted mass at rest in a pathetically vertical position, seeming to strain toward its former glorious height. The jum-

The destruction of the Ferris wheel by dynamite charge, St. Louis, 11 May 1906. *Courtesy Missouri Historical Society.*

ble of gears, wheels, and steel, now nothing more than decaying scrap, would in time be replaced in future amusement attractions by plastics, computer chips, and electronics.

☐ The White City's Planning Legacy

Perhaps the most lasting influence of the World's Columbian Exposition was its demonstration of the efficacy of unified and comprehensive planning. The White City was the first presentation of a model modern city where all services, including transportation, sanitation, water, power, and protection, could be systematically organized to insure maximum comfort, safety, efficiency, and beauty in an urban environment. It gave impetus to the City Beautiful movement, which would become the cause of the exposition's ruling architect, Daniel Burnham. It also showed the way to entrepreneurs more than 50 years later who would want to develop amusement areas that eliminated the chaos, confusion, danger, seaminess, and filth of existing concessions. Most notably, Walt Disney would embrace the unified and complete planning concept, with its reliance on technology, that was so brilliantly incorporated by the World's Columbian Exposition.

More than two years before the opening of the exposition, the comprehensiveness of the planning effort was evident in the advertising campaign. Moses P. Handy, as director of the Department of Publicity and Promotion, designed and produced the first large-scale international advertising and marketing campaign in American history. An Eastern newspaper man, experienced in the power of the press to mold public opinion, Handy assembled a mailing list comprising 30,000 U.S. and Canadian newspapers, 5,000 foreign newspapers, state legislators and officials, foreign ministers and commissioners, and prominent men and women in the United States. Three months after the department was formed in 1890, Handy and his staff were writing and distributing a weekly descriptive newsletter that was mailed to newspapers throughout the country. The newsletter provided high-quality, carefully written articles prepared in standard newspaper form and printed in 14 foreign languages, which could readily be transferred to the pages of local newspapers. The newsletter stimulated the interest of potential visitors and also attracted domestic and foreign exhibitors to the exposition. For those people for whom a visit to the exposition was never a possibility, Handy's articles established the exposition as a symbol of American idealism and progressive aspirations. For over two years, the department distributed around 60,000 documents per week. Publishers throughout the world were requested to send their clippings and articles about the exposition to the Publicity Department, where Handy maintained scrapbooks, which were generated at the rate of 450 pages per day. In addition to the newsletter, Handy produced brochures, circulars, pamphlets, and books in all major languages, as well as lithographic views of the grounds and buildings in every stage of construction. As a result of the unceasing work of Handy and his staff, "the people of all countries were made perfectly familiar with the scope and magnitude of the exposition a year before its opening."[29] The advertising campaign for the exposition presaged Madison Avenue.

Even the photography of the exposition was controlled and planned to foster the imagery of authority and grandeur. Charles Dudley Arnold, the director of the Photography Division, produced all of the official photographs. He insisted on monumental platinotypes composed for an audience of the cultural elite. Although he concentrated primarily on documenting the elegance of the buildings and sculpture, human figures appearing in the photographs were exclusively well-dressed, upper-class Americans. Needless to say, his lens never ventured near the Midway Plaisance. Unlike the exposition organizers, Alfred Stieglitz, the esteemed American photographic artist, found Arnold's work problematic. He "saw the prevailing photographic style as sterile and conservative, and its linkage to undemocratic forces as fundamentally unhealthy to artistic progress in the medium."[30]

Exposition planners found innovative solutions to transportation needs both to and within the exposition site. Chicago's excellent railroad system with connections to the rest of the nation was an essential factor in the choice of that city as site of the exposition; however, developing means to transport hundreds of thousands of people to the exposition grounds each day required major planning. A terminal was built just to the rear of the Administration Building to provide a direct rail connection from central Chicago and to create the major entrance through the golden-domed Administration Building directly onto the Court of Honor. A dispute with railroad companies over rates left the terminal largely unused, however, and most fairgoers entered the exposition through the midway. Instead of the inspiring golden dome they were greeted by the frivolous Ferris wheel.[31] Despite this snafu, by opening day several different modes of conveyance to the exposition were available: Michigan Avenue streetcars, the Illinois Central Railway, or steamers operated by the World's Fair Steamship Company. Organizers bragged that 300,000 people could be transported to the exposition and returned home each day.

It was within the exposition grounds that truly innovative transportation systems were created. The major mode of conveyance was the first "elevated" intramural railway. Powered by the new wonder, electricity, the railway made the 13-mile trip around the grounds in 45 minutes and had a capacity of 16,000 people.[32] It obviously inspired Chicago's elevated "Loop," built in 1897, and was the precursor of the monorails and other such systems that circle some contemporary amusement parks. Even more astonishing was the electric-powered "movable sidewalk." A platform made up of a series of low railway trucks moving at three miles per hour led riders to a second section, where another platform lined with benches proceeded at six miles per hour. Completely covered by an awning, the movable sidewalk carried passengers down the Casino Pier and back on a mile-long track. The first such passenger-carrying platform, it was the forerunner of similar walkways in airports and other locales where tired feet are common and efficient, directioned movement of people is necessary. Marine transport was also plentiful in the White City. Electric launches carrying up to 30 passengers, made prescribed courses around the grounds, while smaller boats and gondolas were plentiful for private excursions.

Since the planners wished to demonstrate that public transport could accommodate the needs of a vital city, private vehicles of all kinds, including bicycles, were prohibited from the exposition grounds. Deliveries of food, drink, and other supplies to concessions and exhibits were made after hours. The White City was kept free of commercial noise and confusion, yet visitors had ample and pleasant means of travel throughout the extensive grounds.

The electric railroad and moving sidewalk were only two manifestations of the use of electricity at the fair. In fact, the World's Columbian Exposition presented the most impressive use of electrical energy in the 19th century. The Paris Exposition in 1889 had been the first fair to be lighted by electricity, but in Chicago its use was increased tenfold. The White City's electrical plant had to provide three times the energy needed to light the entire city of Chicago.[33] As a showcase, it demonstrated the potential of a new technology that was incomprehensible and novel to most people. The planners meticulously integrated the use of electricity throughout the exposition and designed all buildings with the artistic use of illumination in mind. The Westinghouse Company beat out Thomas Edison's General Electric Company for the exposition's massive lighting contract resulting in the use of alternating current, a new method that was safer and more efficient than the more common direct current. Westinghouse's main generating plant, located in Machinery Hall, contained 16 generators producing 8,955 kilowatts, driven by 15 engines equaling 13,000 horsepower.[34] Even the Ferris wheel was liberally enhanced by sparkling illumination from its 2,900 incandescent lamps.

John P. Barrett, in charge of electricity for the exposition, made sure that nearly everything that moved or glowed was powered by electrical energy. In his own words, he felt the exposition "brought electricity to the people in the light of a servant not as an awful master. . . . it created an impression of stability and soundness among the thinking element of the people that will mean wider commercial development in the near future." Importantly, the presentation of electricity at the exposition "dissolved much of the mystery that had pervaded its domain."[35]

The World's Columbian Exposition was a pioneer in comprehensive planning for sanitation, sewage, protective services, and the provision of comfort facilities. Sanitary engineers installed a Pasteur-Chamberland filtering system to provide pure drinking water. Other water needed for decorative fountains, restrooms, fire protection, and mechanical devices was furnished by two enormous Worthington pumps capable of pumping 12 million gallons daily. Throughout the exposition grounds there were 4,011 public toilets, an enormous improvement over the 250 at the Paris Exposition in 1889 and the 900 at the Philadelphia Centennial Exposition in 1876. These water closets were appreciated by "fairgoers who boosted Chicago's annual beer consumption to an all-time high in 1893." More sober visitors could make ample use of an abundance of drinking fountains. For the first time at any fair, a Bureau of Public Comfort catered to the needs of the visitors, providing medical services, waiting rooms, and a Rooming Department to facilitate hotel and rooming-house accommodations.[36]

The entire exposition grounds were swept every night, and regulations that severely limited the distribution of advertising handbills and other materials helped control litter. Even the types of foods sold were determined with cleanliness in mind; for example, only shelled peanuts were available. Elaborate provision was made for the disposal of garbage and sewage. The Engle system, an experimental procedure, chemically treated the sewage at a cleansing station to reduce it to solids, ran the effluent off into the lake, and burned the solids under pressure in a furnace with a capacity of 100 tons a day.[37] Much later, technologically advanced systems for garbage and sewage disposal at Walt Disney World would take their cues from the example of the White City.

The White City even had its own fire and police departments. The elite corps of Columbian Guards kept order without intimidation among the throngs of visitors and monitored the cleanliness of concessions. In accordance with the racial attitudes of the exposition's leaders, no blacks were allowed to serve in the Columbian Guards. Because the buildings were temporary and heavily wired for electricity, fire was a major hazard. Planners located hydrants throughout the grounds and distributed nearly 2,000 hand extinguishers. One catastrophic fire did occur: originating in the chimney of the Cold Storage Building, it resulted in the deaths of 13 firemen and 4 other workers, as well as injuries to many others.

The success and the legacy of the World's Columbian Exposition was not solely the result of the spectacle of the Court of Honor or even the fun and exotic enticements of the Midway Plaisance. The achievement of the White City's urban design was equally reliant on more mundane considerations of transportation and sanitation systems. It suggested, on both artistic and practical levels, that technology joined with art and a progressive spirit could create a garden city out of the wilderness. Its contradictions abounded, focused most obviously on its impermanence, its exclusion of urban reality, and the boundaries that

absolutely limited its utopian manifestations. The White City's dichoto-
mies led Henry Adams to note, with remarkably perceptive simplicity,
that "Chicago asked in 1893 for the first time the question whether the
American people knew where they were driving."[38] History reveals that
we continue to steer toward illusion, to rely on the possibilities of
utopian perfection as a means to circumvent the undesirable aspects of a
reality we knowingly create. But as Alan Tractenberg concludes, "For a
summer's moment, White City had seemed the fruition of a nation, a
culture, a whole society: the celestial city of man set upon a hill for all
the world to behold."[39] We continue to make pilgrimages toward artificial, festal enclaves where reality is kept at bay by formidable barricades
and technology serves to create ever more wondrous contrivances. But
no matter how futuristic the novelties may appear, our fantasy amusement retreats, both in design and in purpose, remain essentially off-
spring of the White City.

3

Coney Island and the Enclosed Park
Steeplechase, Luna, and Dreamland

Why, surely, Coney is all the wonders of the world in
one pyrotechnic masterpiece of coruscating concentration . . . strange Isle of Monsters, Preposterous Palace of
Illusion, gigantic Parody of Pleasure.
—Richard Le Gallienne, "Human Need of Coney Island"

FROM THE 1890S UNTIL THE ADVENT OF
Disneyland Park in the mid-1950s, Coney Island was the embodiment of
the American amusement park tradition. While Coney, unlike the
White City, never attempted to raise the cultural sophistication of its
millions of visitors, the "pyrotechnic insanitarium" provided a release
from the swelling pressures of crowded, dingy urban areas as well as
increasingly mechanized and regimented industrial work. The essence
of Coney Island was its juxtaposition of mechanical amusement devices
with an atmosphere of illusion and chaos. The precision and predictabil-
ity of gears, wheels, and electricity created a fantasyland of disorder, the
unexpected, emotional excess, and sensory overload. This brilliant paradox that was Coney, besides generating fun and frolic, allowed members
of the growing urban working class, many of whom were immigrants or
born of immigrant parents, to assimilate and participate in a culture ever
more dominated by the machine.[1]

Coney Island was once an idyllic ocean shore of sand dunes, clam

beds, and windblown scrub that stretched for five miles at the foot of
Brooklyn. Before the Civil War, Walt Whitman often frequented the
beach during the time he worked for the Brooklyn *Eagle*. He reveled in
the solitude that allowed him to swim naked and race up and down the
sand: "There is a dream, a picture that for years has come noiselessly up
before me . . . a stretch of interminable white-brown sand, hard and
smooth and broad, with the ocean perpetually, grandly, rolling in upon
it, with slow-measured sweep, with rustle and hiss and foam, and many
a thump of low bass drums."[2]

A group of 40 Dutch immigrants first settled the land, granted by
the Dutch director general in 1643, and called it "Konijn," the Dutch
word for "rabbit," because of the hordes of bunnies on the dunes. The
colonists' negotiations for the land with the native Canarsie Indians
culminated in the signing of a deed in 1654 by Guttaquoh, who conveyed the island to the settlers for payment amounting to a multitude of
beads (wampum), three guns, a kettle, a blanket, and three pounds of
gunpowder.

The events that would by the end of the 19th century transform
Coney into a crowded, exotic playground where the ocean was rarely
visible began in 1829 with the building of the Shell Road and a hotel, the
Coney Island House, by the Coney Island Road & Bridge Company. By
the 1850s horse-drawn streetcars were running to Coney from Brooklyn, and in the early 1870s steamers carried visitors on a two-hour trip
from the city for 50¢. The most significant development, which increased Coney's clientele from the thousands to the millions, was the
completion of Andrew Culver's Prospect Park & Coney Island Railroad
in 1875. Finally there was rapid and dependable transportation from
Brooklyn for 35¢. The railroad carried a million passengers the first
year and 2 million the second.[3] Three massive hotels were built between
1877 and 1880; the Manhattan Beach and the Oriental catered to the
upper class, while the even larger Brighton Beach was built for the
rapidly expanding middle-class clientele.

Along with the multitudes of pleasure seekers, the criminal element also discovered Coney Island. Gamblers, con artists, and prostitutes established themselves largely in the westernmost portion of the
beach, which became known as "the Gut." Their activities were tolerated for a fee by the "boss" of Coney Island, John Y. McKane. By 1884
McKane was a one-man government, serving as police chief, town super-
visor, head of the board of health, and, for appearances, superintendent
of Sunday schools. His positions gave him the authority to lease land
for concessions, award contracts, sanction illegal land deals, and in general reward his unsavory friends. The flamboyant McKane, who sported

a diamond-studded police badge as well as a gold-handled cane, along with diamond rings, cuff links, and shirt studs, flaunted his power by fixing elections; he reportedly influenced the elections of presidents Cleveland and Harrison by stuffing the Gravesend and Coney Island ballot boxes. In November 1893 McKane made the fatal mistake of attacking and jailing poll watchers sent by the state to oversee the election. He flagrantly disregarded the influence of reformers and as a result was indicted and sentenced to Sing Sing by early 1894. The departure of McKane, along with massive fires in the nearby West Brighton midway district in the mid-1890s, opened up the beach for legitimate forms of diversion and a new venture, the enclosed amusement park.

☐ Steeplechase Park

An unprecedented era of mass entertainment began in 1897 with the opening of George C. Tilyou's Steeplechase Park. While at the World's Columbian Exposition on his honeymoon, Tilyou, entranced by the Ferris wheel, had tried to purchase it on the spot. Disappointed, he ordered a smaller wheel to be built and delivered to his plot on Coney Island. Having been raised on Coney, Tilyou had witnessed the growing success of technological amusement devices, such as the first merry-go-round in the 1870s, the erection of the 300-foot observation tower in 1881, and LaMarcus Thompson's Switchback Railway, which made its appearance in 1884. When Paul Boyton opened his modest Sea Lion Park in Coney Island in 1895, the first enclosed amusement park with an admission fee, Tilyou recognized the formula with which he could exclude the seamier, rowdy element of Coney Island, and at the same time consolidate his scattered mechanical devices and other concessions to create an amusement extravaganza.

His success was based on a cogent understanding of the needs of Coney's visitors. He explained once to an interviewer that "what attracts the crowd is the wearied mind's demand for relief in unconsidered muscular action. . . . We Americans want either to be thrilled or amused, and we are ready to pay well for either sensation."[4] Every element of Steeplechase Park was designed to sweep away restraints and propel the crowds into extroverted intense activity. Tilyou also knew that many of the Coney revelers were young, single, and seeking a brief release from repressive sexual mores. He therefore designed contrivances that threw young bodies into intimate but innocent contact or lifted long skirts to reveal shapely legs never glimpsed on a city street.

Steeplechase Park, Coney Island, ca. 1903. Painting by Leo McKay. *Courtesy Museum of the City of New York.*

By enclosing his park he cleverly excluded the gamblers and the prostitutes while maintaining an atmosphere of thrills and sexuality packaged in law-abiding respectability.

Tilyou proclaimed Steeplechase Park "the Funny Place," and its emblem was a huge devilish jester with broad cheeks, hair parted in center and flying out in wings to either side, and sporting a massive grin with no less than 33 teeth. The funny face promised irresponsible and somewhat diabolical fun. The oceanside entrance set the tone for the Steeplechase experience; visitors had to pass through the Barrel of Love, a 10-by-30-foot revolving, highly polished wooden drum that rolled unwary revelers off their feet and frequently into rather suggestive if careless contact with total strangers, hopefully of the opposite sex.

Tilyou set a 25¢ entrance fee at the gate to the 15-acre park. Once inside, visitors could enjoy all the attractions as much as they desired. Thus the "pay-one-price" ticket was invented. The central attraction of Steeplechase Park and the ride from which it took its name consisted of eight wooden double-saddled horses that raced along an undulating track from starting gate to finish line. Horse racing had been popular at Coney Island for years, and Tilyou imitated its thrills for the multitudes. Importantly, the double saddles allowed a gentleman and a young lady to ride together with the man's arms snugly around the woman's waist. Unlike a roller coaster, the ride created a genteel intimacy that was appealing on warm summer evenings. Tilyou's $37,000 investment to build the ride was abundantly rewarded. By the park's third season, over a million people rode the Steeplechase, and its popularity continued to grow into the new century.[5]

Other attractions were "blowholes" of compressed air that sent skirts flying upward, distortion mirrors, and rides such as the Human Roulette Wheel, the Whirlpool, and the Human Pool Table, where motion threw willing bodies in all directions and control of one's limbs was completely lost. A 1938 article in *Fortune* magazine, "To Heaven by Subway," contains illustrations by Robert Riggs that accentuate the sensual ambiance of Steeplechase Park. Crowded riders, depicted with ample, undulating curves and powerful muscles, are thrown in all directions at the mercy of Tilyou's contrivances.[6]

Of even greater psychological and social interest, however, was what happened to couples after they dismounted from a ride on the Steeplechase horses. The only exit led through dim, labyrinthian passages to a brightly lit stage dubbed the "insanitarium." Here the unsuspecting but hesitant pair was eyed by a clown and a dwarf while snickers from a large audience could be heard. Suddenly a gust of wind whipped the young lady's skirt around her ears while the clown aimed a rod producing an electric shock between the legs of her beau. As he clutched his wounded parts and the lady tried to reassemble her attire, the crowd's howls increased the couple's humiliation. Their ordeal was far from over, as they still had to endure whacks with slapsticks, more blowholes, and a pile of barrels ominously tottering just above their heads. Stripped of any self-conscious dignity, they finally limped offstage to join the audience and laugh at the next victims.[7]

Tilyou's brilliance was in transforming his patrons into the entertainment. All the visitors to Steeplechase Park unwittingly became the means by which social proprieties were shattered. Sudden disorientation, loss of balance, exposure of flesh, unaccustomed and rather intimate contact with strangers of the opposite sex, public shame, and strenuous physical activity resulted in a tremendous sense of release. Escape and illusion were also part of the formula. Steeplechase Park contained a cyclorama show that transported visitors by spaceship on a voyage to the moon. Tilyou had seen Frederic Thompson's and Elmer "Skip" Dundy's "Trip to the Moon" at the Pan-American Exposition in Buffalo, New York, in 1901. At Steeplechase Park, Thompson and Dundy recreated the elaborate fantasy ride, where visitors were launched in a spaceship with convincing motion to disembark on a moon complete with caverns, grottos, giants, and midgets, as well as prancing moon maidens distributing green cheese. This juvenile entertainment demonstrates that Steeplechase Park provided not only an escape from a mundane, earthly existence of cares and routine drudgery, but also a means to flee from adult pressure back to the innocence of childhood.

Steeplechase Park made people "take the brakes off." Their muscles were loosened and their inhibitions shattered mostly by simple mechanical contrivances designed to strip visitors of all means of control. The added lure of "sanitized sex,"[8] sanctioned by its public nature, made Steeplechase Park irresistible to turn-of-the-century New Yorkers. It is noteworthy that Tilyou's contrivances were extremely simple. The hilarious fun of his park arose from the visitors, who themselves were the show. One observer cogently explains that Steeplechase Park "believes half the world likes to show off and the other and less daring half is perpetually interested in the performance. And it believes that pretty legs, however trite, are never dull, and that ugly ones are always funny."[9]

Tilyou, the consummate showman, was hardly fazed by a devastating fire that reduced his Elysium to ashes in 1907. The next morning he posted a sign reading:

> I had troubles yesterday that I have not today.
> I have troubles today that I had not yesterday.
> On this site will be erected a bigger, better Steeplechase Park.
> Admission to the Burning Ruins—10 cents.[10]

Steeplechase Park, surviving not only fire but also the Great Depression, two world wars, and radical cultural change, remained in operation into the 1960s. After Tilyou died in 1914 his 18-year-old son, Edward, took over the management of the park. The Steeplechase horses, now deserving the stature of amusement icons, continued to run for a while at the now defunct Pirate's World in Dania, Florida.

Tilyou was an entertainment genius whose vision has been a preeminent formative factor in American amusement. As such he overshadows even Walt Disney, who spectacularly augmented but essentially built on Tilyou's foundation of enclosure and exclusion, psychological insight, and the merger of technology with fun.

☐ Luna Park

Following the 1902 season Frederic Thompson and Skip Dundy decided to pull their "Trip to the Moon" out of Steeplechase Park and build their

Luna Park, Coney Island, ca. 1905. *Courtesy Museum of the City of New York.*

own wonderland. They bought Paul Boyton's Sea Lion Park and expanded it into a lavish 22-acre, million-dollar amusement center, which they named Luna Park. Thompson, who had been an architecture student, recognized the powerful entertainment potential of architectural forms and abandoned all restraint and convention in his creation of a lavish, sumptuously ornamental, electric Bagdad. On opening night, 16 May, 1903, visitors were stunned by swirling pinwheels and crescents, blazing spires and turrets, minarets, sculpted fantastic animals, and shows depicting strange lands and peoples, all incredibly ablaze with 250,000 electric lights, at the time the greatest concentration of electric power ever attempted. The *New York Times* described the effect of Luna's opening night as follows:

> About 45,000 men, women and children strolling along Surf Ave. from 8–1 last night stopped at one point along this varied thoroughfare and rubbed their eyes and stood in wonder and pinched themselves to see if there was not something wrong somewhere. Yawning on the dingy pleasure thoroughfare was a monster arch, covering half a city block. The interior of this arch was a solid mass of electric lights and rising many feet into the air were four monster monoliths, traced in electric lights and surmounted by great balls of fire, which shed light over the island.

One stunned visitor is reported to have exclaimed "Ah, God, what might the Prophet have written in Revelations, if only he had first beheld a spectacle like this!"[11]

While Tilyou encouraged sexual titillation and exhibitionism, Thompson and Dundy set out to appeal to desires for unrestrained extravagance, the magnetic wonder of the fantastic, the vitality of ceaseless motion and lush illumination. The result was a sensual, enticing architecture described by one historian as "Super-Saracenic or Oriental Orgasmic."[12] Influenced by the World's Columbian Exposition, Thompson used plaster staff, the malleable properties and economy of which allowed him easily to produce marvelous curving structures of an astounding monumental grandeur. While the Columbian Exposition buildings conveyed solidity, discipline, and a formal stasis appropriate to authority, Thompson's spires and colonnades promoted release, dynamic motion, overwhelming transformation, and above all, exotic illusion. The partners also strove to recreate the most popular if officially denigrated attraction of the Columbian Exposition, the midway. Luna Park's entertainments included the Eskimo Village, the Canals of Venice, a Dutch windmill, a Japanese garden, and illusion rides including "A Trip to the Moon" and "Twenty Thousand Leagues under the Sea." Luna was the place where millions of city dwellers, immured in drab tenements, dulled by the plainness and thrift of daily life, and made tense by the programmed and restrictive labors of mechanized work, could indulge themselves in opulent splendor and unrestrained physical activity, while being constantly bombarded by the bizarre and fantastic.

Thompson and Dundy had learned from Tilyou that an enclosed park effectively eliminated criminal and sordid elements. In an article, "Amusing the Million," Thompson wrote, "ninety-five percent of the American public is pure and good, and it is the public that it pays to serve. . . . I haven't any use for the bad five percent. As a showman I don't want them to come near my enterprises." He publically advertised Luna Park as "the place for your mother, your sister, and your sweetheart." As early as 1904 the financial advantage of the enclosed park had impressed many observers, one of whom offered the following simple economic analysis: "It was learned that decent people have in the aggregate more money to spend than the dissipated, even tho they spend it more sparingly; that eleven dimes were more than a dollar and that a show which can take in the whole family pays better than a show where only one would go."[13]

To their formula of clean fun and lush, carnival architecture, Thompson and Dundy added live entertainment shows. Sensing that their clientele's attention span could not be pressed beyond about 15 minutes, they developed events that were spectacular and swift. A large herd of show elephants performed special stunts, including sliding down the shoot-the-chutes. Regularly scheduled "disaster" extravaganzas included "Fire and Flames," the repeated burning of a four-story apartment building complete with a cast of firemen, rescue squad, and dwellers caught in the flames; recreations of the Johnstown flood of 1889 and the Galveston flood of 1900; and the eruption of Mt. Vesuvius and resulting fall of Pompeii. Best of all was "A Trip to the Moon," which cost the handsome sum of $72,000 to build in 1903 but garnered $250,000 in receipts in three years. These illusions created at the beginning of the century are clearly the conceptual harbingers of such extravaganzas of the early 1990s as Universal Studio Hollywood's "Earthquake: The Big One" and "Star Trek Adventure" and Disney's "Star Tours."

Luna's success was even more spectacular than the park itself. Although Thompson and Dundy had to borrow money to make change on opening night, within two hours 43,000 people paid 10¢ each to enter the gates. By August they had recovered their entire initial investment. The next year, 4 million visitors paid for the Luna experience, and attendance continued to climb through the first decade of the new century. The achievement of these attendance figures becomes even more astonishing when they are compared to attendance at parks in the early 1990s, when only the top four theme parks in the United States can draw more than 4 million visitors a year (Walt Disney World Resort, Disneyland Park, Universal Studios Hollywood, and Knott's Berry Farm).[14]

One Thompson-Dundy "event" that exemplified the bizarre atmosphere of Luna Park was the public execution of Topsy, an elephant who had become cranky and uncooperative in advanced age. The euthanasia was to be effected by feeding the elephant poisoned carrots, but Topsy stubbornly refused to ingest enough of the tainted vegetables. Undaunted and perhaps immediately recognizing the opportunity for continued publicity, Luna announced Topsy's execution by electrocution to be performed the following weekend. This method, quite apropos considering Luna's dependence on electricity to create its wonder, was gruesomely successful, as witnessed by a huge crowd of thrill seekers.[15]

In 1907 Russian writer Maxim Gorky saw in Luna Park an illusion where lights, noise, and crowds stunned visitors into a dazed stupor. In his eyes, the narcotic amusement "rocks and roars and bellows and turns the heads of the people. . . . their nerves are racked by an intricate maze of motion and dazzling fire. Bright eyes grow still brighter, as if the brain paled and lost blood in the strange turmoil of the white, glittering wood. . . . if people come here to be amused, I have no faith in their sanity." Yet in spite of himself and his generally gloomy nature, he responded to Luna with intense emotion and a sensation of wonder, as evidenced in his effusive description of Luna at night: "A fantastic city all of fire suddenly rises from the ocean into the sky. Thousands of ruddy sparks glimmer in the darkness, limning in fine, sensitive outline on the black background of the sky, shapely towers of miraculous castles, palaces and temples. Golden gossamer threads tremble in the air. They intertwine in transparent, flaming patterns, which flutter and melt away in love with their own beauty mirrored in the waters. Fabulous and beyond conceiving, ineffably beautiful, is this fiery scintillation."[16]

Thompson and Dundy manufactured their fiery exotic wonderland by means of the magic of electricity and mechanical technology. The architecture, the shows, and the rides were meticulously designed to contribute to the fast-paced motion and the foreign, opulent atmosphere. The rides, especially, were a kind of rebellious transformation of transportation, energy, and assembly-line technologies into fun machines. Rides such as Thompson's Tickler, which featured spinning cars rolling jerkily down a winding alleyway as they caromed into each other, deliberately reversed the production and efficiency purposes of engines and gears, creating instead sensations of loss of control, extravagance, and unrestrained movement.

An intriguing exception to the dominant aura was the Premature Baby Incubators. No sideshow anywhere on Coney Island matched the run of the incubators, which lasted from 1904 to 1943 under the direction of Dr. Martin Arthur Couney. The close similarity of the doctor's surname with that of the locale of his "show" only adds to the incredible history of the exhibit. Trained in Paris, Dr. Couney developed the first mechanical baby incubator in the 1890s. Faced with limited funds and an apathetic medical profession, he financed his work by displaying his apparatus at international expositions. From the Berlin Exposition in

1896, where his exhibit was called *Kinderbrutanstalt,* or child hatchery, he traveled to Rio, Moscow, and finally to America. Couney decided to settle in the United States, since there seemed to be a major exposition occurring every year or so. Unable to interest the American medical profession in his work, he accepted Thompson and Dundy's offer to bring his exhibit to Luna Park.

Couney combined two seemingly opposing qualities: showmanship and scientific integrity. Though his arrival at Coney Island generated indignant outcry from such groups as the Brooklyn Society for the Prevention of Cruelty to Children, the medical profession pronounced his methods sound, resulting in sanction by the American Medical Association. Even when the efficacy of Couney's methods became accepted and imitated, there was generally no room in hospital facilities for premature babies born to less than wealthy parents. Thus the Premature Baby Incubators, though a sideshow, filled a genuine medical need.

Couney never compromised the care he provided for the newborns. His exhibit was a miniature hospital complete with up-to-date equipment and qualified nurses. Visitors entered a large, immaculately clean room where a lecturer provided technical details about the machines. Oxygen was supplied to the babies through a tube, enabling their lungs to function to a sufficient degree. A system of hot-water pipes connected to a boiler and regulated by thermostat provided heat, and an electric motor pulled air in from an outside pipe rising 40 feet above the building and through a triple filter system to remove impurities. A glass chimney attached to each incubator held a small suction fan furnishing a complete change of air every five seconds. Couney employed four or five wet nurses so that his babies could receive natural mother's milk. The nurses were treated with solicitous care as members of his family, but any nurse caught eating the junk food of Coney Island, such as soda pop, hot dogs, or cotton candy, was immediately fired.

Couney never accepted a fee for treating a premature baby in his incubators. His overhead costs were high, averaging about $150 a day in the 1920s and 1930s. At 20¢ per visitor, he needed heavy attendance every weekend just to maintain the exhibit. His success was astounding. He saved over 6,500 babies of the approximately 8,000 brought to him, the smallest weighing 705 grams. The babies remained under Couney's care for two to three months and then were sent home. For many years Dr. Couney's "graduates" held reunions at Coney Island.[17]

The extraordinary popularity of the Premature Baby Incubators is worthy of commentary. Freaks were a major attraction everywhere on Coney Island, but it was more than morbid curiosity that drew visitors to the incubators. Women made up most of the clientele, especially those who were childless. Some returned daily or weekly to follow the progress of particular infants. Other visitors, generally with little education, were probably somewhat transfixed by the technology. By seeing how the gadgetry worked, they could participate in a medical milieu that was otherwise firmly closed and mysterious to them. Importantly, machinery was seen to save lives miraculously every day. For millions of witnesses, technology, generally felt to be an incomprehensible force generating fearful power over their lives, was seen to be a savior.

The death of Skip Dundy in 1907 was a devastating blow to Luna Park. Thompson, left on his own, no longer had Dundy to check his drinking tendencies. He died an alcoholic in 1919. A group of businessmen then took over Luna, but refused to put money back into the park even for standard upkeep. Luna, built largely of staff, paint, wood, and light bulbs, quickly began to crumble and lose its fiery glitter. Two major renovations in 1935 and 1941 failed to lure the public, and Luna succumbed to a devastating fire in 1946.

☐ Dreamland

The third important enclosed park to appear at Coney Island is noteworthy for its failure. Hoping to cash in on the financial success of Steeplechase and Luna parks, politician William H. Reynolds joined with a few other venture capitalists to develop an even bigger and more spectacular park. In 1904, at a cost of $3.5 million, they opened Dreamland, with classic-styled buildings, columns, and statuary, all painted virgin white. Its 1 million bright electric lights outshone Luna's 250,000. Dreamland's 375-foot Beacon Tower, pure white with 100,000 lights, dwarfed Luna's multicolored spires. The massive entrance lured customers with a monumental, nearly nude female sculpture whose pulchritude was legitimated by "The Creation," a quasireligious show immediately inside the gates that recreated the first chapter of Genesis five times a day. The park also boasted two shoot-the-chutes and an immense 25,000-square-foot ballroom covered by a massive seashell.

Reynolds and his partners attempted to create an amusement park with a veneer of culture. Dreamland mirrored Chicago's White City with the addition of now standard amusements behind the pristine facade. To accentuate the "educational" atmosphere of the enterprise, the cashier booths and many concessions were run by young girls wearing white college gowns and mortar boards. What could not be made "refined" could at least be made bigger. Dreamland's "Fighting the

Flames" employed 4,000 characters, and its Lilliputian Village was inhabited by 300 midgets.

But Reynolds had miscalculated; Coney's clientele was not impressed or intrigued by cultural pretense. They wanted fun, chaos, and exotic illusion, not refinement. Gate receipts could not support the lavish initial outlay or a staff made top-heavy with political appointments. The owners, politicians and businessmen rather than showmen, failed to put together a successful entertainment formula.

Nevertheless, Dreamland finally did provide perhaps Coney's greatest spectacle. On 27 May 1911 a pot of tar came in contact with an electrical short in the Hell's Gate ride, sparking a conflagration that engulfed most of the Coney Island strip, completely destroying Dreamland as well as many other landmark attractions. That night, Coney was a genuine "pyrotechnic insanitarium," with uncontrolled flames leaping higher than any of Coney's towers, animals screaming from within cages where they were trapped to burn to death, and crazed lions from Captain Bonavita's show running with burning manes through the streets. The demise of Dreamland only increased the crowds at Coney, drawing practically all of New York out to the beach the next day to witness the ruins.

☐ New York City Demographics

Coney continued to draw well over a million people a day on summer weekends in the early decades of the 20th century. Its success naturally paralleled unprecedented population growth in the New York City area between 1850 and 1940 (see table 1). The tremendous influx of population, increasing from not quite 700,000 to over 7.5 million in only 90 years, was largely the result of the great waves of immigrants flocking to New York during this period. A burgeoning mass of souls sought release from the pressures of tenement life by fleeing to the Coney dream world.

The age distribution for residents of New York City in 1910 reveals that the population was predominantly young (see table 2). Coney's attractions were designed to appeal to the largest segment of the population, the 15-to-30-year-olds who were seeking romance and unrestrained thrills. Coney's popularity declined in later years as the New York City population also aged. By 1950 the dominant population group consisted of persons aged 25 to 54 years. With marriage and family as well as sobering age, the allure of Coney's brand of fun faded.

Industrialization and the rise of organized labor dramatically re-

Table 1. New York City Population by Borough, 1850–1940

	1850	1860	1870	1880	1890	1900	1910	1920	1930	1940
Manhattan	515,547	813,669	942,292	1,164,673	1,441,216	1,850,093	2,331,542	2,284,103	1,867,312	1,889,924
Brooklyn	138,882	279,122	419,921	599,495	838,547	1,166,582	1,634,351	2,018,356	2,560,401	2,698,285
Bronx	8,032	23,593	37,393	51,980	88,908	200,507	430,980	732,016	1,265,258	1,394,711
Queens	18,593	32,903	45,468	56,559	87,050	152,999	284,041	469,042	1,079,129	1,297,634
Staten Island	15,061	25,492	33,029	38,991	51,693	67,021	85,969	116,531	158,346	174,441
Total	696,115	1,174,779	1,478,103	1,911,698	2,507,414	3,437,202	4,766,883	5,620,048	6,930,446	7,454,995

Source: Barbara Shupe, Janet Steins, and Jyoti Pandit, *New York State Population 1790–1980: A Compilation of Federal Census Data* (New York: Neil-Schuman, 1987), 200–1.

Table 2. New York City Population by Age, 1910 and 1950

Age	1910 Population	% of Total Population	1950 Population	% of Total Population
< 5	507,080	10.6	665,889	8.4
5–9	438,263	9.2	535,039	6.8
10–14	422,431	8.9	443,599	5.6
15–19	457,616	9.6	467,065	5.9
20–24	531,868	11.2	598,718	7.6
25–29	499,149	10.5	665,245	8.4
30–34	422,450	8.9	638,249	8.1
35–39	382,225	8.0	668,845	8.5
40–44	309,891	6.5	642,065	8.1
45–49	246,103	5.2	590,622	7.5
50–54	191,091	4.0	556,389	7.1
55–59	122,206	2.6	450,515	5.7
60–64	94,387	2.0	364,482	4.6
65–69	62,444	1.3	274,343	3.5
70–74	39,285	0.8	170,654	2.2
> 75	33,592	0.7	160,238	2.0
not reported	6,802	0.1	—	—
Total	4,766,883		7,891,957	

Source: Ira Rosenwaike, *Population History of New York City* (Syracuse, N.Y.: Syracuse University Press, 1972), 188.

duced the hours of the work week during the years between 1890 and 1925 (see table 3). There was more time for leisure activities and a bit more money in pockets that could be spent on recreational pursuits. In 1903–5 a study of wage earners' budgets in New York City determined that a family with the average income of $836 per year spent $13.17 annually for recreation. This did not include "drink," which totaled an additional $20.76.[18] Expenditures for recreation rose to $33 in 1918, when annual income averaged $1,505 for city workers. In 1935 the portion allocated for recreation saw only a modest increase to $38, since the Great Depression kept annual incomes low, at an average of $1,518 for city laborers.[19]

Table 3. Average Weekly Hours of
Work in the United States, 1890–1925

Year	Weekly Hours
1890	60.0
1895	59.5
1900	59.0
1905	57.7
1910	56.6
1915	55.0
1920	51.0
1925	50.3

Source: U.S. Bureau of the Census, *Historical
Statistics of the United States: Colonial Times to 1970* (Washington,
D.C.: Government Printing Office,
1975), ser. D765-778, D779-793.

The year 1910 marked Coney Island's high point as an amusement
mecca. The prosperous amusement parks were flanked by some respectable restaurants and rather exclusive bathhouses. A good Sunday crowd
could approach a million people. In 1920, however, the subway extended
to the area, making Coney accessible to the masses for only a nickel.
The millions instantly turned into tens of millions of visitors, who
demanded amusement at subway prices. The decline was inevitable,
despite remarkable attendance figures, such as the 2.5 million revelers
who came on one hot day in 1947. Although the subway was a major
ingredient in Coney's decay, there were other contributing factors, to be
discussed in the following chapter. Coney Island and most other amusement enterprises in the United States before 1950 were the victims of
radically changing social and economic patterns. Still, in its heyday
Coney Island was an intoxicant that turned all the values of its time
upside down, replacing an outmoded Victorian gentility with a mass
culture engendered by the machine and industrialization. Coney's
amusement shattered all expectations of normality and paradoxically
turned engines of work into joy machines, spectacle, and chaos.

4

From Trolley to Automobile
Rise and Decline of the Traditional Amusement Park, 1900–1950

The leisure-seeking public is as fickle as trout.
—Alan Bailey, "The Pitfalls of the Pleasure Dome"

THE FINAL DECADE OF THE 19TH CENTURY witnessed the development of electric trolley lines in most larger American cities. Charles J. Van Depoele initiated use of the underrunning trolley pole, a device consisting of a contact wheel mounted on the end of a pivoting pole and held against the power wire running overhead. This method of current collection, which became nearly universal, sparked the boom in construction of street railway systems.

The companies that built the trolley lines were directly responsible for the establishment of the amusement park as an American institution. Electric power companies often charged transit firms a flat monthly rate regardless of how much or little electricity was used. Thus the street railway owners sought to increase riders during the slow weekends and evenings. The ingenuous solution was to create a lure at the end of the line, a pleasure park for leisure enjoyment. Beginning as shady picnic groves often located near a body of water, the parks rapidly expanded with the addition of regular entertainments, mechanical amusements, dance halls, sports fields, boat rides, restaurants, and other resort facilities. Various sources report the existence of between 1,500 and 2,000 amusement parks in the United States by 1919.[1]

The parks almost instantly became a financial bonanza for the transit companies. As early as 1898 one observer noted that the amusement centers actually lessened the cost of day-to-day transportation: "The summer-excursion business is depended on to make the undertakings profitable. The ordinary traffic may possibly pay operating expenses, but the dividends come from summer travel. . . . In the great cities, even, the summer traffic shows an enormous increase over that of winter."[2]

As early as 1902 an article in *Cosmopolitan* magazine reported that a large pleasure park near a city could draw 50,000 people on a summer holiday or Sunday. Blending "natural and artificial diversions," the parks became "meccas" for the working classes and the "middle millions." But the pleasure parks were not just an urban entertainment: by the turn of the century they had gained popularity as "centers of recreation for clusters of small communities which may be linked by the electric current." One such park in Massachusetts was Whalom, located on the lake of the same name. The recreation center for Worcester and Fitchburg, as well as several smaller towns along the trolley line, it boasted a theater costing $30,000 to build and $5,000 a week to maintain, yet a reserved seat ticket could be obtained for a mere 10¢. The street railway company that owned and operated Whalom generally collected $35,000 more in revenues during the park season than during early spring, autumn, or winter.[3]

Much of the pleasure of excursions to the parks was the leisurely and festive journey in the open trolleys on summer weekends and evenings. Some companies would advertise evening "specials," when cars would be gaily illuminated with colorful lights and musicians on board played popular band music. The peaceful open electric cars were in obvious contrast to the smoke, cinders, and noise of the steam railroads. At the usual fare of 5¢, with free admission to the pleasure park, the trolley park excursion became irresistible to the multitudes—upper class, middle class, and poor alike. The wonder and enjoyment of the summer trolley ride is fondly remembered by Robert Coates in the *New Yorker*:

> The trolley approached the park in just the right way—slowly through the city, then faster as it gained the suburbs, faster still in the open country beyond (the salt marshes, if it was a seaside resort; it was there that one got the first whiff of that tangy salt-rock-and-seaweed smell that was to flavor the rest of the day). . . . By then—and how can I recapture the feeling of feverish anticipation that would by then have taken hold of us?—one could hear . . . the click-click of the roller-coaster safety cogs as

Water toboggan, an early version of the flume ride, Cedar Point park, Sandusky, Ohio, 1890. *Courtesy Cedar Point park.*

> the cars were hauled slowly up the long starting incline, the screech and blare of the merry-go-round, and the crack of shots from the shooting galleries.[4]

In the early 1900s every major city boasted one or more trolley parks: Cincinnati's own Coney Island, Cleveland's Euclid Beach, Boston's Revere Beach, Chicago's Cheltenham Beach, Palisades Park in New Jersey near New York City, Denver's Manhattan Beach, Pittsburgh's Kennywood Park, St. Louis's Forest Park Highlands, The Chutes in San Francisco, and perhaps the best of all, Willow Grove Park near Philadelphia. The early picnic groves, enlivened by a band pavilion and perhaps some boat rides, almost immediately began to incorporate the features that contributed to Coney Island's mass appeal. By 1910 almost every amusement park had a carousel, a Ferris wheel, a roller coaster, a penny arcade, and fireworks displays. The parks emphasized band concerts and other entertainment such as balloon ascensions, and some boasted massive dance halls.

Most of the trolley parks prohibited alcoholic beverages or games of chance. Repulsed by the tawdry atmosphere of Coney Island and located in much more conservative, church-going communities, the parks were designed to encourage family patronage. Church-sponsored picnic groups formed the staple clientele. Visitors prepared for a day at the park by donning their Sunday best. Photographs taken in amusement parks during the first two decades of the century show men dressed without exception in suits, ties, and hats, while all of the women appear to have just stepped out of church.[5] Philadelphia's Willow Grove Park, the largest park of the era, had as its focal point a pavilion that could seat up to 10,000 people rather sedately enjoying the music of John Philip Sousa's band and gazing at soft electric lights over the lake.

While attire remained formal, forms of amusement intensified. Mechanized fun machines, with their fast pace and noise, easily found secure space in all of the pleasure parks for the same reasons they had succeeded at Coney Island: they reflected an industrialized society and allowed everyone to participate in the new technologies of transportation, gears, steel, and electricity. On a more immediate, tangible level, the roller coaster and other rides stimulated the delicious sensations of danger and speed. The mechanized rides satisfied three irresistible cravings of the riders: "a chance to wonder, a chance to shudder, and a chance to be scared out of their wits."[6]

☐ Social and Economic Transitions

There were more factors involved in the phenomenal growth of amusement parks in the first two decades of the 20th century than simply the ingenuity of transit company owners and the seductive force of mechanical rides and glittering electric lights. Social, cultural, and economic changes created more leisure time, a rise in discretionary income, and new attitudes regarding the spending of both time and money.

The Saturday "half day" and the "continental" Sunday holiday became standard during the early years of the century in most manufacturing industries. The number of weekly work hours in manufacturing reduced slowly but steadily from 1890 to 1925, as reflected in U.S. Bureau of the Census data. At the same time, average annual earnings for workers in manufacturing and service industries, such as railroads, street railways, telephone and telegraph companies, and power companies, dramatically increased. Table 4 documents the 192 percent increase in annual earnings that accompanied the 19 percent reduction in working hours between 1890 and 1925, both largely the results of industrialization, unionization, and the economic stimulus generated by World War I. The most dramatic decrease in working hours and the greatest increase in earnings occurred during and immediately after World War I, as reflected in the figures for 1915 and 1920. Average annual earnings for clerical workers in manufacturing industries and railroads show a similar 172

Table 4. Average Working Hours and Hourly and Annual Earnings for Low-Skilled Wage Earners in Manufacturing Industries, 1890–1925

Year	Weekly Hours Total/Union/Payroll	Earnings/Hour Union/Payroll	Annual Earnings
1890	60.0/54.4/62.2	$0.324/0.149	$439
1895	59.5/53.5/62.3	$0.327/0.141	$416
1900	59.0/53.0/62.1	$0.341/0.152	$435
1905	57.7/51.1/61.1	$0.378/0.168	$494
1910	56.6/50.1/59.8	$0.403/0.188	$558
1915	55.0/48.6/58.2	$0.439/0.212	$568
1920	51.0/45.7/53.5	$0.884/0.561	$1358
1925	50.3/45.9/52.2	$0.989/0.493	$1280

Source: U.S. Bureau of the Census, *Historical Statistics of the United States: Colonial Times to 1970* (Washington, D.C.: Government Printing Office, 1975), ser. D765–778, D779–793.

percent growth, rising from $848 in 1890 to $1,011 in 1900, $1,267 in 1915, $2,160 in 1920, and to $2,310 in 1925 (source same as table 4, series D779–793). The impressive gains in earnings were, however, significantly offset by inflation during and following the war. The consumer price index rose from 30.4 in 1915 to 60.0 in 1920, an increase of nearly 100 percent (1967 = 100, source same as table 4, series E135-166).

Earnings and hours alone, of course, do not reflect the general economic status of the society. It is necessary to determine if the amount of discretionary income—monies not required for housing, food, utilities, and attire—altered during this period. Then, the amount of the discretionary income devoted to recreation must be considered. Table 5 registers the national percentages of income expended for food, housing, and attire, and the balance available for other purposes, from 1909 to 1925. Housing essentials include rent; the expense of occupying an owned home; nondurable household supplies such as soap, fuel, and ice; electric power; gas; laundry; and telephone. While the percentage of income allocated to housing and clothing remains relatively stable, that designated for food shows a significant decline after 1920, while discretionary income shows a corresponding increase. Throughout the period, the proportion of income available after budgeting for the necessities of life is substantial, culminating in nearly 50 percent of income in 1925.

Table 5. National Percentages of Income Expended for Food, Housing,
Attire, and Available Balance, 1909–1925

Year	Food	Housing	Attire	Available Balance
1909	33.1	14.7	13.2	39.0
1914	32.9	14.0	11.9	41.2
1919	33.2	10.6	13.2	43.0
1922	26.8	12.7	14.2	46.3
1925	25.5	12.5	12.1	49.9

Source: Julius Weinberger, "Economic Aspects of Recreation," *Harvard Business Review*
15 (Summer 1937): 458.

How did the new century's citizens spend their available money?
Medical and personal care, transportation, insurance, alcohol and to-
bacco, education, and religious and welfare activities all competed with
recreation for consumption expenditures (see table 6). An apparent drop
in spending for alcoholic beverages coincides with the implementation
of Prohibition in 1917 as a war measure, two years before enactment of
the Eighteenth Amendment. Spending for "recreation," as defined by
the Census Bureau (see table 6), increases moderately as monies out-
layed for alcohol seem to subside. There is also a noticeable transferal of
resources to medical and personal care during the same time period. The
largest area of expenditure, however, is on transportation. By 1914 mass
production was turning out motor cars for as little as $400; more impor-
tantly, improvements eliminated the prohibitive maintenance expenses
of previous years. The 2 million automobiles of 1914 became 9 million
by 1921, only to double in numbers again by 1926.[7] Apparently, the
automobile became more desirable than booze. Since, as is documented
in table 7, the automobile was often used for recreational travel, analysis
of expenditures for recreation should embrace transportation as well as
the Census Bureau's "recreation" category.

Although statistics related specifically to amusement parks as distinct establishments were not segregated in census data until 1935,[8] we
can trace the ways consumers spent money on recreation during earlier years (see table 7). Julius Weinberger's analysis suggests that by
1920 vacation travel and motion-picture attendance were preferred recreational pursuits in the United States. The increase in spending for
motion pictures accompanies a noticeable lessening in outlay for phono-
graph equipment and recordings, and also a leveling of spending for

Table 6. Percentage of Total Consumption Expenditures Allotted to
Selected Products and Services, 1909–1925

	1909	1914	1919	1923	1925
Recreation	2.9	3.0	3.6	3.9	4.0
Alcohol	6.2	6.0	3.3	2.3	2.4
Tobacco	2.2	2.2	2.4	2.2	2.1
Medical	3.6	3.6	4.3	4.5	4.6
Transportation	5.2	6.4	8.1	9.8	10.6
Insurance	0.06	0.07	0.07	0.10	0.11
Education	1.4	1.5	1.2	1.2	1.2
Religion/Welfare	2.8	2.5	2.4	1.9	1.8

Source: U.S. Bureau of the Census, *Historical Statistics of the United States: Colonial Times to 1970* (Washington, D.C.: Government Printing Office, 1975), ser. G470–494.

musical instruments and sheet music. Significantly, the advent and great popularity of the movies does not affect the dramatic rise in vacation and pleasure travel. The automobile, with all its leisure travel possibilities, became the American public's chosen vehicle for pleasure following World War I.

American preferences in amusement were characteristically passive. Viewing motion pictures, driving or riding in automobiles, and reading require only a minimum of physical exertion. Amusement parks, though fast-paced and crammed with activity, similarly catered to the tendency of their clientele to take their amusement sitting down. Strolling through the park and standing in line for rides provide rather sedate activity, and mechanical rides, in which nearly all passengers take a seat, leave riders breathless, but from the thrills of speed and height rather than physical exercise. The reveler gets the sensation of exertion without much muscle strain.

From 1900 to 1920 the amusement park was a perfect embodiment of the American spirit. It provided a delightful escape from drab, routine city existence while incorporating most of the favored modes of recreation. New transportation technologies, cleverly transformed into mechanical rides, provided the sensations of speed and danger while actually maintaining admirable records for safety. People of all classes, including the vast immigrant population, could mingle with little regard for the strict social distinctions or mores of the time. Thus the parks reflected the increased democratic character of society. In fact, some observers saw the

Table 7. Estimated Consumer Expenditures for Selected Recreational
Products and Services, 1909–1925 (in millions of dollars)

	1909	1914	1919	1921	1923	1925
Amusement Admissions						
Motion Pictures	—	—	—	460	514	561
Theaters, Concerts	—	—	—	67	122	170
Other[1]	—	—	—	127	189	195
Total	286	327	574	654	825	926
Nightclubs[2]	—	—	4	26	22	21
Social/Athletic Clubs	20	24	41	62	72	87
Firearms	29	31	64	34	58	44
Music/Instruments						
Sheet Music	10	12	25	22	22	22
Pianos	109	103	204	141	222	212
Phonographs/Records	26	54	339	209	238	125
Photographic Equipment	15	24	45	38	41	43
Radio Receivers	—	—	—	—	28	196
Books/Magazines	95	120	182	220	251	299
Sporting Goods/Attire	17	51	78	95	131	130
Toys and Games	20	32	65	60	91	79
Vacation Travel[3]						
Trunks/Suitcases	32	31	74	54	73	71
Auto Operation	59	115	568	515	709	983
Railroad/Air Fares	126	156	265	258	258	240
Other (Domestic)	150	200	350	400	450	550
Foreign Travel	130	140	40	150	375	495

1. Includes amusement parks as well as dance halls, billiard parlors, bathing beaches, sporting events, race tracks, fairs, etc.
2. Includes expenditures for admission, food, entertainment, but not alcoholic beverages (Prohibition in effect).
3. Weinberger calculates recreational and vacation use of automobiles, railroads, airways from estimates by the American Automobile Association, and by analyzing summer month passenger revenues for railroads and airlines for a number of normal years.

Source: Julius Weinberger, "Economic Aspects of Recreation," *Harvard Business Review* 15 (Summer 1937): 452, 454, 456.

parks as fulfillment of the promise of Canaan. One sage, noting the trend away from tawdry, raucous parks toward "clean, innocent amusement" in the late 1920s, witnessed "an almost holy joy" emanating from the revelers at the "New Jerusalem" of Rye Beach park and was convinced that amusement parks had a better opportunity than the churches "to prepare an entire nation for Heaven." Others felt transported to the "garden of Eden" upon entering the imposing gates of a park.[9] Despite their "celestial" aura, perhaps the actual key to the success of amusement parks during this era is their reflection of the mechanization and efficiency of industrialization while serving, as John F. Kasson has pointed out, as a "safety valve, a mechanism of social release and control that ultimately protected existing society."[10]

Because most parks of the period, especially those in the Midwest, were modeled on Coney Island, moral guardians made efforts to eliminate the sordid activities they associated with New York's "Bagdad by the Sea." For instance, Kansas City's two amusement centers, Electric Park and Forest Park, were extremely popular despite the watchful regulatory eyes of Recreation Superintendent Fred McClure and Board of Public Welfare investigator Fred R. Johnson. The two parks, easily accessible by streetcar, entertained 1,336,000 people during the 120-day season in 1911, a remarkable figure in light of Kansas City's population of only 248,381 in 1910. The cost of admission was 10¢ at Electric Park and 5¢ at Forest Park. Once inside, each person spent an average of 20¢. Annual revenue for the parks for the 1911 season was $319,996 for Electric Park and $77,208 for Forest Park.[11]

In his article "Mass Commercial Amusements in Kansas City before World War I," Alan Havig discusses the abundant information on commercial amusements in Kansas City that is contained in publications of the city's Board of Public Welfare and Recreation Department. McClure, braced by a conservative morality untarnished by 20th-century social change, strictly disapproved of the two parks' "immoral" climate. He admitted that the bathing pools did "furnish a great deal of pleasure for the people," but prudishly warned that "unsupervised bathing results in undue familiarity." In the dance halls, "prostitutes and men seeking prey mingle with those seeking innocent amusement." The rides, too, encouraged moral depravity, since they " 'usually disarrange the clothing' and throw members of the opposite sex into close proximity in darkened enclosures." McClure apparently saw no harm, however, in such blatantly racist games as Forest Park's "Coontown Plunge" and "Nigger Baby Rack." Similarly, Fred Johnson proclaimed "public dances, questionable picture shows, poorly regulated amusement parks and burlesque houses" to be "prolific sources of corruption." By 1913, Johnson's roving inspectors allowed only those dances "that did not involve close positions of the body, the undue exposure of the limbs, improper swinging of hips or shoulders, or the improper placing of the hands upon the partner."[12]

Rowland Haynes, a field secretary for the Playground Association of America who conducted in-depth recreation surveys of several Midwestern cities,[13] was convinced that the economic and moral future of Kansas City depended on "the efficiency of its workers."[14] Since efficient job performance required satisfying leisure time, city officials led by McClure and Johnson tried through legal regulations, educational efforts, and other means to stem the growth and influence of what they considered to be degrading, unartistic, and crassly commercial mass amusement enterprises. Despite their efforts, the amusement parks, motion pictures, and other entertainments flourished simply because of their magnetic appeal to the multitudes. Still, as chapter 5 examines, Kansas City's puritanical atmosphere of social control, moral righteousness, and sexual repression would have its influence. It served as the early, formative environment of Walter Elias Disney.

☐ Post-1920: Abandonment, Resurgence, and Decay

The years following World War I marked the zenith of prosperity for the traditional amusement park in America, with around 2,000 parks located in or near most cities in all areas of the country. As early as 1921, however, the parks began a steady decline. Many factors battered the parks, primarily the automobile craze and the accompanying rise in extended, independent leisure travel; the lack of space for automobile parking facilities at urban parks; Prohibition; a wide-ranging railroad strike in 1921; three successive years of bad summer weather in the 1920s; the selling of the parks by the transit companies to private individuals; and the Great Depression at the end of the decade.

In the 1940s and 1950s the affluent urban population began to flee to the suburbs, to be replaced by blacks, rural poor whites, Hispanics, and other minorities. Many habitual patrons did not wish to share their parks with the new clientele. The television set, providing "free" entertainment in the safety and comfort of the home, entered most households in the 1950s, transforming the living room into the preferred center of entertainment. Families paid fewer visits to amusement parks and other public leisure facilities.

Table 8. Number of Amusement Parks, Receipts (in millions of dollars),
and U.S. Population (in millions), 1920–1967

Year	Number of Parks	Receipts	U.S. Population
1920	1800-2000	na	106.0
1935	303	9.0	127.3
1939	245	10.1	130.9
1948	368	38.7	146.6
1954	400 (est.)	—	162.4
1958	650 (est.)	—	174.1
1963	997	105.9	189.2
1967	786	174.1	198.7

Sources: U.S. Bureau of the Census, *Census of Business, 1935, 1939, 1948, 1954, 1958, 1963, 1967* (Washington, D.C.: Government Printing Office, 1937, 1942, 1952, 1956, 1961, 1966, 1970); "Amusement Parks Unveil Their Winter's Work," *Business Week,* 15 May 1954, 185; U.S. Bureau of the Census, *Historical Statistics of the United States: Colonial Times to 1970* (Washington, D.C.: Government Printing Office, 1975), ser. A29–42.

U.S. Bureau of the Census statistics do not accurately document the stagnation of amusement parks through the midcentury. Although in 1935 the Census Bureau began to provide statistics for amusement parks as a separate business category, during the 1950s the Bureau combined data on parks with that for amusement device concessions— shooting galleries, kiddielands, picnic grounds, and games of skill and chance. That decision may have been spurred by the decline in the number of parks in preceding decades (see table 8). Separate classification resumed in the 1963 *Census of Business,* probably in response to the rise of the new theme parks, beginning with Disneyland Park in 1955. Some major traditional parks that created the culture of amusement parks prior to Disneyland are listed in Appendix A.

A closer look at Olympic Park in Irvington, New Jersey, and Riverview Park in Chicago demonstrates that social changes and increasing affluence paradoxically led to the irreversible decay of most of the traditional parks by the 1950s. The survival of a few traditional parks into the 1980s and beyond, however, prompts an examination of two noteworthy examples, Kennywood Park near Pittsburgh and Cedar Point in Sandusky, Ohio, to identify the ingredients that have contributed to nearly a century of continued commercial success.

☐ **Olympic Park, Irvington, New Jersey**   The following
account of the history of Olympic Park is derived from the pleasant 1983
chronicle in words and pictures by Alan A. Siegel, *Smile: A Picture
History of Olympic Park 1887–1965*.[15] Becker's Grove, as Olympic Park
was first known, opened in 1887 at a time when the Newark Law and
Order League was vigorously campaigning for the suppression of Sunday drinking in the beer gardens and lager parks frequented by the city's
German and Irish immigrants. Located about half a mile from the Irvington horse car line, the Grove was owned and developed by John A.
Becker, an affluent member of Newark's German community. In the
early years, the Grove boasted a dancing pavilion, bowling alley, rifle
range, and ball field. As early as 1889 the Newark *News* could report
that around 5,000 people visited the Grove on a fine Sunday. Reflecting
the puritanical traditions of the city leaders, the paper grumbled about
the free-flowing lager: "Everything went on smoothly until about 2
o'clock when the beer began to take effect, and all the afternoon young
men and boys could be seen lying about the grove in an intoxicated
condition. A number of women, some not more than 12 or 14 years of
age, were hardly able to stand up."[16] Proper Newark was outraged.

In 1897 Frank Buehler, a Springfield brewer, leased the Grove from
Becker and began to add improvements, including electric lights and an
enlarged restaurant. By this time, the Irvington and Hilton trolley
brought clientele from downtown Newark right to the park's gate for a
nickel. Entertainment focused on musical concerts and open-air dancing, but unlike most other amusement parks, there were no mechanical
rides in this sylvan setting. Competition from new parks opening after
the turn of the century and boasting rides, Wild West shows, menager-
ies, and lavish use of electric lights, led to the transferal of Becker's
Grove to brothers-in-law Christian Kurz and Herman Schmidt. They
added a midway, an essential part of amusement parks since its phenomenal success at the World's Columbian Exposition, a circus, mechanical rides, a miniature railroad to transport patrons around the park,
extravagant landscaping, 2,000 incandescent lamps, and two gilt lions,
13 feet in height, majestically stationed just inside the entrance. Opening in 1904, the new park was renamed Olympic Park in honor of the
Olympic games held that year in Saint Louis.

Though they billed it as "The Eldorado of Essex County," Kurz and
Schmidt designed Olympic Park for rather mild family enjoyment, with
attractions that would appeal to all age groups. The tranquillity of the
picnic grove and the elegant restaurant still prevailed over the few
mechanical rides, the circus, the beer garden, and the small midway. For
1905 more extensive improvements were evident, including a new ball-

room, a theater seating 2,500, an electric merry-go-round, a roller coaster, and brilliant fireworks displays each evening. By 1909 *Billboard*, the magazine of the amusement industry, labeled Olympic Park "one of the finest, shadiest and most accommodating parks in the East, easy to reach by trolley." An average of 10,000 people were paying the 10¢ admission charge daily, and season income was reaching a half million dollars.[17] Success was primarily due to constant renovation of the park's facilities, vigilant efforts to keep the park clean, and the attractiveness to a "better class" of patrons who enjoyed the opera house, theater, concerts, dining, and dancing. "The Classiest Family Resort in America" required gentlemen to wear coat and tie and expected children to wear their Sunday best. Waiters in the restaurant, all German-born, wore white shirts and black bow ties. A 1909 Olympic Park brochure firmly states, "Representatives of the rowdy element will not be tolerated. Games of chance and buncombe of any and every sort are tabooed. Only clean and wholesome amusements are permitted and proper sanitary conditions prevail throughout."[18]

Olympic Park's fortunes took a nosedive in 1914 when, at the height of a fire that destroyed most of the park, its guiding genius, Herman Schmidt, suffered a stroke that left him unable to speak. In 1915 the park was lost at a sheriff's sale to the Home Brewing Company, which had also acquired Forest Park Highlands in St. Louis by similar means. The park survived this turn of events because Henry A. Guenther, a principal stockholder of Home Brewing who was charged with the management of the park, discovered a real fondness for running the enterprise and bought Olympic Park outright in 1919, four months before Prohibition. The park would remain in the Guenther family until it closed in 1965. By 1921 Guenther had transformed the park into a Coney Island funland with the Palace Sanitarium, a fun house, and a multitude of sideshows and fast rides. Unlike Coney Island, even after Prohibition Olympic Park would remain "dry" until its closing day 44 years later.

Although attendance grew to a peak of over a million visitors in the 1930 season, by 1933 receipts were down 25 percent in the wake of the Great Depression. Faced with rapidly diminishing attendance and income, the park turned to special events to lure clientele. An emblem of the Depression, the dance marathon, was first staged at Olympic Park beginning in September 1932. Advertised to last 3,500 hours, by mid-December 11 of the 58 original couples were still dancing for the prize money, $500 for the winning duo down to $160 for the couple finishing fifth. On the final day in February 1933, with five bandaged couples, some of them on crutches, still on the dance floor, the promoter skipped town with the prize money. This gruesome spectacle of couples dragging each other around the dance floor or collapsing from life-threatening exhaustion was a tremendous attraction. Spectators bused in from as far away as Philadelphia paid the extravagant Depression-era admission fees of $1.00 for weeknights and $1.50 on Friday and Saturday evenings just to watch the dancers. Marathon participants were allowed a half hour every day to leave the hall for some fresh air, and 15 minutes each hour to attend to personal needs and sleep. Another marathon beginning on 23 January 1935 lasted four months and featured Red Skelton as emcee. Two of the fatigued couples were married on the dance floor in front of the spectators.[19] The dance marathon replaced the midway freak show as a lure for the voyeuristic tendencies of the local citizens.

The outbreak of World War II in 1939 began an economic upsurge that put more spending money in people's pockets. Although war rationing from 1942 to 1946 made new rides and parts to repair aging ones scarce or impossible to obtain, the Guenther family brought the crowds back to Olympic Park by faithfully maintaining the park's facilities with a new coat of paint each spring, by expanding the peaceful grove, which was attracting throngs of war-weary picnickers who had acquired a new respect for quiet relaxation, by admitting servicemen free of charge through the 1947 season, and by doubling the size of the parking lot. Standards of conduct were strictly maintained despite the growing social liberalism sparked by the war. In 1945 the park announced that no female over the age of 15 would be admitted wearing shorts, and males were still required to wear ties. In 1949 Olympic Park receipts totaled $700,000, due largely, *Billboard* magazine contended, to the park's unstinting provision of free entertainment shows.[20]

Despite its ability to recover in the 1940s, irreversible decline began in the early 1950s when state antigambling laws forced the removal of all games of chance and pinball machines. "Wheels" of chance at this time accounted for no less than 40 percent of the park's revenues. Henry Guenther vigilantly policed his concessions to ensure their absolute honesty and replaced "wheels" with games of skill, but to no avail. In 1956 the New Jersey Supreme Court ruled that games of chance were illegal even if prizes were awarded on the basis of player skill, thus immediately shutting down three dozen such games at Olympic Park.

Guenther attempted to counter television's threat by installing a "Tele-Theater" in 1952 with seven large television screens in continuous operation day and night. But the size of the screens alone was not enough to intrigue customers who could see the same shows in their homes. The Tele-Theater closed by the end of the 1953 season.

By the mid-1950s the civil rights movement forced a change in the

Guenther family's unwritten policy of excluding blacks. Previously it had been generally known that blacks were unwelcome, and few had attempted to enter the park. The same decade saw a relaxation in the dress and conduct codes and the Guenther family's declining interest in upkeep of the languid park. The more affluent population of Essex County had more exciting leisure options, as effectively conveyed in a 1964 article in the Newark *Evening News:* "The roller coaster or the putt-putts don't mean so much to a suburban teenager who has his own car by the time he graduates from high school. He has new frontiers— the shore, the lakes and New York City."[21]

In 1965 Olympic Park's last season began with an incident that graphically depicts the decay of urban amusement parks (as well as the cities they served). On the first of May, 400 to 500 Newark youths went on a rampage in the park, wrecking amusement equipment and stealing prizes and other merchandise. When chased out the gates, they extended their riot to neighboring residential areas, smashing windows and vandalizing property. The resulting publicity effectively kept leisure fun-seekers away from the park for the rest of the season. The rapid growth of the Newark–Essex County suburban area made the prime real estate on which Olympic Park was situated too valuable to remain primarily a hangout for gangs of urban youths entertained more by vandalizing the rusting rides and concessions than by patronizing them. Following continual rumors and speculation, the Guenthers sold the land to urban developers.

Even after the park's demise, the spirit of Olympic Park endures in its spectacular Liberty carousel, originally built in 1914 by the Philadelphia Toboggan Company. Henry Guenther purchased the ride in 1928 from Belle Isle Park in Detroit. Its 60-foot circular base carried 80 magnificently carved wooden horses created by Daniel C. Mueller, one of the premier carousel artists in America. Its band organ, decorated in gold leaf, featured cymbals, drums, and four graceful dancers twirling to the music. When Olympic Park closed, Walt Disney preserved and redesigned the carousel for eventual installation as the focal point of the medieval courtyard in Fantasyland at Walt Disney World Resort.[22]

☐ **Riverview Park, Chicago**   The history of Riverview Park in Chicago provides a striking contrast to that of Olympic Park. While Olympic Park deliberately maintained its tranquil atmosphere, with emphasis on the picnic grove, formal restaurant, and ballroom, Riverview Park embraced the speed and pandemonium of mechanical rides, especially the "scream machine" roller coasters, which became the rage in the Roaring Twenties. Riverview actually became the testing ground for the leviathan skeletal "woodies"; major builders John Miller, Harry Traver, Frederick Church, and Fred Pearce all set up offices in the park and traded ideas and construction techniques.[23]

Riverview first opened its gates in 1904 as the German Sharp-shooter Park, a hunting preserve owned by the Schmidt family. In 1906 Wilhelm or William Schmidt commissioned a merry-go-round for the park to provide some diversion for wives and children left to wait while husbands and fathers were shooting. Carved and manufactured by the Philadelphia Toboggan Company, as was Olympic Park's carousel, the 70 prancing horses unfailingly carried their adoring riders for 60 years until Riverview closed in 1967. After languishing in a warehouse in Illinois, it now graces Six Flags over Georgia in Atlanta. Around the same time in the early years of the century, George Schmidt came home from his travels in Europe bursting with enthusiasm about the amusement parks he had visited. Beginning with George's return, the park expanded to become heralded in the 1920s as "the world's largest amusement park."[24] By then it was served by four streetcar lines.

There were as many as 11 and no fewer than 6 roller coasters in Riverview during most of its existence. At least 25 other major rides joined the coasters to ensure an atmosphere of screaming speed and unceasing din. The newest and most daring rides were always featured on Riverview Park's two-mile midway. Considered by many coaster enthusiasts to be the "ultimate" roller coaster, the Bobs, designed and built by Frederick Church, Harry Traver, and Thomas Prior, opened at Riverview in 1924. Despite Chicago building code regulations limiting the height of tracks to 72 feet, the Bobs claimed a first hill that was 87 feet high. Its 3,253 feet of track covered 16 hills and 12 curves, including a possibly exaggerated 67-degree drop. It was savage, as is apparent from the reaction of one fan who "endured" the ride:

> The first hill is yet to be scaled. And then you see it, soaring unbelievably, so steep that you are nearly on your back once the train begins the ascent. . . . Down! Up! Fierce screeching turns! Banking so steeply that we crash screaming against each other, now tearing straight on, the undersides of the tracks we've been on seconds before just inches above our heads, then wrenching left, shooting ahead, then dipping down and up thinking, Geez, if I hadn't been holding on . . . then into the twisting bowels of the Bobs again thinking, that's the turn that's in the ads, That's the turn! and on and on and on, lights flashing and the night a wild windstorm as we're twisting, swerving, swooping, wrenching, rearing, roaring towards the end.[25]

After 43 years of ferocious rides, for an estimated 30 million people,[26] the Bobs was bulldozed in 1967 when Riverview closed. Its demise is unfortunate, since only the memories of its riders can fortify its status as "ultimate scream machine" against the claims of contemporary coasters.

The other especially notable coaster at Riverview was the Fireball, which first appeared as the Blue Streak but was redesigned many times before its final metamorphosis loomed on the scene in 1963. It circumvented the building code by burrowing beneath the ground to achieve a terrorizing drop of 90 feet to a pile of rocks, ducking underneath them at the last second. Its fire-engine red cars traveled through a menacing dark tunnel that threatened riders just at the base of the first drop. The park's advertisement of a 100-miles-per-hour speed on the Fireball was exaggerated, but the actual speed of about 65 miles per hour exceeded that of most contemporary coasters.

Despite the ferocity of the thrill machines and the park's status as a testing ground for new rides, Riverview maintained a superb safety record, one of the best in the industry. Only six people lost their lives at Riverview and only two of the deaths were considered to be the fault of the rides or the park. Most of the accidents on roller coasters have always been due to the foolhardiness of riders who feel compelled to exhibit their bravado by standing up in the speeding cars.

The spectacular rides were not sufficient to secure the continued success of urban Riverview, which began a rapid decline in the early 1960s. The park became the grounds for racial and gang conflicts as well as hordes of city youths bent on vandalism and robbery. The penny arcade was an easy target; gangs would smash machines for a handful of coins. Chicago's population soon stayed away from the rough, dangerous atmosphere of Riverview. A similar fate doomed many other parks, most notably Glen Echo, near Washington, D.C. Like Olympic Park, Riverview became, as the city grew up around it, a prime location for development. On 3 October 1967 Riverview was sold for $6.5 million, a sum that today would not even rebuild the Bobs.[27] Following the sale, all of the rides, including the seven roller coasters, were reduced to mournful piles of broken wood and steel by bulldozers, to be replaced with a shopping center, a factory, and parking lots.

☐ **Kennywood**   In 1898 the Monongahela Street Railway company leased a country picnic grove from owner Anthony Kenny, whose family had originally purchased the land for "five pounds, ten shillings, six pence and a barrel of whiskey."[28] Located 12 miles from Pittsburgh, Pennsylvania, on a bluff overlooking the Monongahela River, the Kenny property became a popular picnic site as early as the 1860s.

It was financier Andrew Mellon, founder of the Mellon National Bank, who chose the name Kennywood for the trolley park. Mellon, one of the owners of the Monongahela Street Railway, recognized the value of the goodwill the Kenny family had created over the years by allowing area residents free access to the groves for picnicking and leisure activities. The railway company designed the park with buildings and rides surrounding an artificial lake dotted with islands and wooden walking bridges. There was a dance pavilion, a merry-go-round, and a casino, as well as landscaped gardens and shady groves of trees. While most parks of the period erected hastily constructed buildings that appeared to be little more than framework and roof, Kennywood's structures were substantial, and in fact the casino and merry-go-round buildings are still in use nearly a century after their construction. The park's first hand-carved merry-go-round, built by the master, Gustav Dentzel of Philadelphia, had stationary animal figures, since the jumping mechanism had not yet been invented. Twenty-seven years later, William Dentzel, Gustav's son, built a magnificent, four-row merry-go-round with prancing steeds that has been preserved with dedication by Kennywood and still entrances riders today. In 1977 the carousel was registered as a historic landmark by the Pittsburgh History and Landmarks Foundation.[29]

The trolley ride to Kennywood for Pittsburgh residents provided thrills nearly equal to those within the park itself. The line ran through the steel mill areas of Homestead and Duquesne, then climbed a winding route with curves right on the edge of cliffs overlooking the Monongahela River Valley. On the return trip in the evening darkness, the fires from the blast furnaces of the steel mills created a spectacle of industrial prowess that rivaled the park's own wondrous display of light. Since the street railway paid a flat fee for all electricity used, Kennywood was laced with thousands of sparkling incandescent bulbs. By 1900 picnickers were entertained by music emanating from the magnificent bandshell constructed by the Mellons at a phenomenal cost for the period of $15,000. One of the first figure-eight roller coasters was built by Fred Ingersoll, a Pittsburgh native, at Kennywood in 1902. The coaster joined other attractions, including rowboats, tennis courts, a dining hall, a shooting gallery, a Ferris wheel, a bowling alley, and the Old Mill toboggan ride.[30]

As the street railways began to merge and the Monongahela Railway joined with the Pittsburgh Railways Company, ownership and management of Kennywood changed hands repeatedly during the early years of the century. In 1906, eager to divest itself of the amusement park business, the Pittsburgh Railways Company leased the park to Andrew Stephen McSwigan, Frederick W. Henninger, and A. F. Meghan. A major factor in Kennywood's success has been continued control and management by the Henninger family from 1906 to today.[31] The new owners recognized that picnickers were their stable clientele, but that thrill rides and entertainment would be the lures to attract the picnic trade. On 30 May 1919 the park hosted a picnic jointly sponsored by Carnegie-Illinois Steel and the Duquesne community that was attended by 30,000 people.[32] While many other parks in the Pittsburgh area closed when the trolley companies relinquished ownership, Kennywood survived because of aggressive and dedicated management.

To counter Coney Island and other amusement parks' unsavory reputation, McSwigan and Henninger, both men of strict moral convictions, advertised and rigorously adhered to their slogan, "No fakes, no liquor, no gambling, and no disorder." Their park was kept clean and moral to a fault. A 1914 brochure says of the unbending park police force, "Courteous uniformed police are always present to suppress the slightest semblance of disorder." The partners were distressed by bathing-suit fashions following the opening of the swimming pool in 1925. Guards were instructed to enforce prohibitions against one-piece suits. A member of the McSwigan family warned swimwear manufacturers in a 1932 column in the *Pittsburgh Catholic* that pool owners were outraged by "such indecencies as the modern bathing suits bring. . . . the current tendency in bathing suits has already gone too far."[33] Henninger and McSwigan were prime movers in the founding of the National Amusement Park Association, now the International Association of Amusement Parks and Attractions. Through their influence, McSwigan and Henninger established the upholding of high ethical standards as an enduring criterion of the association.

In 1920 the building of large roller coasters began in Kennywood when leading coaster engineers John A. Miller and Harry C. Baker, who had just established a partnership, were hired to design a new high-speed coaster. The Jack Rabbit, at a cost of $50,000, employed the newly invented system of wheels underneath the tracks to hold the cars on track, an innovation that allowed steep drops; the Jack Rabbit boasted a heart-stopping 85-foot double-dip drop through a ravine. John Miller on his own built the Pippin in 1924, using another ravine at the opposite end of the park. Miller's Racer, in which two tracks allow cars to race side-by-side, was completed in 1927. The only continuous-track racing coaster still in existence today, Kennywood's Racer is a gem of symmetry, perhaps the most beautiful traditional woodie that fans can still see and experience.[34] In the late 1960s, at a cost of $200,000, Andrew Vettel remodeled Miller's Pippin to create one of the greatest coasters ever built, the Thunderbolt. This coaster looks relatively tame to observers because the deep ravine is cleverly hidden by trees and fences. Midway through the ride, cars whirl through turns in opposing directions, disorienting the rider, who then suddenly plunges down the ravine in double-dip dives of 80 and 90 feet. Robert Cartmell rated Kennywood's Thunderbolt the "ultimate coaster" in his 1974 survey published in the *New York Times*.[35] Cartmell also credits Kennywood Park as a significant force behind the survival of the roller coaster, since Kennywood continued to build and maintain its marvelous coasters when most of the woodies were being abandoned and bulldozed.[36] The park became known as the "Roller Coaster Capital of the World."

Kennywood remained fairly stable during the Great Depression. Even in 1933, when business dropped 63 percent from the 1929 high, upkeep and entertainment were not cut, and the relaxing picnic facilities, roller coasters, dance bands, and swimming pool continued to attract loyal clientele, who found a meticulously maintained park despite the depressed economy.[37] A kiddieland was added in 1947 in response to the baby boom. It was the 1950s, with competition from television and the renewed growth of the automobile as the primary mode of transportation, that forced Kennywood to change with the times or decline along with almost all of the traditional parks. Fortunately, the Kennywood management was up to the challenge. They cleverly and effectively turned the popularity of television, their chief rival for leisure time, to the park's advantage, first by running advertising spots on local stations during the most popular children's programs, and then by presenting television stars in appearances at the park. Captain Video and his Video Ranger appeared in 1953, as did Clarabell, Princess Summer Fall Winter Spring, and Chief Thunder Chicken from "The Howdy Doody Show." Superman George Reeves, Lassie, Gabby Hayes, Captain Kangaroo, the Cisco Kid, and Zorro all performed at the park, but the biggest draw of all was the Lone Ranger, who rode in the park on his horse, Silver, on 27 August, 1957.[38] Henninger and McSwigan were right on the mark when they gambled that everyone would want to see in the flesh the personalities viewed on the little screen in their homes.

Because Kennywood was located well beyond Pittsburgh's urban growth area, it could also survive the cessation of the Number 68 streetcar service in 1958. A widened boulevard leading into the park, better highways, and available land for parking facilities encouraged automobile traffic. After the Pennsylvania Railroad dropped all excursion trains to the park in 1960, the automobile became the only mode of access to Kennywood. Lack of access by public transportation was a blessing for the park, enabling it to avoid the destruction, danger, and vandalism generated by urban gangs in other parks. The management could maintain Kennywood's clean, safe, relaxing family atmosphere, though it could not continue to enforce its traditional dress customs as shorts, T-shirts, sneakers, and even short shorts replaced the suits, ties, and Sunday dresses of earlier years.

Fred Henninger died in 1950 and his partner Andrew McSwigan passed away in 1964 after a long illness, but Henninger's three sons enthusiastically took over management of the business. Through the 1960s, when even the biggest parks were closing, Kennywood added a new ride every year, including the $100,000 Turnpike, where riders operate little cars that can travel at a maximum speed of 12 miles per hour to traverse a course complete with bridges, underpasses, and a miniature Gulf service station. Modeled after a ride at Disneyland Park, the Turnpike appeals to young would-be drivers anxiously awaiting adulthood and their chance to get behind the wheel of a real automobile. For those preferring nostalgia, by the middle 1960s the Gateway Clipper offered a cruise service from the Pittsburgh docks up the Monongahela River to Kennywood in McKeesport.

The park's established reputation readied it for its greatest expansion in the early 1970s. The park's first million-dollar-plus ride was the Log Jammer, a water flume built by Arrow Development Company in 1975. It has maintained its high ridership over the years, with a per-hour capacity of 1,400 people. The third generation of the dedicated Henninger family led the mid-1970s development of the park, adding extensive landscaping, new rides, restaurants, and "theme" characters such as Kenny Kangaroo. The 1980s commenced with the space-age roar and speed of the Laser Loop, built by West German Anton Schwarzkopf and marketed by the international amusement ride manufacturer Intamin AG of Switzerland. The coasterlike "shuttle loop" jets out of the loading station, attaining a speed of 54 miles per hour within five seconds, whips through a vertical loop, climbs an incline of 139 feet at a 70-degree angle, then suddenly stalls out at the top with no track ahead, only to speed backward down then up another incline, stall out again, and finally burst back to the station.[39] Riders experience a near weightlessness quite similar to that felt by astronauts.

In spite of the high-tech rides and borrowings from theme parks, the management still views Kennywood as a local and limited regional family picnic park. Its survival when most other traditional amusement parks have closed, even those similarly emphasizing rides and coasters like Riverview, is due primarily to two factors: dedicated, continuous family management that for nearly a century has consistently put profits back into the park in order to ensure constant change and meticulous maintenance, and location well beyond the urban limits of Pittsburgh, which has ensured that Kennywood would not be a victim of urban development pressures, racial tensions, or gang violence. Its rural site allowed Kennywood to structure the park for the automobile culture with an appealing balance of exhilarating thrill rides, entertainment, the serenity of picnic groves, and the nostalgia of preserved tradition, most evident in a magnificent carousel from a bygone era of craftsmanship.

☐ **Cedar Point, Sandusky, Ohio**   Located at the tip of a seven-mile peninsula that separates Sandusky Bay from Lake Erie near the city of Sandusky, Ohio, Cedar Point began as a summer resort as early as 1870, when Louis Zistel, a German immigrant cabinetmaker, opened a beer garden, dance floor, and bathhouse. Unlike most of the parks of the period, it was not situated near a major city. Instead, it lies about 60 miles west of Cleveland and 60 miles east of Toledo. Its rural setting, in the center of the Detroit-Cleveland-Akron-Pittsburgh transportation corridor, would be a major factor in its continued prosperity for more than a century.[40] Entrepreneur and showman George A. Boeckling acquired the resort in 1897 and immediately began to build a midway with rides and other amusements. With a flair much like that of George Tilyou and Thompson and Dundy of Coney Island, Boeckling was the force behind the creation of Cedar Point as one of the nation's finest resorts. Since Cedar Point boasted one of the best sand beaches in the North, Boeckling wisely developed the area as both a resort and an amusement park. In 1905 he built the magnificent Hotel Breakers, containing 600 rooms and a grand lobby graced by chandeliers created by the Louis C. Tiffany studios in New York and stained glass windows crafted by Tiffany glass cutter Louis Buser.

Although the hotel was elegant, the amusement park and midway were pure Coney Island. Boeckling installed incandescent lights with lavish abandon, staged vaudeville acts, and even permanently imported a tribe of Philippine natives who were, in showmanship style, billed as "headhunters." Like Coney Island, the bizarre architecture and ornamentation were a jumble of spires, domes, and minarets, all seemingly placed in disorienting confusion. One of Boeckling's most successful publicity spectacles was pioneer aviator Glenn "The Birdman" Curtiss's 1910 flight from Euclid Beach Park in Cleveland to Cedar Point, a distance of 64 miles. Occurring only seven years after the Wright Brothers' first sputtering flight in 1903, Curtiss's feat eclipsed the distance record of 25 miles over the English Channel then held by French aviator Louis Bleriot. The result was national acclaim for Curtiss, who would become a prominent manufacturer of aircraft in the early days of avia-

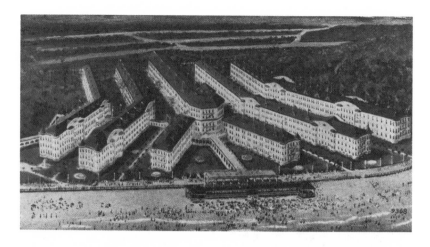

Hotel Breakers, Cedar Point park, Sandusky, Ohio, 1905. *Courtesy Cedar Point park.*

tion, and priceless, enduring publicity for Cedar Point. The park boasts another landmark in American history, for it is said that Knute Rockne and teammate Gus Dorais perfected football's forward pass on the Cedar Point beach while working as lifeguards in 1913. By 1903 Boeckling's yearly profits were $110,000, rising to $400,000 in 1908, and well surpassing $1 million each summer in the 1920s.[41]

Cedar Point was unique among the early parks in that it was not a trolley park. Visitors traveled to the park by steamship and by railroad. Steamships provided daily runs in the summer months from both Cleveland and Detroit, while railroad excursions, often sponsored by industrial companies or churches, brought a steady clientele. Not until 1914 did Boeckling, well aware of the growing popularity of the automobile, build a concrete highway traversing nearly the entire peninsula. Cedar Point provided the quintessential amusement park experience with its up-to-date rides, unceasing vaudeville entertainment, freak shows, fun houses, games of chance, penny arcades, festive lights, garish architecture, band concerts and dances, and holiday foods, all promoting an exotic aura where everyone abandoned themselves to uninhibited fun. In 1918 the new Leap Frog Railway, billed as the longest and largest scenic railway (roller coaster) in America, dazzled and thrilled war-weary summer visitors. But there were also quiet, restful lagoons, classic fountains and sculpture, cooling shade trees, and performances by

Glenn Curtiss completing his record-breaking flight from Euclid Beach park, Cleveland, to Cedar Point park, Sandusky, Ohio, 1910. *Courtesy Cedar Point park.*

highbrow artists such as opera singers Enrico Caruso and Nellie Melba at the Hotel Breakers. By the 1920s Cedar Point deservedly basked in the summer sunshine as "The Queen of American Watering Places." The 1929 season opened spectacularly with the inauguration of the Cedar Point Cyclone, a roller coaster built by Harry Traver. Publicity claimed it was "scientifically built for speed," and its steep descents and sharply banked turns made it a Midwest legend.

The 1930s brought not only the Great Depression but also the death of Cedar Point's guiding genius and owner, George Boeckling, in 1931. The park began a rapid decline similar to that of most other parks in the country but perhaps quickened by the unwillingness of Boeckling's heirs to invest steadily in capital improvements or even in significant maintenance of the facilities. Steamship and rail lines continued to service Cedar Point, but with reduced schedules. The repeal of Prohibition in 1933 resulted in increased attendance and some rejuvenation of the park and concessions. When roller skating became a craze, the Coliseum dance floor was converted to a huge skating rink. But the crowds that came to Cedar Point during the World War II years to listen and dance to the big bands of Glenn Miller, the Dorsey brothers, Stan Kenton, and other top bandleaders, could not help noticing the peeling

Scenic Railway, Cedar Point park, Sandusky, Ohio, ca. 1920. *Courtesy Cedar Point park.*

paint, weeds, trash, and inoperable, rusting rides. Rumors of a polio epidemic kept the public away in the early 1950s. Even the Hotel Breakers could not compete with new motels that offered private baths, air-conditioning, and television to the traveling motorist.

Cedar Point's location would save it from the fate of nearby Euclid Beach Park in Cleveland. Like Olympic and Riverview parks, Euclid Beach would succumb to the urban pressures of development and racial tensions, finally closing in 1969 after decades of decline.[42] But Cedar Point's site would intrigue Toledo municipal-bond dealer George A. Roose, who initially viewed the scenic peninsula as a valuable location for an exclusive residential-marina development. Roose's plans would be foiled, however, by the unprecedented action of the Ohio State legislature, which insisted that the area remain a public recreation resort. Governor Frank Lausche vowed the state would condemn the property and purchase the land at a "fair price" if Roose pursued his development plans. In 1957 Roose and Cleveland banker Emile Legros did acquire controlling interest in Cedar Point Park for the sum of $313,000, but the partners announced that they would not only preserve the park but also develop it into the "Disneyland of the Midwest."[43]

Surprising even himself, George Roose became fascinated with Cedar Point as he spent the 1958 season in residence studying all aspects of the operation. Deciding that the park would need a major investment to survive, Roose and his associates purchased total control in January 1959. With large loans from the Cleveland Trust Company, Roose began a $1.2 million facelift for the 1959 season, including a partial refurbishing of the Hotel Breakers, new midway rides and attractions, a marina, and, significantly, a new causeway to replace the narrow road that had been a bottleneck to automobile travel. Though profits were modest in 1959, in the same year the Cleveland Real Estate Board appraised Cedar Point's value at $6.6 million.[44]

Roose and Legros were well aware of the unprecedented success of Disneyland Park following its opening in 1955; therefore, after the 1959 season, they hired the firm of Marco Engineering, whose president was a former general manager of Disneyland, to produce a comprehensive five-year plan for Cedar Point. Noting its ideal location within easy driving distance of six major cities, the developing interstate highway system, rising affluence, the emphasis on family recreation that could be expected to follow the baby boom, and the continued increase in leisure time, the Marco report recommended that substantial investment in capital improvements, complemented by effective management and promotion, would result in substantial dividends for the owners.[45]

Unlike the Disney and theme parks, which were conceived and totally designed before construction began, the new Cedar Point did not suddenly rise from the ashes of its past. Roose and Legros wisely built on the traditions already in place by devoting each year's profits to the modernization and improvement of the existing park. They were careful, however, to incorporate many of the key elements in Disneyland's success, namely, extreme cleanliness, family appeal, clean-cut employees, guest services, and effective, widespread advertising. Press releases billing Cedar Point as the "Ohio Disneyland" announced plans to invest $16 million in a glorious restoration of the park. The owners were careful to create an atmosphere of nostalgia by retaining much of the old Cedar Point. The Hotel Breakers, modernized to include air conditioning and private baths but retaining its original classic form, was placed on the National Register of Historic Places in 1982. A guest at the hotel in the 1990s pleasurably experiences turn-of-the-century ambiance, genteel leisure, and a tangible aura of bygone seaside summer culture. The Grand Pavilion, built in 1888, has been preserved and expanded to serve as a convention center and cafeteria. A grove of cottonwood trees surrounding the hotel has been left untouched. Sculpture, massive antique iron flower urns, lampposts, and gargoyles have been integrated into the modern park. One tradition has been abandoned, however—racial segregation. Like most major resorts, Cedar Point had excluded blacks from its hotels, but in 1961 the National Association for the Advancement of Colored People recorded a complaint against the Cedar Point management and forced the removal of the outdated policy.[46]

By 1961 attendance was up to 1.5 million with a gross income of $3.5 million. Attendance at the park rose from 970,000 in 1959 to 1.5 million in 1963 and more than 2.5 million in 1967. In 1965 it was estimated that the 2 million visitors spent an average of $3.75 apiece for a day at the park. Roose actualized one of his own dreams when he built an authentic narrow-gauge steam railway using restored antique locomotives. The Cedar Point & Lake Erie Railroad carried its first passengers in 1963, powered by locomotives originally built in 1902 and 1911. Even after the retirement of George Roose and the subsequent death of Emile Legros in 1975, the new, energetic leader, Robert L. Munger, Jr., maintained the strategy of continuous investment in the facilities, devoting $37 million to improvements from 1969 to 1979. Besides new restaurants, shops, and such, a Frontier Trail theme area opened in 1971, and terrorizing roller coasters began to dominate the grounds and horizon in the 1970s.[47]

The park's emergence as a theme park in the late 1970s and 1980s is chronicled in chapter 6. In 1989 Cedar Point ranked number nine among the top theme parks in the United States in attendance, attracting 3.15 million visitors.[48] Its attendance surpasses that of such nationally advertised parks as Six Flags over Georgia, Opryland, Six Flags Magic Mountain, and Busch Gardens' Old Country in Williamsburg, Virginia. Cedar Point is now an updated park where much of the chaos and garishness is gone, along with such earlier vulgarities as freak shows and exhibitions of primitive natives. Instead, modern thrill rides and conveniences grace an atmosphere where the traditional amusement park can be subtly sensed and the gentler times of a bygone era are cleverly superimposed on today's technologies.

□   The Closing of Crystal Beach Park: Memories
     Shattered by an Auctioneer's Hammer

Labor Day 1989 witnessed the last screams from riders of the famed Comet roller coaster as the 101-year-old Crystal Beach Park on the shores of Lake Erie in Crystal Beach, Ontario, closed forever. A $7 million capital improvement plan initiated in 1986, which included re-conditioning the beach house and the entertainment center, the addition of a beach club, and even the revival of ferry service on the *Americana* from Buffalo, New York, was not enough to save the traditional 80-acre park. The Comet, Crystal Beach's 1946 wooden coaster, had through the years retained its Top Ten status as one of America's best coasters, as rated by the American Coaster Enthusiasts. The park also boasted the Giant Coaster, built in 1916, one of the last two remaining side friction coasters in existence.

Owners Joseph Biondolillo, Ed Hall (the son of the park's founder, G. C. Hall), and Rudy Bonifascio blame the park's sudden demise, after a century-long span as a favorite summer outing destination, on the competition from new theme parks. Located close by are Fantasy Island on Grand Island, New York, Darien Lake Park in Darien Center, New York, Canada's Wonderland in Maple, Ontario, and Marineland in Niagara Falls, Ontario. The owners recognized that a $20 million investment would be necessary to return the park to competitive status, but that even then a lack of land for adequate parking space would limit attendance. The owners plan to convert the property into a marina complex.[49]

Crystal Beach had been in decline for years. Loyal fans rightly blame the owners and managers for the closing of the park. Almost everything had become shabby and inoperable: the Laughing Lady was silent except for her unoiled creaking limbs; real cobwebs infested the Magic Palace fun house; a pop-up corpse sported duct tape on its head; the brightly painted colors of Kiddyland had faded; the magnificent white and gold merry-go-round had long been dismantled and the hand-carved wooden horses, lions, and tigers sold to the highest bidders; and the sounds of the big bands had faded away decades ago. But memories will be cherished for years to come. Many folks remember pleasant summer cruises to the park on the *Canadiana,* the huge open ferry that would skim across Lake Erie from Buffalo to Crystal Beach. Forty-something parents recall getting lost in the fun house, being scared senseless on the Comet, stealing kisses in the Old Mill, and eating scrumptious sugar waffles. A young mother admits, "The bumper cars were my all-time favorite, but I didn't realize it until I was there with my children and saw the looks on their faces as they came full speed ahead into Mom." Older folks talk of roller skating during the Great Depression and dancing to the big bands of the 1940s. Even in the late 1980s, many traditionalists found Crystal Beach far more appealing than its glitzy theme park competitors. It's "a bit worn out but more

Auction announcement for Crystal Beach Amusement Park, 17 October 1989.

comfortable and cheaper than the new model." "It's junky, but there aren't a lot of lines." "You need $100 a day for [Canada's Wonderland]. We can spend the whole day here for $35."[50]

On 17 October, 1989 the auctioneer's hammer fell on every scrap of Crystal Beach from benches, statues, and signs ("Next Dance," "Men Must Wear Shirts," "Hall's Original Crystal Beach Suckers") to the antique electric cars, the Big Eli Ferris wheel, the Flying Bobs, the Laff-in-the-Dark, and the magnificent Comet. Nostalgia seekers did not have a chance, as professionals from around the country raised bids well beyond the sentimental price of memories. Jane Vollmer, a former lyricist for the Duke Ellington band, hoped to bid on a piece of memorabilia to preserve in the Ellington Room at the Smithsonian Institution, but her dreams were dashed by the high "price of the past."[51] The Comet was bought by the owner of other amusement parks and, reportedly, it may soon be reassembled to thrill riders in a Lake George, New York, park.

The Comet roller coaster at Crystal Beach park, Crystal Beach, Ontario, Canada. Photograph by S. A. Amatrano.

5

The Disney Transformation

Disneyland Park: A Sanitized, Electronic Actualization of the American Dream

The epos of Disney is "Paradise Regained."
—Sergei Eisenstein[1]

ON 17 JULY 1955 AN AMERICAN ICON WITH perhaps no match in popular culture exploded into being amid the orange groves of Anaheim, California, irrevocably altering the course of the amusement industry. Disneyland Park, created from the imagination and psyche of Walt Disney, would become a compelling vision of "paradise regained" for the American public in the latter half of the 20th century. This place of fantasy, fortified against the intrusion of the real world by a massive barrier, actualizes a perfect world of pleasure where electronics, plastics, and psychology are harnessed for fun and escape from the fetters of adulthood. Its ingenious juxtaposition of advanced technologies with a nostalgic atmosphere of simpler times and locales preserves an ideal vision of American history. With phenomenal success it mirrors the desires of its "guests" regarding the shape of the future.

□ Walter Elias Disney

Who was this grass-roots genius, Walter Elias Disney, who possessed such a precise, intuitive identification with the impulses and dreams of the ordinary American? Among the several biographies of Disney that have been published, the most comprehensive and objective are Richard Schickel's *The Disney Version: The Life, Times, Art, and Commerce of Walt Disney,* and *Disney's World* by Leonard Mosley.[2] While there is no need to duplicate available detailed biographies here, discussion of formative elements in Disney's younger days will assist in understanding the personal motivations shaping Disneyland and the resulting complex, omnipresent cultural effects of the Disney phenomenon.

Walter Elias Disney was born on 5 December 1901 in the bedroom of the modest family home at 1249 Tripp Avenue in Chicago. Named in honor of his father and the local Congregational minister who baptized him, Walt was the fourth son of Elias and Flora Disney. Something of a drifter, father Elias had been lured from the Kissimmee area in central Florida (ironically, precisely where Walt Disney World Resort would be built) to Chicago by the construction boom associated with the World's Columbian Exposition, where he secured work as a carpenter and furniture maker. Walt's brother Roy had been born during the exposition in 1893 and very nearly was named Columbus by a father grateful for the livelihood made possible by the world's fair. It is intriguing to speculate on the influence recollections and tales of the Columbian Exposition transferred from parents and older siblings may have had on the younger members of the Disney family. Brothers Herbert, Raymond, Roy, and Walt were joined by sister Ruth Flora in 1903, whose arrival may have influenced Elias's decision to flee from raucous, violent, and lawless Chicago in order to preserve his family from corruption.

The impassively stern and excessively frugal Elias purchased a farm in Marceline, a small community of 3,000 people about 100 miles from Kansas City. The family settled on the farm, near the main line of the Atchison, Topeka & Santa Fe Railroad, in the spring of 1906, when Walt was five years old. Within a few months the two older brothers, Herbert and Raymond, ran off back to Chicago and by all accounts never were brought back into Walt's life or any of his business ventures. Meanwhile the young Walt was enchanted by the farm, especially its animals, both wild and domesticated, by the local railroad, and by the town of Marceline, whose Main Street would be idealized years later as Main Street, U.S.A., the entrance to Disneyland.

It has been assumed that Disney embraced the animals around the farm as playmates because of a lack of companionship in his family. The forbidding Elias was an active advocate of corporal punishment who never allowed his sons an allowance or any type of plaything. Roy was much older and too busy working on the farm, while mother Flora, exhausted by chores and broken in spirit by her despotic husband, had no time for her young son.[3] Walt never learned to play the games of a boy; instead he anthropomorphized pigs, chickens, rabbits, field mice, and other creatures into his personal friends. His best "friend" was probably Porker, the sow he would jump astride and ride until thrown off into the mud.

Although Walt would later romanticize this period in his animated films and in the amusement parks, the times were actually brutally hard for the family. Successive years of crop failure, along with outbreaks of swine fever and typhoid from tainted water, resulted in the loss of the farm. Because of his endless chores, Disney may have viewed the raw, natural earth as a challenge that drove him to tame, transform, and order the land to create something productive and useful.

In the summer of 1910, with Walt at the threshold of his impressionable teens, the family moved to Kansas City. Psychologically immured within his successive failures, father Elias became even more tyrannical, resulting in his two sons' contributing most of the work toward running his extensive newspaper route. Though Roy and Walt were dragged out of their beds at 3:30 in the morning all year round to deliver newspapers, they received no wages or allowances. Walt Disney's adolescent years were ruled by a repressive, increasingly cruel father who was incapable of love or affection. Elias's rigid self-righteousness, extreme conservatism, and suppression of emotion was mirrored in the strict moral climate of Kansas City during the years the Disneys remained there, 1910–17. As discussed in the previous chapter, Recreation Superintendent Fred McClure and Board of Public Welfare investigator Fred R. Johnson diligently regulated all types of amusement to dispel any transgressions from a puritanical, sexually repressive policy of social control.

Given the ages of brothers Roy and Walt, it seems most likely that they must have at times slipped away from Elias's tyranny to revel in the unbridled joys of one or both of the Kansas City amusement parks, Forest Park and Electric Park. Both of the boys held part-time jobs kept secret from their father, thus earning spending money of their own. The amusement parks of Kansas City no doubt offered a brief release from the bleak daily lives of the toil-weary adolescent Disney boys. Walt enjoyed one summer of freedom as a candy salesclerk on the Santa Fe Railroad, traveling between Kansas City and Chicago. He would sometimes ride in the coal car right behind the locomotive and leisurely watch the countryside go by. For a boy whose life had been dominated by backbreaking work, the steam railroads would become even more splendid in his memory.

Disney openly admitted that during his adolescent years girls were

of no interest; in fact they were simply a "nuisance." He is reported to
have commented, "I was normal, but girls bored me. They still do.
Their interests are just different."[4] This attitude may well have been
formed by the nearly total lack of affection in his family. Only with his
brother Roy is there any evidence of companionship and attachment.
His childhood and adolescence were totally dominated by work—there
was no time for frivolous attention to girls. And there apparently was
no sexual awakening in his formative years.

Following a brief stint as a Red Cross driver in France at the end of
World War I, young Walt left the parental home for good to join his
brother Roy back in Kansas City. Walt was hired as an apprentice by a
small advertising agency, Pesmen-Rubin, where he met and began a
collaboration that would last nearly the rest of his life with the shy
draftsman Ubbe Iwwerks, who at Disney's suggestion slightly shortened his name to Ub Iwerks. When both were laid off, Walt decided he
and Ub should go into business together as commercial artists. With
$250 Walt had saved from his Red Cross days, the two partners opened
Iwerks & Disney.

After only a few months, temptation came Disney's way in the
form of a $40-a-week offer from the Kansas City Film Ad Company, a
venture that made one-minute animated cartoon advertisements for
showing in local theaters. Disney was fascinated by the extremely primitive animation techniques, and both he and Iwerks viewed the salary as
a comparative fortune. Though the partners split up, the separation was
brief, as Iwerks joined the company within a few months. Iwerks was
the technical genius from the beginning. Influenced by his friend's
books on cinema and art, Disney patronized the Kansas City Public
Library, where he had access to books and articles on cartooning and
film animation. He became familiar with the work of perhaps the most
innovative filmmaker of the time, Georges Méliès, who had merged live
actors with sketched backgrounds in his 1902 film *Le Voyage dans la
lune* (The trip to the moon) and with newspaper cartoonist Winsor
McCay, whose pioneering 1909 cartoon *Gertie the Dinosaur* ran briefly
in Kansas City movie theaters. Gertie was probably the first animated
creature to have a personality—she smiled, laughed, danced, and even
wept when she accidentally trod on a friendly mouse.[5]

Soon Disney and Iwerks were making their own cartoon shorts
with a borrowed camera in Disney's garage. The satirical shorts on local
topics were sold to the owner of a local chain of movie theaters and
dubbed Newman's Laugh-o-Grams. Success allowed Disney to raise
some funds for the production of a pair of more ambitious seven-minute
cartoons, *Puss in Boots* and *Red Riding Hood*. He and Iwerks risked all

they could borrow or beg on the production of one more film, *Alice's Wonderland*, using a real-life Alice, a six-year-old moppet, filmed in front of a background of animated cartoon animals. But *Alice* was too late to save Disney's business, and he filed for bankruptcy in the spring of 1923.

An official legend tells it, in July 1923 the 22-year-old Disney boarded the train for Los Angeles, where Roy Disney was then living, with only $40 in his pocket (from the sale of his camera) and one print of the *Alice* film.[6] With money borrowed from Roy and his uncle Robert, who also lived in Los Angeles, Walt, doing all the work himself, produced another Alice film, *Alice's Day at Sea*, and sent it off to New York film booker Margaret Winkler. When a check for $1,500 and a contract for a series of six *Alice in Cartoonland* films arrived for Walt, Disney Productions was officially born. Disney quickly convinced Ub Iwerks to come to Los Angeles for a promised salary of $40 a week. For the next few years Roy, Walt, Ub, and a few "inkers," as the women who inked in the drawn cartoon frames were known, continued to produce *Alice* episodes, but production costs always came close to or surpassed receipts. Although crude, the *Alice* films clearly revealed Disney's major talents, that is, his apt blending of live and animated action and his uncanny ability to recognize and exploit the potential of a technological advance.

Roy's marriage to longtime sweetheart Edna Francis, and Walt's resultant loss of his roommate and cook, served as the catalyst for Walt to look around for a wife. She was close by: one of the inker girls in his shop, Lillian Bounds. They were married on 13 July 1925 after a brief and lackluster courtship. Both Mosley and Schickel report that Disney developed a toothache on his wedding night aboard a Pullman train and spent the time not with his bride but with a porter polishing passengers' shoes.[7]

At about the same time as their marriages, Walt and Roy decided to draw out their meager savings to build a new, spacious studio on Hyperion Avenue. When the facility was completed, Walt changed the name of the concern from Disney Productions to Walt Disney Studio. It was from this point that Roy was forced to take a backseat while Walt took charge. On a train trip from New York back to Los Angeles, Walt reminisced on a pet mouse he had kept in his Kansas City office and began to sketch a perky rodent with pointed snout and round belly. Mortimer, soon to become Mickey Mouse, was born. Iwerks and other Disney employees were quick to see the facial resemblance between Walt and Mickey.

Plane Crazy and *Gallopin' Gaucho*, the first Mickey Mouse cartoons, appeared in 1928 to polite but unenthusiastic audiences. In late 1927, just before Mickey's debut, the first talkie, *The Jazz Singer,* opened in New York. Disney immediately jumped on the new technologies for sound and vowed that the third Mickey Mouse film would boast elaborate sound effects and music. Disney himself served as and remained the preadolescent, high-pitched voice of Mickey as first heard in *Steamboat Willie,* ready for release by the fall of 1928.

The original Mickey was not quite as cuddly as the contemporary version. *Time* magazine in 1954 described the original rodent as "a skinny little squeaker with matchstick legs, shoe button eyes and a long, pointy nose. His teeth were sharp and fierce when he laughed, more like a real mouse's than they are today." Mickey's disposition, too, matched his teeth; he was "cocky and cruel, at best a fresh and bratty kid, at worst a diminutive and sadistic monster."[8] Mickey not only became rounder and cuter over the years but also quickly became well-behaved, for Disney soon recognized that audiences were unwilling to accept a transgressive cartoon mouse-hero. Mickey should be on a pedestal; Donald Duck would soon become the repository of mischief and anger. But Mickey remained a large-eared alter-ego for his creator, in voice, facial appearance, and most notably in subtle psychic traits. David I. Berland, in his psychological study of Disney, "Disney and Freud: Walt Meets the Id," analyzes the mouse and his creator: "Mickey is sexless. . . . Because of his sexual neutrality, sexual envy and jealousy do not occur in the unconscious of the viewer, making Mickey a safe identification object. Perhaps Disney was aware of the importance of this sexual neutrality when he appointed himself as Mickey's voice, the voice of a sexually ambiguous prepubescent child."[9] The indifference and violence of Walt's youth shaped the adult man whose only passion was ceaseless work and who never stopped trying to create an idyllic, if illusory, eternal childhood free of anything threatening, including forces that contribute to growth.

From the birth of Mickey, the Walt Disney Studio stayed in high gear, producing along with the mouse cartoons the *Silly Symphonies, The Skeleton Dance, The Three Little Pigs,* and many others, but always at costs that were barely recouped. Disney's next project, however, would change his fortunes forever, a full-length cartoon feature film. In the fall of 1934 he brought his animators together and outlined the scenario of *Snow White and the Seven Dwarfs.* Once again Walt's dreams would take every cent of the Disney brothers' money and much more. While Disney's *Snow White* would become the apotheosis of innocence, the ordeal of its production was anything but. In the nearly five years of *Snow White*'s production, the studio staff grew from 150 employees to 750, with the addition of mainly lower-level animators and inkers. There was a great deal of commitment and enthusiasm around the studio, with artists confident they were in the forefront of a new art form; the boss himself, still in his early thirties, was full of exuberance and inventive ideas. However, in time Disney's endless, demanding production quotas, long work hours, and miserly pay created a quiet resentment. Workers were frustrated by the strict specialization of tasks. The artistic price was the loss of individual initiative and a withholding of a certain amount of creativity. Still, *Snow White*, which premiered in Hollywood on 21 December 1937, became one of the most successful films of all time. Its first run earned over $8 million for the Walt Disney Studio; more importantly, it established Disney as the foremost animation artist of his time.

During the war years, Disney turned to making war films for the Department of Defense. *Victory through Air Power* was designed to demonstrate the power and effectiveness of large-scale strategic bombing. It was dramatic, with hordes of planes majestically filling the skies, and it conveyed the power of the American war machine. But critic James Agee perceived its detachment from the effects of bombing and its romantic attitude toward the technology of war: "I noticed, uneasily, that there were no suffering and dying enemy civilians under all those proud promises of bombs; no civilians at all, in fact. . . . this victory-in-a-vacuum . . . is so morally simple a matter . . . of machine-eat-machine."[10]

☐ Disneyland Park

During the studio's relatively fallow war years, Disney was nurturing his vision of a new venture, an amusement park different from all other such parks, where there would be none of the dirtiness, sham, deterioration, and menacing atmosphere that dominated all existing amusement enterprises. Roy Disney bluntly refused to support Walt's scheme with funds from the heavily indebted studio, and Walt was forced to raise the money himself for his dream, already named Disneyland. Cashing in an insurance policy provided funds for a field survey of existing amusement parks in the United States and abroad. Walt was particularly impressed with the orderly and relaxed aura of Tivoli Gardens in Copenhagen and with Greenfield Village, a historical park in Dearborn, Michigan, that celebrates American entrepreneurial ingenuity.[11]

Because of Roy's firm unwillingness to support Disneyland Park with studio funds, Walt financed his newly created WED Enterprises in

1952 with his own meager resources and established a small staff of designers, whom he immediately dubbed "imagineers," to develop plans, designs, and models for the park. In the same year, he commissioned Stanford Research Institute to analyze available sites in the Los Angeles region. From the survey of parks, Disney and his crew established some basic criteria for the design of Disneyland: a single entrance; a coherent, orderly, sequenced layout within which elements would complement each other rather than compete for attention; wide, leisurely walkways; extensive landscaping; plenty of food and entertainment; attractions unique to Disney; efficient, high-capacity operations; and a large custodial staff sufficient to keep the park spotless. Disney's production of the animated film *Peter Pan* (1953) probably sowed some seeds for the design of Disneyland. Perpetual boy Peter's mystical Never Never Land is an isolated island where no one grows up and where one adventure leads into the next. With the design plans underway, Disneyland became an obsession to which Disney devoted nearly all of his attention, refusing even to consider any new films. In the early 1950s, he said in an interview in the Hollywood *Citizen News:* "The park means a lot to me. It's something that will never be finished, something I can keep developing, keep 'plussing,' and adding to. It's alive. . . . When you wrap up a picture and turn it over to Technicolor, you're through. . . . The park . . . will keep growing. The thing will get more beautiful year after year. And it will get better as I find out what the public likes."[12]

The Stanford Research Institute targeted the orange groves near Anaheim in Orange County as the most advantageous area for construction of the park. The projected Santa Ana Freeway would make it less than a half hour's drive from Los Angeles, the air was free of smog, and the land was much cheaper than in the populated sectors. Stanford also produced a feasibility study recommending an initial investment of $11 million. By opening day, costs would rise to $17 million. Initial funds were obtained by leasing agreements with American corporations and refreshment purveyors who agreed to develop exhibitions and restaurants in the park. Among them were American Motors, Kodak, Kaiser Aluminum, Trans World Airlines, Pepsi, and Monsanto. Disney insisted on five-year leases with the first and fifth year's rent paid in advance. With millions of dollars still to be raised before construction could start, Disney conceived of his most inspired arrangement. He turned to television for both financial sponsorship and promotion. Spurned by both CBS and NBC, Disney found the fledgling American Broadcasting Company more receptive, especially to his promise to produce a weekly hour-long television program for seven years, titled "Disneyland," in return for ABC's financial investment in the park. Walt engineered a deal for half a million dollars in cash and a guarantee for $4.5 million. ABC purchased 34 percent of Disneyland, Inc.; Disney himself retained about 17 percent of the stock; Western Printing and Lithographing, in return for the continued rights to print all Disney books and comic books, secured almost 14 percent; Walt Disney Productions bought 34 percent.[13]

The summer of 1954 saw the uprooting of orange trees on the 160-acre plot in Anaheim, and in the fall the television program "Disneyland" hit the airwaves and promptly climbed to the top of the Nielsen ratings. Construction took place inside a permanent 25-foot-high earthen berm built to isolate the park from intrusions from the outside world and to seal in a world of controlled illusion, fantasy, and perfectly engineered harmony. As virtually every American would come to know, inside the 25-foot barrier materialized five worlds, all joined at a central plaza: Main Street U.S.A., Adventureland, Frontierland, Fantasyland, and Tomorrowland.

Opening day, 17 July 1955, was far from carefree and controlled. Workers had toiled 24 hours a day for weeks to prepare the park for the scheduled televised inauguration. Rivers ran dry immediately after being filled, necessitating last-minute rebottoming with clay; concrete was still being poured as Walt faced the live television cameras; a plumbers' strike resulted in a shortage of drinking fountains; some of the asphalt paving in the streets was still steaming, "trapping" high-heeled shoes; more than twice the maximum projected attendance of 10,000–15,000 people turned up, half of them gate crashers; Fess Parker as frontier hero Davy Crockett was soaked by ill-timed sprinklers as he made his grand entrance on horseback. On the following day a gas leak erupted in Fantasyland, spewing flames right through the asphalt; the riverboat *Mark Twain* nearly capsized during the overloaded maiden voyage; and gate-receipt money was transported in fire buckets to the office and quickly to the bank to cover the payroll. Closely following the opening, a 15-day heat wave of 100° temperatures nearly dried up the cash flow and gravely threatened the park's continued existence. Unlike the perfect control and organization later evident in the Disney parks, the birth of Disneyland was chaotic, and the press was not tolerant. Unaware of the untimely plumbers' strike, the press focused on the lack of drinking fountains as a ploy to sell soft drinks. One journalist bemoaned the collapse of his own fantasies: "Walt's dream is a nightmare. . . . I attended the so-called press premier of Disneyland, a fiasco the like of which I cannot recall in thirty years of show life. To me it felt like a giant cash register, clicking and clanging, as creatures of Disney magic came tumbling down from their lofty places in my daydreams to peddle and perish their charms with the aggressiveness of so many curbside barkers."[14]

But Disney learned quickly from those early problems. In the first year, visitors paid the entrance fee only to face additional charges for each attraction. The resulting continual need to dig into pockets was annoying, tended to overload the most popular attractions and isolate others, and slowed the loading, thus significantly reducing capacity. Disney soon initiated the sale of books of tickets graded A to C (later A to E) to be used for the various classes of attractions. The ticket books allowed visitors to forget about money once inside the park and spread the crowds out to many of the less spectacular but enjoyable features. The ticket books would eventually be replaced by an all-encompassing single admission fee. Disney also vowed that never again would there be an inadequate number of drinking fountains, restrooms, and waste containers. Such facilities would be installed all over the Disney parks and would even provide architectural interest, as they were cleverly designed to blend into and contribute to the atmosphere of each "land." Outsiders who had been contracted to provide security, crowd control, operation of parking lots, and custodial services were found not to have the proper friendly attitude toward the Disneyland guests, and their tasks were not performed with sufficient thoroughness. All were soon replaced with staff hired by the park and trained in "Disneyland University."

Disneyland's shaky start was fleeting. Within six months over a million "guests" had entered the magic land, and by the end of the first year Disney Productions was able to pay off loans totaling $9 million. *Barron's* reported in 1956 that the average visitor spent $4 inside Disneyland, including $1.20 for rides and 80¢ for food.[15] Nearly 4 million people came through the gates in 1956, and the park itself from then on financed all expansion, change, and upkeep. The 50-millionth visitor would enter the turnstiles in July 1965; within the first 10 years, attendance had come to equal a quarter of the total population of the United States. The public demonstrated, with their attendance and their wallets, that the Disneyland amusement formula perfectly reflected their desires for entertainment and escape. One of the park's primary attractions is that it allows visitors to walk right into and experience the historical environments and fantasy worlds they passively watch on the television screens in their living rooms. They can immerse themselves and participate in the worlds that tantalize them nightly but from which the television screen separates and limits them to the status of observers.

In the first decade alone, Disney spent an additional $36 million beyond the initial investment on his precious park.[16] The weekly television show, "Disneyland," catapulted ABC to the status of the third major network. By 1990, 35 years after its opening, Disneyland Park retains its stellar position as the second top attraction in terms of attendance in the United States, drawing over 14 million visitors, second only to Walt Disney World in Florida.[17]

Disneyland Park is the prototypical theme park, where control is the overriding element not only in the design but in the experiencing of the park. Total control of space, movement, and mood create a succession of visual stereotypes so profound in effect that they quickly achieve the status of national popular images. Everything about the park, including the behavior of the "guests," is engineered to promote a spirit of optimism, a belief in progressive improvement toward perfection. Elements within the park achieve mythic, religious significance as treasured icons protecting us against infusion or assault by evil in any form, including our own faults. Beginning with the assassination of John Kennedy in 1963, events have continually cast doubt on America's faith in its providential role as the leader in the quest toward the perfectibility of man. Individually, Americans have been faced with progressively worsening social and urban problems, a government lacking moral integrity, a chaotic and competitive working world, and the severing of the family unit. Paradoxically, self-doubt and loss of faith have not rendered Disneyland obsolete but have instead engendered the sanctification of the park as a Mecca, a holy city, where the values of hope, goodness, perfection, and order are protected and can be instilled in its guest pilgrims. Disney management is aware of the park's power to transmit confidence. John Hench, reflecting on his 50-year career with Disney, has stated, "Actually, what we're selling throughout the Park is reassurance. We offer adventures in which you survive a kind of personal challenge. . . . We let your survival instincts triumph over adversity. A trip to Disneyland is an exercise in reassurance about oneself and one's ability to maybe even handle the real challenges of life."[18] The role of the park as pilgrimage center would be intensified in Walt Disney World Resort, as discussed in chapter 7.

By the entry through the railroad station, guests are transported to Main Street, U.S.A., an ideal midwestern town at the turn of the century. Of all the Disneyland attractions, Main Street has generated the most comment and architectural imitation. It has inspired the design of shopping malls, the historic restoration of countless town centers across the nation, and the design of people-oriented proposals by city planners. James Rouse, the developer of Baltimore's Harborplace and Boston's Faneuil Hall Marketplace, as well as some pioneering suburban malls, has credited Main Street and Disneyland with providing much of the inspiration for his projects.[19]

Main Street, U.S.A., is, of course, an idealized caricature. Its gingerbread Victorian streetscape of railroad station, city hall, ice cream parlor, firehouse, barber shop, movie theater, candy store, apothecary, emporium, and more, all perpetually newly painted in a pastiche of soothing, blending tones, never existed in reality. The turn-of-the-century Main Street was dingy from the dust and mud of dirt roads, cluttered by competing signage, and composed of a hodgepodge of shabby architecture where economy and utility ruled rather than a desire for beautification. Disney's Main Street, then, is not so much a memory as it is an archetypal ideal, "a kind of universally true Main Street—it's better than the real Main Street of the turn of the century ever could be," as architect Paul Goldberger has explained.[20] It is a rose-colored visual image that successfully stimulates a feeling of nostalgia for a simpler, more relaxed past and serves as a preferred substitute not only for the dingy reality of such streets as they existed in the past but also for the disillusionment and shortcomings of one's own hometown.

The obviousness of the false fronts, the inability to explore interiors beyond the commercial stores located on the ground floors within the facade result in an atmosphere of theater, a feeling of presence within a movie set. The visitor is obliged to move in one direction, from frame to frame, in order to traverse the street-passage. The perfection of the structures, vigilantly overseen by caretakers, reinforces their unreality, their existence in a realm above that occupied by the ordinary, imperfect creatures who stroll by and longingly peek in windows. The visitor is just passing by, unable to live in this idyllic province where time has stopped. That is its magic. It makes us smile, feel safe and at ease in a perfect place while at the same time infusing us with hope that our own flawed environment can be improved.

While Disney embraced the totality of planning and the creation of pervasive visual symbols that were the essence of the World's Columbian Exposition, he chose to glorify the ordinary, small-town origins of the common citizen rather than to contrive an aristocratic, elegant realm suitable for a ruling class. He thus elevated the democratic spirit and America's unique civilization while at least visually dismissing elitism and European cultural borrowings. But just like Chicago's White City in the previous century, the darkest aspect of Main Street is its enshrinement of Anglo-American imagery to the total exclusion of immigrant and ethnic infusions. Main Street, U.S.A., exudes prosperity, shuns pluralism, and is a haven for white America. It has a railroad, an emporium, and a city hall, but no church and no school. The values depicted are those of civic rule and commercialism, not spiritual aspiration, mental enrichment, or personal growth. It is popular culture sanitized of its most creative and energetic elements, static in time, and reserved for the financially comfortable. America's prejudices and monetary ambitions are endorsed and encouraged.

Once the central plaza at the end of Main Street is reached, nostalgia gives way to futurism and adventure. Disney's "lands" retain the exoticism of Coney Island but none of the sensuality and chaos. Because Disney was not interested in the sexual element of the human condition, his "adventures" are not designed to titillate or bring riders into unavoidable intimate contact, as did nearly all of Coney's rides and stunts. Fun in Disney's worlds results from transport into mysterious fantasy realms, the illusion of potential danger, and admiration for the wondrous and clever workings of plastic and electronic technologies. Adventureland presents the everlasting human quest for exploration. Frontierland celebrates the American desire for freedom and facility for harnessing nature as man's servant. Tomorrowland is a showcase for our technological sophistication and daring. Fantasyland, with its actualization of fairy tales, is the least effective realm. It may be unable to engage its guests because the presented myths are not American in origin or spirit. The tales are originally European in derivation and meaning, and the dominant symbol, Sleeping Beauty's castle, has no firm place in American culture. The fairy tales are familiar, but they are not derived from nor do they reflect the American experience.

The individual adventures, such as the "Jungle Cruise," "Tom Sawyer Island," "Snow White's Adventures," the "Submarine Voyage," and the "Haunted Mansion," offer escapism from the ordinary along with a pleasurable participation in perfection. It can be suggested that the adventures, within which each rider is placed in a conveyance, either a boat or a cab, and transported on an unchanging, established route, are a form of manipulation that eliminates individuality and spontaneity. Riders calmly surrender their freedom, however, because they are constantly stimulated without the necessity for thinking, acting, or making choices. They are relaxed, content, and amazed.

Much of Disneyland's technological wonder emanates from Disney's pioneering work in audioanimatronics. Put simply, audioanimatronics produces three-dimensional animated characters with sound and movement operated by means of electronics and computers. Bringing a character to life begins with the sculpting of a clay figure, followed by the making of plaster molds. A character's skin is carefully cast from Duraflex, a vinyl-like material that stands up to weather, oils, and gases. Extremely intricate and precise movements are designed for the figure and programmed into a computer control system located under Main Street, U.S.A. Nearly all of the attractions in Disneyland Park are automated, which allows them to be repeated countless times during the day. The human attendants serve more as decoration than as functional components. In the late 1970s it was estimated that each robot show at Disneyland costs approximately $6 million, not including the technological (computer) support controlling it.[21] Because the attractions are fully automated, tens of thousands of people can be moved through a limited space without jams and long lines. Disneyland's success in transporting enormous numbers of people as well as in designing loading areas that keep waiting guests in constant motion are revolutionary and continue to have substantial impact in the design of transportation systems in all venues.

The audioanimatronic attractions have one drawback—guests can't touch them. Touch is poignantly absent from the Disney attractions. The systems of transport through the adventures or attractions are carefully designed to place all elements other than the transport vehicle itself beyond the outstretched arms of any rider. Even within the park as a whole, most components are man-made rather than natural, so anything that can be grasped by human hands generally has a sameness of texture. A curious guest only reduces the illusion by feeling and touching.

The Disneyland experience has been caustically criticized, especially from academic-oriented critics. In 1958 Julian Halevy grumpily complained: "Romance, Adventure, Fantasy, Science are ballyhooed and marketed: life is bright-colored, clean, cute, titivating, safe, mediocre, inoffensive to the lowest common denominator, and somehow poignantly inhuman." Comparing Disneyland and Las Vegas, he analyzed their effect in intellectual terms: "Both these institutions exist for the relief of tension and boredom, as tranquilizers for social anxiety, and . . . both provide fantasy experiences in which not-so-secret longings are pseudo-satisfied. Their huge profits and mushrooming growth suggest that as conformity and adjustment become more rigidly imposed on the American scene, the drift to fantasy release will become a flight."[22] John Ciardi in 1965 found Disneyland "depthless," an "artifice in which the real cannot survive," referring to the artificial fish in the "Submarine Voyage," where chemicals required to keep the water clear would kill real fish.[23] These academic observers are even more unwilling to recognize and respond to the delights and wonders of the new forms of amusement than was Maxim Gorky when he visited Coney Island early in the century.

In a much more balanced and open-minded assessment, Richard Schickel, in *The Disney Version*, recognizes the manipulative aspects of Disneyland. "The trick is not to harass the visitor into spending but rather to relax him to the point where the inner guardians of his frugality are lulled into semiconsciousness. It works." Schickel is also troubled by the all-American, conservative, standardized look of the attendants and the early practice of barring entrance to long-haired youths or anyone dressed in an eccentric manner. These practices demonstrate "corporate fear" of minority subculture groups and a "maniacal desire to keep the eccentricities of individualized expression . . . away from its door." But Schickel finds much to admire in Disney's marvel. The sanitation effort is unparalleled, with no apparent regard for the profit margin. The wide walks, abundance of shade trees, lakes, ponds, and water rides create an extremely pleasant atmosphere even on hot Southern California summer days. The curving, shaded walks encourage a leisurely pace, "a sense of ease and well-being" even when crowds are huge. And there is always a small discovery, a surprise around every bend. Schickel explains Disney's ability to understand the needs of the common person: "What the average, middle class American wants and has always wanted of art and of the objects he mistakes for art, is the fake alligator that thrills but never threatens, that may be appreciated for the cleverness with which it approximates the real thing but that carries no psychological or poetic overtones. . . . you carry away not some dark phantom that may rise up someday to haunt you but an appreciation of the special-effects man's skill."[24]

The dream, then, of Disneyland Park is escapism from problems, responsibilities, and the threats of reality. It is an idyllic, isolated place where there is no sex, no violence, no social problems, no need to work. As Sergei Eisenstein said in a commentary on Disney's films, Disney "bestows . . . precisely obliviousness, an instant of complete and total release from everything connected with the suffering caused by the social conditions."[25] At the same time, due to its founder's relentless optimism, Disneyland celebrates the American dream of progress through technology. By means of innovative and enterprising technological advances, the park demonstrates that America can achieve its providential role as creator of the promised land. The perfectibility of man is seen as achievable through technology and democracy. As John Bright perceptively notes, it is "a little like Christianity without Christ."[26]

☐ Economics and Demographics

The revenues generated by Disneyland Park and the publicity created by the weekly television show catapulted Walt Disney Productions from a struggling firm that barely matched income with costs to a megacorporation with income over $160 million and net profits over $20 million by 1970, before the creation of Walt Disney World Resort. The net profits line in figure 1 is indicative that much of the income

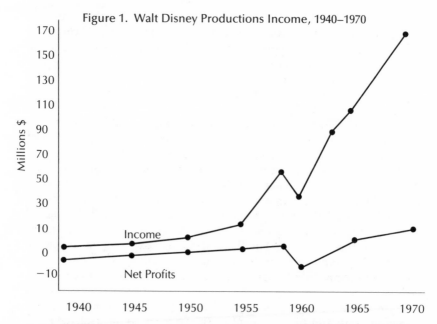

Figure 1. Walt Disney Productions Income, 1940–1970

Source: *Moody's Industrial Manual* (New York: Moody's Investors Service, annual editions, 1956–71); John MacDonald, "Now the Bankers Come to Disney," *Fortune* 73 (May 1966): 141.

was reinvested in the enterprises. The downward blip between 1959 and 1960 was the result of losses from Disney's only box-office flop, the film *Sleeping Beauty*. Revenues were sent zooming upward in 1965 by the record-setting movie *Mary Poppins*, along with the growing success of Disneyland.

In the 15-year period from 1955 to 1970 Disneyland's share of the total Disney revenues rose to nearly 50 percent, and yearly profits of all the Disney enterprises surged from $1 million to over $20 million.

Another factor influencing Disneyland's success, beyond the genius of Walt Disney and the magnetic appeal of the park, was the post–World War II baby boom. Between 1940 and 1965 the number of children under 15 years of age increased from just under 33 million to over 59 million, an increase of nearly 80 percent.

The tremendous augmentation of disposable personal income between 1940 and 1970 was, perhaps, as much a contributing factor to Disneyland's success as the population boost. In terms of current prices, disposable per capita personal income increased nearly 500 percent, or

Table 9. Disneyland Revenues as Percentage of Total Revenues of Walt
Disney Productions, 1955–1970 (in millions of dollars)

Year	Disneyland Revenues	Total Revenues	% Revenues from Disneyland	Net Profits Walt Disney Prod.
1954		11.6		0.73
1957	—	35.8	—	3.6
1959	17.1	58.4	29.3	3.4
1960	18.1	50.9	35.5	−1.3
1962	20.1	75.6	26.5	5.3
1964	32.8	86.7	37.8	7.1
1965	35.4	109.9	32.2	11.4
1967	52.4	117.5	44.6	11.3
1969	70.3	148.4	47.4	15.8
1970	82.0	167.1	49.1	21.8

Source: *Moody's Industrial Manual* (New York: Moody's Investors Service, annual editions, 1954–71).

Table 10. U.S. Population (in thousands), 1930–1970, and Percent Increase
from Previous Five-Year Period

Year	Total Population	% Increase	Children under 15	% Increase
1930	123,077		36,003	
1935	127,250	3.4	34,383	−4.5
1940	132,122	3.8	32,942	−4.2
1945	139,928	5.9	34,578	4.7
1950	151,684	8.4	40,808	15.3
1955	165,275	9.0	48,715	16.2
1960	180,671	9.3	56,076	15.1
1965	194,303	7.5	59,250	5.7
1970	204,879	5.4	57,889	−2.3

Source: U.S. Bureau of the Census, *Historical Statistics of the United States: Colonial Times to 1970* (Washington, D.C.: Government Printing Office, 1975), ser. A29-42.

Table 11. Annual Disposable Personal Income, Expressed in Current Prices and Constant 1958 Prices; Percent Increase over Previous Five-Year Period, 1940–1970

Year	Current Prices	% Increase	Constant 1958 Prices	% Increase
1940	$ 573		$1259	
1945	$1132	97.6	$1642	30.4
1950	$1364	20.5	$1646	.2
1955	$1666	22.1	$1795	9.1
1960	$1905	14.3	$1883	4.9
1965	$2436	27.9	$2239	18.9
1970	$3376	38.7	$2610	16.6

Source: U.S. Bureau of the Census, *Historical Statistics of the United States: Colonial Times to 1970* (Washington, D.C.: Government Printing Office, 1975), ser. F17-30.

slightly over 100 percent in terms of constant 1958 prices during this period. While population, especially the number of children, began to decrease dramatically after 1960, enhanced growth in disposable income made significantly more funds available to smaller families for leisure activities. Disneyland Park has never been adversely affected by the decrease in children after the boom of the 1950s because its strongest appeal is to adults rather than children. Adult admissions consistently outnumber those for children at a ratio of four to one, and 50 percent of the guests are repeaters.[27]

In part to celebrate the 35th anniversary of Disneyland, Walt Disney Company announced in January 1990 a billion-dollar expansion of the Southern California attraction. Calling the 1990s the "Disney Decade," Michael Eisner, chairman and chief executive officer of Walt Disney Company, detailed plans, including the addition of two new theme areas, Hollywoodland and Mickey's Starland; a total rehabilitation of Tomorrowland, with a network of skyways making possible a second-story level; and many new attractions: a "Young Indiana Jones Adventure," a "Little Mermaid" ride, an "Alien Encounter" ride, a "Dick Tracy's Crime Stoppers" attraction, a "Toontown Trolley" simulator ride, a "Baby Herman's Runaway Baby Buggy" ride, and a "Great Movie Ride." New live shows are in the works based on the Muppets, for which Disney acquired the character rights in 1989, and on the Dick Tracy comic-book personalities.[28]

6

Theme Parks
Pleasure Zones Where Time and Space Are Relative

If you can't afford to go to Kenya next year, it's waiting
for you just outside Tampa.
—Billboard advertisement for Busch Gardens' Dark
Continent

Facsimile parks did not suddenly ap-
pear across the landscape following Disneyland Park's immediate success. In fact, American entrepreneurs were uncharacteristically slow to
recognize and copy the Disney formula with any degree of success.
Although Disney publicists predicted that at least 20 parks designed
from the Disney model would appear within five years, the succeeding
decade witnessed mostly failed ventures. Denver's Magic Mountain,
scheduled to open in 1958, was aborted largely because of financing by a
cartel of backers who collectively lacked any enthusiasm for the amusement business. They overextended promotional advertising, but no substantial construction ever materialized. Pleasure Island, an 80-acre park
near Boston built at an initial cost of $4 million, lacked the Disney
attention to detail and technical expertise. The focal attraction, a 70-foot
giant whale designed to leap menacingly from the waves, never became
operational. Thrill rides were soon brought in to attract crowds not
impressed by the faux locales, which along with a reconstruction of a
whaling harbor included a Pirates' Island and a Western town dubbed

Cactus Flats. Pleasure Island managed to survive only by sizing down to a small traditional amusement park.

In 1958 Pacific Ocean Park, in Santa Monica, California, was purchased by the Hollywood Turf Club and the Columbia Broadcasting System (CBS). A $16 million investment transformed the pier park into a marine wonderland where visitors entered through Neptune's Kingdom, replete with waterfalls and mermaids, to enjoy such attractions as the Double Diving Bell (glass water bubbles riding out over the ocean), a "Flight to Mars," the Sea Serpent roller coaster, a sea animal show performed in a 2,000-seat amphitheater, and a South Sea Island theme area, complete with a banana train ride and simulated tropical storms and volcanic eruptions. But the first-class attractions created high overhead costs, which were not adequately recouped by the low admission price of $2.50. Faced with a resulting shortfall in operational funds, the management neglected routine maintenance. The ocean air also contributed to rapid deterioration. Bankruptcy closed the park in 1968.[1]

The most spectacular and newsworthy failure was Freedomland, U.S.A., built in the middle of Bronx, New York. Designed by a former head of the Disneyland design team and backed by several corporate investors at a fabulous cost of $33 million, the park opened in June 1960, acclaimed by influential business publications as the "East Coast's answer to Disneyland." Laid out in the shape of the United States, the park featured many sectors: Little Old New York (circa 1850), a New England fishing village, a stern-wheeler ride around the Great Lakes, a Civil War battlefield, the Chicago fire, New Orleans Mardi Gras, a western train robbery, San Francisco's Chinatown, and even that city's Great Earthquake. Like Disneyland, Freedomland had no thrill rides; instead its publicity billed it as an educational experience that "brings history to life" by recreating "the scope of the American Adventure." But the 60,000 people who pushed through the gates on opening day encountered a park in various stages of incompletion with attractions that stimulated yawns rather than excitement or laughter. The uninspired live-action events, which were generally nonparticipatory, failed to entertain or to teach. Perhaps Freedomland's most crucial flaw was its lack of mass-media exposure, an oversight unthinkable to Disney, who recognized the importance of linking Disneyland to televised family entertainment. Within a few days of opening, the park did receive media attention, but of a negative nature. A highly publicized stage-coach accident injuring ten people seemed to solidify the popular perception that the park was not worth the $3.50 admission fee. Freedomland, U.S.A., operated in the red for three years, then in desperation brought in thrill rides to supplant the pseudo-historical sectors, but still it lost millions before it quietly closed in 1964.[2] Even if the park had not been a victim of its own shortcomings, it is likely that its location would have killed it. No urban park has been able to guarantee the safety, cleanliness, and order essential to a successful family attraction.

☐ Emergence of the Concept

Despite the failures, the trend of corporate ownership of entertainment complexes emerged. The prospect of massive capital investment, unthinkable for the traditional family-owned parks, could be realized through corporate ownership, making possible the instant erection of fully developed and minutely planned amusement enterprises.

The first successful venture based on the Disney model was Six Flags over Texas, between Dallas and Fort Worth. Built by real estate developer Angus Wynne, the 35-acre enclosed park opened in 1961 with six theme areas, representing the six flags that have waved over Texas: Spain, France, Mexico, the Republic of Texas, the Confederacy, and the United States. In a departure from Disneyland, thrill rides were liberally planned into each sector, serving as active promoters of the segmented environment. A log flume bounces through Spanish rapids, a runaway mine train races through the Confederacy, and a wild roller coaster zooms above the United States. Entertainment was an important ingredient in the Six Flags parks from the beginning, with a multitude of stationary and roving shows as well as big-name featured performers.

Six Flags over Texas raked in the crowds and the money during its inaugural year and in succeeding years, but the business community remained hesitant and financially conservative in the wake of the Freedomland disaster. The Six Flags backers were willing to gamble on their success formula by starting a park chain, Six Flags, Inc., and building two new parks, Six Flags over Georgia, near Atlanta, and Six Flags over Mid-America, near St. Louis.

Six Flags over Georgia, which opened in 1967, embodies the emerging theme park concept and maxims for success. The result of corporate strategy and investment, the Georgia park, like its precisely engineered siblings in Texas and Missouri, is located in a large metropolitan area but well outside the boundaries of public transportation from the urban neighborhoods. Its all-inclusive ticket price, $4.50 in 1967, rising to nearly $20.00 by 1989, entitles guests to free access to all rides and attractions. This ticket concept was, at the time, distinct from Disney's coupon system; now the industry standard, it allows as many repeat encounters with rides and shows as a guest desires. With convenience and spectacle outweighing strict fact, the six sectors reflect in their architecture and atmosphere six historical influences in southeast history: England, France, Spain, the Confederacy, Georgia itself, and the United States.

Six Flags over Georgia, on the interstate highway system, encourages the patronage of families simply because an automobile is needed to reach the park. Cleanliness and hospitality further promote the family atmosphere, and the park even offers a picnic area with attractive landscaping and facilities. A staff largely comprised of college students, gayly costumed in accordance with the sector in which they are assigned, run the rides, attractions, and refreshment concessions, as well as maintain the grounds and quickly remove litter. Hans Peters, a prominent Hollywood art director, collaborated with Six Flags architects to design the park. As a result opening day saw exotic and romantic locales: quaint villages, a covered bridge, Fort DeSoto, a logging camp, a riverboat expedition complete with savage beasts and threatening redskins, the enchanted woodland of Okefenokee with adorable animated animals, the Happy Motoring Freeway, the Petsville petting zoo, and the Crystal Pistol Music Hall.

From the outset, thrill rides were given center stage at the Six Flags parks. The same basic rides appear in each park, although they are cleverly outfitted to fit into the sector in which they are located. The log flume and white-water rafting rides have become increasingly popular, making it difficult to believe that they are essentially the same as the turn-of-the-century shoot-the-chutes at Coney Island's Luna Park. The roller coasters have become terrifying monsters of speed and gravity-generated loops and drops. In the early 1990s, Six Flags over Georgia embraces the slogan "Land of Screams and Dreams" to advertise its coasters. The Great American Scream Machine, a classic wooden coaster with an 85-foot drop, rose from the previously tranquil lake in 1973 and claimed the title of the world's longest wooden coaster. Steel coasters allow extravagant freedom in design and terror; Six Flags contracted the Swiss firm of Intamin AG to create the Mind Bender, a magnificently swirling triple-loop coaster that made its awe-inspiring appearance in 1978. The Z Force, with its narrow cars twisting and rolling through a series of tight turns and swooping dives, thrilled its first brave riders in 1987.[3]

With their emphasis on exciting rides, cleanliness and meticulous maintenance, the free-access ticket, first-rank entertainers as regularly scheduled features, and a picnic grove for quiet, relaxed leisure, the Six Flags parks stretched the original Disneyland concept. The predictable year-by-year financial success of the three parks set the stage for the burgeoning of the industry in the 1970s. By their fast-growing patronage, American consumers express their delight and enthusiastic interest in the theme park entertainment formula. They also demonstrate their embrace of the theme park experience as one of the few participatory activities in American twentieth-century culture that the whole family can enjoy together.

Before construction can begin on a theme park, investors, generally corporate owners or in rare cases a group of independent entrepreneurs, must engage in detailed market studies, zoning and land acquisition dealings, and environmental impact assessments. Site determination is a primary key to the development of a park. Planners and investors must determine the population within radiuses of 25, 50, 100, and 150 miles of a potential site. The routing of the existing interstate highway system plays its role, since most theme parks are bonded to the automobile as the primary means of access. Investors learned from the demise of the traditional parks in the first half of the century that an urban location was usually a death sentence. The baby boom of the 1950s dictated that the family would be the most lucrative target market but that parents with children in tow would not be lured to an urban attraction where crime, unsupervised youth, and rowdy elements would have ready access.

Another factor affecting site choice is, of course, land values. The extensive acreage required by theme parks made unimproved, relatively cheap land well beyond the urban corridor most attractive. A park rising from a former "wasteland" invests its own wonder. The resulting attraction is more than a transformation of inhospitable space, it is a creation of a new land, a magical kingdom that through the power of technology vanquishes the untamed wilderness.[4]

During the 1970s, when most of the two dozen major theme parks were built, owners invested $40 million to $50 million in each park. The final product in each case was a pleasure zone completely engineered and planned down to the smallest detail. A safe, controlled leisure environment, cloistered by distance and barriers from the fearful, chaotic, and generally decaying city, is the result. The overall design requires five or six contrasting sectors loosely connected to some unifying idea. Architecture, costumes, landscaping, shows, and attractions within each sector are carefully coordinated to provide a pervasive, if relatively brief, "experience."

The sector structure can be seen as a reflection of the segmented nature of television entertainment. Television has become such a pervasive element in American culture that most Americans are comfortable with the rapid changes in time and place that occur each evening on the television screen. Just like television programs, which last for a half hour or an hour, then make way for a different setting and dramatic situation, the theme park creates a series of startlingly diverse environments to be experienced in a single day. Transition zones between events are not expected and probably would be ineffective. Our computer culture, too, trains us to accept a reality where events occur sequentially but need not be connected to or dependent upon what comes before or after. Theme parks are generally not designed so that sectors are experienced in a prescribed order. Guests are perfectly content to roam from the seventeenth century to a future world or from Europe to Africa in a single step. It is important, however, that the sectors depict either past, future, or exotic lands; no one wants to be confronted with present reality. It is precisely the real world that millions of visitors wish to escape by hopping in their cars and immersing themselves in the total fantasy realms of the theme parks.

Theme parks cleverly exploit the traditional American romance with adventure and travel. At the same time they provide at least the illusion of an educational experience in cultural history. The typical theme park is divided into a fantasy space, a safari land or other type of animal or sea life enclosure, and recreations of historical or international settings. Because many of the theme park owners or designers, like Disney, had backgrounds in the film entertainment industry, the sectors work much like movie sets. The visitor typically allows about an hour per theme, just like an evening in front of the television. The experiential enhancement is in immersion. Theme park guests actually walk into and become part of an exotic land or a historical period. They can experience history and faraway places in three-dimensional immediacy rather than just watch them or read about them. They are sensually bombarded with music, sounds, intricate architecture, a kaleidoscope of color and constant movement. The nonstop sensual engagement assures visitors that they will not be asked to pause to analyze or even connect their experiences. Sensation largely bars cerebral activity while exciting the masses and replacing their stress with comfortable ease.

Millicent Hall, in her insightful conceptual analysis "Theme Parks: Around the World in 80 Minutes," considers a paradox apparent in all of the successful parks: "Everything in the theme park—even the minor events and the employees—is controlled, yet the total package creates the illusion of spontaneity." Hall recognizes the importance of the employees in maintaining the underlying manipulation of the guests. They serve basically as leaders, engaging visitors in the "script" and leading them on their way. To Hall, this reliance on leaders reveals "how alien the average theme park visitor feels in a community environment. He needs guides to help him find his way and to know what to do, because he has opted for the individualism of the ranch house and the automobile over the city center."[5] Thought and decisions are rarely necessary, because visitors are essentially batched through the various attractions. Each attraction is designed much like an assembly line, with long, regimented waiting lines leading to fixed cars or boats, which carry guests on an undeviating path through the event in a set period of time. Guests go in one end and out the other, having engaged in exactly the same sensual program as thousands or millions of other people.

Unlike the traditional amusement parks, which enticed city dwellers with fabulous lights and noise, the theme parks have unimpressive exterior shells or are surrounded by buffer zones of vegetation. There is nothing apparent to beckon the visitor. A structural lure is not necessary, because those who travel to the theme park already know about the marvels behind the fence or the foliage through television and other advertising. Moreover, their automobile trip is already directed to the park; the cost and the time required for a visit eliminate spur-of-the-moment encounters.

The buffer zone, the earthen barrier, or the high fence enforces the atmosphere of isolation so essential to the success of theme parks. Visitors must feel that they are escaping their everyday urban or suburban existence by entering a magic land protected against intrusions from reality. Inside it must be miraculously clean, free of any conflict, with everything in perfect working order. While the types of attractions may change over the years, especially as the baby boomers all turn 40, replacing teenagers as the dominant population group, the formula of isolation, escape from reality, cleanliness, order, and sensual bombardment is likely to remain stable.

These formula factors create, overall, a conviction of safety wedded to excitement. Parks must engineer maximum excitement with the elimination of actual danger. While thrill rides should generate an aura of risk, visitors must be convinced that they are completely safe. A fire or an accident at a theme park will significantly affect attendance in succeeding years until the public can once again feel assured of safety. New Jersey's Great Adventure theme park began to rebound only in 1989 from a fire in 1984 that resulted in eight deaths. In Great Adventure's case, a change of ownership was necessary before public confidence was restored. Detailed standards for amusement rides and their operation have been developed by the American Society for Testing and Materials. They cover testing of components, installation, and operation as well as maintenance, inspection, and quality control programs. They also carefully delineate responsibilities of manufacturers and operators.[6]

Science and technology writer Hal Hellman views park visitors as "sense receptors" who are "sitting back and letting it all happen to us."[7] Theme parks provide few participatory encounters; generally visitors merely observe from a familiar, comfortable conveyance or are transported effortlessly along the peaks, dips, and curlicues of a gravity ride. Even competition is absent. Hellman sees the popular water flume rides to be an exception. Riders get genuinely wet, resulting possibly in a "dampening of that safe little cocoon that has enveloped us."[8]

The desire to turn one's back on reality elevates the stature of artificiality as achieved by computers, electronics, and plastics. The artificial, as it strives to represent the real, perhaps best exemplified in audioanimatronic figures, becomes a source of wonder at the expense of nature. Many people who have visited a theme park have witnessed the disappointment evident in guests when a swan or other animal turns out to be "only real" rather than an electronic robot. One park owner asserts, "We are living in an age when artificiality is fast becoming the norm rather than the exception. If there is a demand for something— whether food for astronauts . . . metals in short supply, or recreational activity—man is creating the commodity artificially."[9]

Long-term survival for a theme park, once it has captured an audience, depends almost completely on its ability to generate repeat visits with regularity. To this end, meticulous, constant maintenance, upkeep, and cleaning is essential, while three marketing strategies are normally followed: a new ride or attraction at least every other year; featured live entertainment, especially big-name performers; and special promotions featuring discount tickets or group rates. Well-managed major theme parks can expect a clear profit of 10 percent to 15 percent after operating expenses and capital expenditures. While attendance and profits are regularly affected by weather, they have proved not to be influenced by economic conditions. In the 25 years since the emergence of theme parks, the major parks have thrived even in recessions, because the need to escape is intensified in economic hard times. During the gasoline shortages of the later 1970s, when the "destination parks," most prominently Walt Disney World Resort, experienced a downturn, the regional theme parks flourished.

☐   Growth of Conglomerate-Owned Parks

In 1970 there were only three theme parks in existence, drawing about 12 million visitors. By the end of the decade, two dozen major theme parks were attracting over 60 million revelers and accounting for about

70 percent of the total amusement park industry revenues of over a billion dollars.[10] Let us look at how several corporate owners have approached establishing theme parks, as well as how they have fared within the industry.

☐ **Taft Broadcasting**   The next successful venture to emulate the Six Flags parks was Kings Island, which opened in 1972 just north of Cincinnati. The owners, Taft Broadcasting, a television and communications conglomerate, had also owned Cincinnati's traditional park, Coney Island. The repeated destruction of that park by seasonal floods convinced Taft to build a new theme park that would incorporate European country sectors; a safari tour; a HappyLand, where the Hanna-Barbera cartoon characters Yogi Bear and the Flintstones would cavort; and a midway-type area designed to preserve the atmosphere and memories of the city's beloved Coney. Taft originally became interested in building a theme park as a vehicle for increased utilization of the cartoon characters of the Hanna-Barbera television shows, which they owned. Therefore, like Disney, Taft had in-place television exposure for its park. From its first full season, Kings Island steadily attracted well over 2 million people each year (see table 12).

The success of Kings Island led to Taft's joining with Kroger Com-

Table 12. Taft Parks Attendance, 1973–1984 (in millions)

Year	Kings Island	Kings Dominion	Carowinds	Canada's Wonderland
1973	2.01			
1974	2.38			
1975	2.58	0.65		
1976	2.49	1.81	0.91	
1977	2.60	1.96	0.98	
1978	2.58	1.96	1.13	
1979	2.62	1.83	1.04	
1980	2.75	1.83	1.10	
1981	2.50	1.68	1.05	
1982	2.82	1.70	1.14	2.19
1983	2.72	1.75	1.19	2.13
1984	2.60	1.91	1.11	2.21

Source: Taft Broadcasting *Annual Reports.*

pany to build a similar park, Kings Dominion, which opened in 1975 near Richmond, Virginia. Its initial $50 million investment placed it right behind the Disney parks in project cost. That same year, Taft and Kroger also purchased an existing smaller theme park, Carowinds, in Charlotte, North Carolina. In 1981 Taft realized the first international venture in the theme park industry by opening Canada's Wonderland near Toronto. The cost of Wonderland, $122 million in Canadian dollars, is indicative of the rapidly escalating financial requirements for theme parks as they moved into the 1980s. In fact, investment costs have become so prohibitive that only the Disney organization has constructed major parks in the United States during the 1980s.

In 1981 Taft bought out the Kroger interest in Kings Dominion and Carowinds, thus dissolving the partnership, because Kroger wished to remove itself from the amusement business. By 1982 the amusement ventures were contributing 36 percent of Taft Broadcasting's revenues and 28 percent of its operating profits (see table 13). Despite the stabil-

Table 13. Taft Parks Revenues, Operating Profit, and Capital Expenditures (in millions of dollars), and Amusement Share of Total Company Revenues, 1973–1984

Year	Revenues	Operating Profit	Capital Expenditures	Parks Share of Total Co. Revenues (%)
1973	17.3	4.6	6.7	24.6
1974	22.3	5.7	7.9	28.1
1975	28.1	6.5	5.7	31.3
1976[1]	28.6	6.4	4.9	30.7
1977	32.1	7.9	3.6	29.4
1978	37.0	8.8	5.2	26.8
1979	41.9	9.0	18.0	25.1
1980	46.2	10.1	47.0	19.6
1981[2]	45.6	9.1	111.0	19.0
1982	130.8	22.4	21.2	36.5
1983	135.3	19.7	24.4	35.5
1984	142.1	17.4	23.5	31.3

1. Kings Dominion's first full year

2. Canada's Wonderland's first year

Source: Taft Broadcasting *Annual Reports*.

ity in revenues and attendance, in 1984 Taft sold all of the parks with the exception of Canada's Wonderland to Kings Entertainment Company (KECO), a leveraged buy-out group, for $167.5 million. Kings Entertainment acquired 80 percent of Canada's Wonderland in 1986 for $90 million (Canadian). Legal ownership of Kings Island changed once again, to American Financial Corporation in 1989. Both parks are still managed by Kings Entertainment, which sold its 80 percent share of Wonderland to a Toronto real estate developer, J.D.S. Investments Ltd., in 1988.[11]

The Taft parks' record profits and attendance in 1982 were the result of several factors. It was the first year of sole ownership of Kings Dominion and Carowinds, as well as the second year of operation of Canada's Wonderland. Two major new rides also made their appearance, the Grizzly at King's Dominion and Rip Roarin' Rapids at Carowinds. While revenues continued to increase in the two following years, profits began to decline due to steadily growing operating costs and capital expenditures. Taft may well have become disenchanted with the theme park segment of its holdings because of high operating costs—constant meticulous maintenance of existing facilities, the high level of management oversight, and the capital expenditures required for major new attractions at each park every couple years to lure repeat visitors.

☐ **Anheuser-Busch**   Adolphus Busch, the patriarch of the brewing family, opened to the public his elaborate botanical gardens in Pasadena, California, in 1903. Although the gardens were closed in 1928 following the deaths of Busch and his wife, the German concept of the pleasant beer garden remained in the corporate consciousness. The corporation's interest in entertainment can be traced back to its sponsoring of the Tyrolean Alps attraction, a reproduction of an Alpine mountain village complete with imitation snow-capped peaks, at the 1904 St. Louis World's Fair. With grandson August Busch, Jr., at the corporate helm, the Anheuser-Busch Corporation developed a magnificently landscaped park of gardens, tropical birds, waterfalls, lakes, and lagoons adjacent to its brewery in Tampa, Florida. The public was invited to tour the brewery, stroll the gardens, and enjoy complimentary beer. Within a few years Busch Gardens developed a wild animal habitat sector with an African theme and animals native to that continent. No admission was charged until thrill rides were added in later years. A second park was opened in Los Angeles in 1966, but was never profitable. Anheuser-Busch converted it to a bird sanctuary and promotion facility for the corporation's beer products in 1976.

Large-scale expansion of the Tampa Busch Gardens, dubbed The

Dark Continent, began in the early 1970s, culminating in a new Moroccan Village complex of restaurants, theme shops, and theater, as well as a sky ride over the African Veldt wildlife sector in 1974. The Dark Continent presently comprises Congo, Timbuktu, Stanleyville, Nairobi, Morocco, and Serengeti Plain sectors. Also in 1974 a new park, the Old Country, opened in Williamsburg, Virginia. Borrowing from the atmosphere of nearby Colonial Williamsburg, the Old Country takes seventeenth-century Europe as its theme, with sectors recreating German, English, and French hamlets picturesquely named Hastings, Banbury Cross, Heatherdowns, Aquitaine, New France, and Rhinefeld, along with Octoberfest. Both the Tampa and Williamsburg parks emphasize the authenticity of the theme areas and rely less on thrill rides than most other theme parks. The big rides have established their presence, however, including the Loch Ness Monster, a twisting, turning, double-loop roller coaster, and the Big Bad Wolf, both in the Old Country, and the Python and the Scorpion, looping coasters in the Dark Continent. The Tampa park boasts two major water rides, Stanley Falls and the Congo River Rapids, while the Old Country has white-water trips on Le Scoot Flume Ride and Roman Rapids.

Table 14. Busch Gardens Parks
Attendance, 1975–1989 (in
millions)

Year	Dark Continent	Old Country
1975	2.4	1.6
1978	2.7	1.9
1980	3.1	2.2
1982	3.1	1.9
1983	2.9	1.95
1984	2.8	1.9
1985	2.9	2.05
1986	2.9	1.97
1987	3.2	1.94
1988	3.4	2.1
1989	3.5	2.1

Source: Anheuser-Busch *Annual Reports; Amusement Business,* 30 December 1989, 88.

Jumps in attendance at the two parks in certain years (see table 14) are generally attributed to the appearance of new attractions. The increase of visitors to the Dark Continent from 1978 through 1980 probably resulted from the expansion of the Stanleyville and Congo sections and the addition of the African Queen jungle boat excursion. Thanks to the Congo River Rapids water ride, the Tampa park achieved an increase in 1982 despite a general downturn in all Florida attractions while tourists stayed home anticipating the opening of EPCOT Center. Instead of a thrill ride, the record attendance at the Tampa park in 1987 through 1989 is ascribed to special visitors in residence—the giant pandas on loan from the People's Republic of China. In contrast, declining attendance is blamed on gasoline shortages in the mid-1970s and the sluggish economy of the early 1980s, or quite specifically on the opening of EPCOT Center in late 1982.[12] In its financial reports, Anheuser-Busch combines the revenues from theme parks with those gained from a few other diversified operations. The parks dominate this reporting sector, however, and the steady rise in revenues is indicative of the increasing success of the parks (see table 15).

The steadily growing success of the Busch parks is due to the unique atmosphere of the Tampa and Williamsburg properties, each of which has attributes that appeal to various age groups, and the willingness of the corporation continually to devote substantial funds to maintenance and capital improvements ($22.3 million in 1982, rising to $64.2 million in 1988). The Busch parks are the most successful of the theme parks in attracting older visitors. Corporation management has recognized that over-40s and retired folks will continue to be the largest population groups during the coming decades, and the parks have been

Table 15. Revenues for Anheuser-Busch's Diversified Operations Sector (Including Theme Parks) 1982–1988 (in millions of dollars)

Year	Revenues
1982	145.1
1983	149.3
1984	169.5
1985	189.6
1986	247.3
1987	263.8
1988	361.8

Source: Anheuser-Busch *Annual Reports*.

developed with their enjoyment in mind. With the September 1989 purchase of six parks from Harcourt Brace Jovanovich, including four Sea World attractions, Cypress Gardens, and Boardwalk & Baseball, Anheuser-Busch owns ten theme parks, more than any other single company. The parks acquired from Harcourt Brace Jovanovich fit well into Busch's emphasis on attracting more mature clientele with marine shows and exhibits and botanical displays.

☐ **Marriott Corporation**   In 1976 Marriott Corporation, a leader in hotel and restaurant operations, entered the theme park industry by opening two identical Great America parks, one in Santa Clara, California, 40 miles south of San Francisco, and the other in Gurnee, Illinois, between Chicago and Milwaukee. Each 200-acre park comprises five theme areas: Hometown Square, Yukon Territory, Yankee Harbor, Midwest County Fair, and Orleans Place. Within the sectors are lots of rides, a cable car, a train, numerous thrill rides, theaters, restaurants and snack bars, gift and craft shops, and roving circus acts and parades. Construction costs for the two parks together were $72,751,000 in 1976.[13] The Great America parks are planned to the last detail to ensure authenticity and isolation for each theme area. Sectors are kept from intruding on each other by shrubbery zones and visual barriers. A 20-foot high embankment ensures that the real world will not intrude in Marriott's fantasy conception of America.

Marriott's particular vision, as actualized in the Great America parks, deserves some scrutiny. Greeting visitors as they enter through the ticket booths is a double-decker carousel, the Columbia, which while setting a mood of peaceful beauty and charm, also exemplifies larger-than-life excess and artificiality. The horses, fiberglass "replicas" of rare carousel figures, are considered by observers to be "characterless."[14] Elizabeth and Jay Mechling view the park as a patterned series of transitions between "Big/Expensive/Dangerous" and "Human Scale/Inexpensive/Safe."[15] The Columbia itself is in contrast with the much smaller carousel at the opposite end of the Santa Clara park, the Ameri-go-round, a "real" 1918 carousel with carved wooden horses. In each sector, a big and dangerous zone is juxtaposed with a small-scale, safe cluster. For example, Hometown Square, an all-American small town circa 1920 with late Victorian architecture, had a monster in its backyard, Willard's Whizzer, with its menacing spiral track and 70-degree banked turns. Yankee Harbor promoted nostalgic reassurance in its quaint fishing village, but right beyond the lighthouse lurked the Tidal Wave, a roaring flume ride with a 60-foot waterfall to be navigated. The Mechlings interpret the Great America experience as a

Table 16. Marriott's Great America Parks: Revenues, Profit, and Capital
Expenditures, 1976–1984 (in millions of dollars)

Year	Revenues	Operating Profit	Capital Expenditures
1976	36.0	2.4	—
1977	68.7	4.7	9.7
1978	75.5	11.8	9.2
1979	83.9	17.5	6.3
1980	84.8	16.6	16.3
1981	94.7	17.7	10.8
1982	82.5	20.0	10.6
1983	86.2	13.0	9.9
1984	40.1	—	—

Source: Marriott Corporation *Annual Reports.*

"performance" by guests in which they alternately place themselves in danger, "survive," and return to safety. The safety zones provide "rewards" for enduring harrowing exploits—food and gift shops. Consumption, then, becomes a reward for risking danger and a relief from anxiety. The authors conclude that people with a "strong achievement motive" are drawn to the risky thrill rides, then reward themselves with food and merchandise. Great America, then, can be viewed as "a training ground for entrepreneurial consciousness and behavior."[16]

Marriott's Great America venture proved to be an entrepreneurial success for several years, but notwithstanding profits approaching $20 million a year, management gradually became uninterested with its fantasy worlds. The revenue, profit, and capital expenditure figures provided in table 16 can shed some light on Marriott's decision to sell the parks in 1984, the same year Taft Broadcasting divested itself of its parks.

Capital expenditure figures indicate that Marriott was not willing to devote extensive resources for maintenance and improvement of the parks. Attendance at the Great America parks began a steady decline from 1979, during the period of economic stagnation, from which it did not revive. Advertisement was perhaps not as vigorous as it could have been, and Marriott apparently did not recognize the continual need for new attractions. Profits took a significant dive in 1983, despite increased revenues resulting from higher in-park per capita expenditures. The parks must have been viewed as an expensive encumbrance to other

Marriott interests. The Gurnee park was sold in 1984 to Bally Manufacturing Company for $113.2 million, and the Santa Clara park followed in 1985, reaping $82 million. Through the Bally purchase, the Gurnee park became Six Flags Great America, under the banner of the Six Flags organization, at the time a Bally subsidiary. In 1989 the Santa Clara Great America Park was purchased by Kings Entertainment, which also owns Kings Dominion and Carowinds.

□ Six Flags and Bally Manufacturing Corporation

Although the four Six Flags parks were built by the independent Six Flags, Inc., all of the parks as well as the company itself were bought by Bally Manufacturing Corporation in 1982 from Great Southwest Corporation, a subsidiary of Penn Central, for the sum of $146,862,000.[17] Bally's other interests include the operation of casino hotels in Atlantic City, Reno, and Las Vegas; the design, manufacture, and sale of gaming equipment such as slot machines and video games; and the operation of fitness centers.

The 1,500-acre Great Adventure theme park in Jackson, New Jersey, was also acquired by Bally. Opened in 1974 under independent ownership, the huge Great Adventure approaches the scale of the Disney parks and is by far the largest of the non-Disney theme parks. When built, Great Adventure was divided into two sectors: the Safari, where more than 2,000 wild animals roam freely and automobiles drive through, and the Enchanted Forest, a theme area that has boasted for periods of time the world's longest flume ride, the world's highest Ferris wheel, and for a fleeting three weeks in the spring of 1989 the world's highest and fastest roller coaster, the Great American Scream Machine (173 feet high, 68 mph), which would be eclipsed by the roaring Magnum XL-200 at Cedar Point park in Sandusky, Ohio. Despite its size and seven 360-degree loops, the Scream Machine is more of a visual than an experiential scare. One rider finds the two-and-a-half minute ride "as stable and serene as a merry-go-round. . . . There is very little centrifugal force . . . no motion sickness."[18] Other problems at Great Adventure are ordinary fast-food-quality fare, long lines not only for the rides but also for a hamburger, and an insufficient number of water fountains, forcing guests to spend substantial cash for soft drinks.

Great Adventure is only beginning to revive from a fire in one of the enclosed rides that killed eight people on 11 May 1984. A New Jersey grand jury returned an indictment of manslaughter, and by 1986 Bally Corporation settled the wrongful death claims out of court for cash payments. Great Adventure, despite its size and location as the only theme park in easy proximity of New York and Philadelphia, has

Table 17. Revenues and Operating Income for Bally and Six Flags Theme Parks, 1975–1988 (in millions of dollars; debit figures in parentheses)

Year	Revenues	Operating Income	Capital Expenditures
1975	79.2	18.1	—
1977	116.8	28.3	—
1979	177.0	34.0	—
1982	258.7	37.8	25.5
1983	301.8	49.8	50.9
1984	331.6	33.6	32.6
1985	356.9	36.9	45.8
1986	369.4	48.6	31.1
1987*	282.3	(11.4)	28.1
1988*	368.7	(30.8)	29.6

*Six Flags, Inc., no longer part of Bally

Sources: Bally Manufacturing Corporation *Annual Reports;* "Six Flags Corp." in *Disclosure* database, 1989; Margaret Thoren, "Fun and Profit: Amusement Parks Shrug Off First Bad Season in Years," *Barron's* 60 (3 November 1980): 68.

never realized its anticipated or expected potential. In 1989 it finally appears in the top 20 amusement parks in the United States, as measured by attendance. After consistently poor attendance since the fire, Great Adventure rebounded in 1989 to rank 14th among amusement/ theme parks.[19]

In 1984 Bally also acquired from Marriott the Great America theme park in Gurnee, Illinois, for $113,210,000. With this addition Bally was operating seven theme parks: Great Adventure, Six Flags Magic Mountain (Los Angeles), Six Flags over Texas, Six Flags over Great America, Six Flags over Georgia, Six Flags over Mid-America, and Astroworld (Houston). Although it had become a giant in the theme park industry, in 1987 Bally sold all of its amusement park holdings and its subsidiary Six Flags, Inc., to Wesray Corporation for $600 million. As a result, Six Flags, Inc., has achieved a more independent status as a standing corporation devoted solely to theme park ownership and management, although under the corporate umbrella of Wesray. Revenues, income, and capital expenditures for Bally's theme park sector during the years of ownership (1982–86) and for Six Flags, Inc. (1975–79 and 1987–88), are provided in table 17.

In the 1980s the large corporations such as Bally, Taft, and Marriott all decided to disengage themselves from the theme park business largely because the parks, acquired as a sideline to other, more dominant interests, demanded expanding resources in the areas of capital expenditures, operating procedures, and managerial attention. These large parent companies found the seasonal nature of park operation and the fluctuations caused by uncontrollable factors of weather, economics, and fuel prices and availability to be a financial burden. For the steadily successful parks, capital expenditures outpaced income levels. Bally may also have been soured by the legal problems and expenses related to the wrongful death suits following the fire at Great Adventure. The Six Flags parks, once again returned to ownership by a company solely devoted to the business of theme parks, are faring well within the industry. The tremendous resurgence of Great Adventure in 1989 is encouraging. Income losses for Six Flags, Inc., posted for 1987 and 1988 are considered to be the effect of expenses incurred in the acquisition of the company from Bally and changes in expense accounting associated with operation as an independent business.[20]

☐ **Harcourt Brace Jovanovich**   In 1977 Harcourt Brace Jovanovich (HBJ) branched out from its publishing interests by purchasing Sea World, Inc., for $51,241,000. To the three existing marine theme parks in San Diego, Orlando, and Cleveland, HBJ added in 1988 a fourth, in San Antonio; like the others, it provides entertainment in the form of shows involving aquatic life and educational exhibits. The array of marine life is surrounded by theme areas: a Japanese Village, a Hawaiian Village, and Atlantis. The parks' marine biologists and staff also conduct research and rescue services for marine life in the wild.

In 1985 HBJ purchased Cypress Gardens in Winter Haven, Florida, an old park in existence since the 1950s featuring botanical displays, boat tours, and water and animal shows. Two years later HBJ opened Boardwalk & Baseball in Haines City, Florida, which takes action sports as its theme and boasts an old-fashioned seashore boardwalk and a baseball stadium. The Kansas City Royals reside and play there during spring training, while a Class A team in the Florida state league plays its games in the park's stadium throughout the summer.

The HBJ theme park holdings prior to 1989 were second in size only to those of Walt Disney Company. Because the parks had a record of steadily improving revenues and profits for more than a decade (see table 18), it may appear surprising that the company decided in 1989 to offer its

Table 18. HBJ Theme Parks: Revenues, Operating Income, and Capital
Expenditures, 1978–1988 (in millions of dollars)

Year	Revenues	Operating Income	Capital Expenditures
1978	78.0	15.3	8.3
1979	86.1	14.1	17.2
1980	103.8	15.4	12.2
1981	117.3	20.1	12.5
1982	119.0	18.1	14.5
1983	128.1	19.2	20.1
1984	143.2	24.0	17.6
1985	170.4	34.2	30.3
1986[1]	223.2	40.1	86.6
1987[2]	295.1	53.0	144.5
1988	388.0	61.9	69.6

1. Cypress Gardens acquired.
2. Boardwalk & Baseball built.

Source: Harcourt Brace Jovanovich *Annual Reports.*

theme park interests for sale. Company officials made that decision in order to reduce the huge debt assumed in 1987 to thwart a hostile take-over attempt by British publisher Robert Maxwell. The top contenders to purchase HBJ's theme parks were Disney, MCA, Anheuser-Busch, and a group of Japanese bidders. On 28 September 1989 Anheuser-Busch announced an agreement to purchase all six of HBJ's parks for $1.1 billion. W. Randolph Baker, president of Busch Entertainment Company, is responsible for all of these parks along with the Busch attractions. Busch quickly closed Boardwalk & Baseball in January 1990.[21]

□ **MCA, Inc.**   MCA, the motion picture and entertainment giant, operates two theme parks, Universal Studios Hollywood, a tourist attraction since 1964, and Universal Studios Florida, which opened in June 1990. The combination of a studio tour and a theme park transports visitors behind the scenes into a working motion-picture and television production studio, where they can walk through and experience replicated movie sets and famous action sequences, as well as watch or

Table 19. Universal Studios Hollywood:
Revenues and Attendance, 1970–1988 (in
millions)

Year	Revenues	Attendance
1970	$ 6.0	—
1973	$ 11.2	1.56
1975	$ 19.3	2.4
1978[1]	$ 38.7	3.3
1980	$ 52.4	3.8
1981	$ 55.2	3.6
1982[2]	$ 50.4	3.1
1983	$ 51.4	2.95
1984	$ 52.7	2.85
1985	$ 64.5	3.27
1986	$ 84.5	3.8
1987	$ 96.9	4.2
1988	$103.5	4.24

1. Revenues from amphitheater performances
   in Universal City included with studio tour
   revenues.

2. Amphitheater revenues no longer included.

Source: MCA, Inc., *Annual Reports.*

participate in the actual filming. Among individual attractions at Universal Studios Hollywood are "Battlestar Galactica," "Castle Dracula," "King Kong," "Miami Vice Live Action Spectacular," "Star Trek Adventure," "Earthquake: The Big One," and "Streets of the World" which recreates the Moulin Rouge, Sherlock Holmes's Baker Street, and a 1950s American avenue. The Universal Studios Hollywood park has been a tremendous success, with attendance and revenues soaring in the 1980s (see table 19). By 1990 the movie studio tour became the hottest concept in the theme park industry. Universal Studios Hollywood maintains its position among the top five theme parks in attendance, right behind Walt Disney World and Disneyland.

In 1988 MCA, in conjunction with Cineplex Odeon Corporation, opened a newly built studio production facility in Orlando, Florida. Plans for a second studio-tour theme park at the Florida facility, with

Steven Spielberg as creative consultant, were on the boards since 1980,[22] but suffered a devastating blow when Disney rushed to complete its Disney-MGM Studios Theme Park attraction in the Walt Disney World Resort complex in 1989. MCA apparently deliberated over its Orlando studio-tour project for too many years, allowing Disney to scoop them.

MCA is currently engaged in an international venture in conjunction with Nippon Steel Corporation to build Universal Studios Japan. Both Steven Spielberg and famed Japanese film director Akira Kurosawa are consultants for the project. In late 1989 MCA announced its plan to build a theme park near London, in partnership with the Rank Organization and British Urban Development.[23]

☐ Parks Owned by Nonconglomerates

While conglomerate ownership of theme parks dominates the industry, some successful parks are still owned and managed by families or small companies formed for the sole purpose of operating a specific park. Two such parks are Knotts Berry Farm in Buena Park, California, and Cedar Point in Sandusky, Ohio.

☐ **Knott's Berry Farm**   Owned and operated from 1940 to the present by the Knott family, Knott's Berry Farm has consistently maintained its place in the top five theme attractions in the United States as measured by yearly attendance. It has steadily drawn over 3 million visitors a year since the late 1950s, breaking the 5 million mark in 1989. In the late 1970s and early 1980s it firmly held its fourth-place position behind the Disney parks and the Universal Studios Hollywood Tour. From 1986 to 1988 it was slightly edged by Sea World in Orlando, but in 1989 it regained its fourth-place position. Revenues in 1989 reached $160 million.[24] Located in Buena Park, California, it is a mere 22 miles from Los Angeles and offers a retreat into a West long displaced by the California megalopolis.

Knott's Berry Farm has evolved over more than half a century. Unlike its neighbor Disneyland Park, it was not created as the result of a conscious plan or a clear vision. The story of its founder and its development is a charming chronicle of the American pioneer spirit and of independent entrepreneurship. Walter Knott, his wife, Cordelia, and their four children arrived in the Orange County farm district in 1920 after hard, unrewarding years homesteading in the Mojave Desert and sharecropping in the San Luis Obispo area. Walter Knott possessed the qualities ascribed to our mythic conception of the western pioneer: an independent, firm self-reliance; a diligent acceptance of backbreaking toil; an unwavering faith in the promise of the land; and devotion to his family. His personality, his optimistic outlook on the future, and his strong family ties are in striking contrast to the psyche and background of his fellow amusement pioneer, Walt Disney, who arrived in Los Angeles three years later, in 1923.

Knott planted a 10-acre berry patch on his Buena Park land and opened a roadside stand. Within eight years, he and his wife had developed their berry market, where plants as well as berry products were sold, and Cordelia served berry pies and hot biscuits in her small tearoom. To bring in some additional cash during the Great Depression, Cordelia began to serve 65¢ fried chicken dinners with rhubarb appetizers, mashed potatoes and milk gravy, boiled cabbage, hot biscuits, and berry pies for dessert. Mrs. Knott's chicken instantly became famous in Southern California, resulting in the need to build a spacious dining room. In the mid-1930s a Department of Agriculture agent told Walter about an Orange County farmer who had cultivated a new berry, a cross between a loganberry, a blackberry, and a raspberry. Rudolph Boysen showed Knott six struggling vines, which, when transplanted to Knott's much richer soil, began to yield excellent fruit. Within three years, the fruit Knott named the boysenberry was bringing in $1,800 an acre.[25]

By 1940 the farm had expanded to 100 acres, the dining room could seat 600, and the grown children were running the market, a gift shop, a flower stand, and a music box museum. The years of struggle for the Knott family were over. With the growing profits, Walter decided to create a living monument to settlers like his grandmother who had crossed the plains in covered wagons. Walter commissioned an artist to make an indoor cyclorama depicting the hard trek through the desert. The finished attraction featured a tableau of alkali flats, distant blue mountains, dimmed lights to suggest nightfall, a chorus in song, and a narrator relating the hardships and dangers of the migration. To house this show in a suitable enclosure, Knott found the abandoned 1869 Gold Trails Hotel in Prescott, Arizona, and had it transported piece by piece to Buena Park, where he installed his cyclorama. Inspired, he scouted old abandoned gold-mining towns for more ramshackle buildings to move to his reconstructed ghost town in the berry patch. Soon, a stagecoach, the Calico Lost Mine train ride, a Haunted Shack, and a replica gold mine where guests could try their luck panning for precious nuggets made their appearance. Ghost Town—conceived and built as a reminder and living museum of California's pioneer heritage—was free to waiting customers of the Chicken Dinner Restaurant.

By the late 1950s the Chicken Dinner Restaurant was serving 4,000 dinners a day in seven dining rooms; some 270 products of the farm, kitchens, and bakeries were sold on site and available through mail-order catalogs; and the Ghost Town trailed through 30 acres. Knott is reported to have expressed his business philosophy as follows: "We'll keep building just as fast as we earn. We'll pay the help and taxes, and plow what's left back into the business. We'll grow slow and steady with no help from anybody else."[26]

Thrill rides invaded the "farm" in 1970, making it a true theme park with three major sectors: the Old West Ghost Town; Fiesta Village, portraying Spanish California; and the Roaring Twenties, a nostalgic traditional amusement area with a 1920s-era airfield. By then admission charges had been instituted. In 1975 the world's first Corkscrew roller coaster made its debut at the Berry Farm. The youngest Knott daughter, Marion Knott Anderson, continued to oversee operations and improvements. The late 1970s brought substantial competition in the Los Angeles area from Magic Mountain in Valencia, new attractions at Disneyland, and the growing popularity of the Universal Studios Hollywood Tour. Knott's Berry Farm countered with a 10-year, $100 million master plan culminating in two massive attractions, which made their debut in 1987 and 1988. The $7-million "Kingdom of the Dinosaurs" ride opened in 1987, featuring a jungle setting with 23 lurking prehistoric beasts that hiss, chomp, and roar at visitors. The 3.5-acre, $10 million "Wild Water Wilderness," a water rapids ride complete with boulders, waterfalls, geysers, and cliffs, was unveiled in 1988, and in the 1990 season a new coaster, dubbed the Boomerang, arrived, manufactured by the Netherlands-based Vekoma International. This monster has three forward-motion upside-down loops and three backward loops, and dumps riders down its steepest hill backward. In 1988 Terry Van Gorder, the president and chief operating officer of Knott's Berry Farm, succinctly articulated the essence of the park's advantage over other theme attractions in the area: "There's an earthy texture to Knott's. . . . Disney is artificial in a way. Knott's is farm-like. It's just more natural, it's just real."[27] Texture is the important distinction here. The Disney parks offer no tactile experience, since touch destroys the illusion, proving a tree trunk or boulder to be plastic, and almost everything is protected by placement beyond one's extended reach. In contrast, many constructions at Knott's Berry Farm are of rough-hewn wood, corrugated metal (in the airfield), tiles, and stucco. A year-long celebration during 1990 marks the 50th anniversary of Walter Knott's purchase of the Knott's Berry Farm land.

☐ **Cedar Point**   As sketched in chapter 4, Cedar Point, well over a century old and located on Lake Erie in Sandusky, west of Cleveland, Ohio, is one of the longest-surviving amusement parks in America. As such it generates much cultural interest, especially regarding its successful conversion into a theme park. After Cedar Point's dynamic earlier owner-managers—George Roose, Emile Legros, and later Robert L. Munger, Jr.—passed away, the park became owned and operated by a partnership, Cedar Fair, L.P., which limits its interests solely to Cedar Point and one other smaller park, Valleyfair, near Minneapolis. Cedar Point is blessed by a location within a market area of 22 million people, within easy driving distance of Cleveland, Akron, Toledo, Detroit, Columbus, Flint, Saginaw, and Youngstown. However, its northern location limits its season to just over 100 days each summer.

Cedar Point's prosperity in the 1960s and early 1970s generated acquisition and takeover interests. August Busch, Jr., of Anheuser-Busch, Inc., visited in 1972, and Taft Broadcasting Company made an official offer in the same year. In 1974 Marriott Corporation made another friendly offer. Roose and Legros terminated both of these negotiations despite offers in excess of $60 million. MCA Recreation Enterprises attempted an unfriendly takeover by offering to purchase a large amount of outstanding shares of Cedar Point stock. Fortunately for Cedar Point, the stock rose to well above the price offered by MCA, effectively squashing the hostile maneuver. Recognizing the threat of such takeovers, the directors authorized the formation of a new partnership comprised of S. Pearson and Son, Ltd., a British firm that owns interests in Madame Tussaud's Wax Museum; Lazard Freres & Company; and Cedar Point president Robert L. Munger, Jr. Cedar Fair Limited Partnership became final in 1983 with director Munger, under whose management as chief executive officer the park had achieved profits in excess of $10 million in 1982.[28] George A. Boeckling's turn-of-the-century "Queen of American Watering Places" had made the transformation to "Cedar Point, the Amazement Park."

"The Amazement Park" is an apt publicity moniker, since Cedar Point has also been dubbed "America's Roller Coast." Under Robert Munger's leadership in the 1970s, Cedar Point began to direct much of its expansion and capital improvements toward the installation of state-of-the-art roller coasters. The Corkscrew was the first of the revolutionary "scream machines" to invade the Cedar Point midway. Appearing in 1976, the world's first triple-looping coaster, featuring two helical curves and a 360-degree loop, sends screaming passengers on a two-and-a-quarter-minute ride with a top speed of 48 miles per hour. Constructed of tubular steel, its $1.75 million price tag makes it seem a bargain in comparison with later coasters.

Built in 1978, the gigantic wooden Gemini racing coaster, with its

The Corkscrew, the world's first triple-looping roller coaster, built in 1976 at Cedar Point park, Sandusky, Ohio. *Courtesy Cedar Point park.*

two parallel tracks, was at its opening the highest and fastest coaster in the world. Its 125-foot height provides a top speed of 60 miles per hour and a vertical drop of 118 feet. Riders cover its 3,935 feet of track, nearly twice as long as the Corkscrew, in 2 minutes, 20 seconds. The massive "woody" is constructed of Western fir at a cost of $3.4 million. Former park owner George Roose, then in his 80s, was one of Gemini's first brave riders. Since then, over 3 million riders experience the stomach-churning racer each season.

Avalanche Run, debuting in 1985, is unique in that the free-wheeling cars are not attached to tracks, but rather travel through metal troughs like bobsleds sliding through an iced course. The 10-person bobsleds depend solely on gravity to zip through the course at about 40 miles per hour. The ride was designed and built by the Swiss firm Intamin AG at a cost of $3.4 million.

The Iron Dragon, like the Corkscrew a visually intriguing ride, features cars suspended below the track and creates an impression of

Table 20. Cedar Point Revenues, Operating Income, Capital Expenditures,
           and Attendance, 1969–1988 (in millions)

Year	Revenues	Operating Income	Capital Expenditures	Attendance
1969	$18.3	$1.6	—	—
1970	$22.6	$2.3	—	—
1975	$34.2	$10.7	—	2.6
1978	$52.7	$18.2	—	3.0
1983	$75.3	—	$1.9	—
1984	$76.8	$18.9	$2.9	3.4
1985	$85.5	$23.5	$7.5	3.7
1986	$96.3	$28.7	$8.5	4.1
1987	$102.8	$30.1	$7.9	4.1
1988	$103.2	$30.1	$8.1*	3.9

*Capital expenditures reached $12 million in 1989.

Source: Cedar Fair and Cedar Point *Annual Reports* and *Securities and Exchange Commis-
         sion 10-K Reports;* Margaret Thoren, "Fun and Profit: Amusement Parks Shrug Off
         First Bad Season in Years," *Barron's* 60 (3 November 1980): 68.

flying as cars sway side to side as they negotiate the swirling course.
Emerging over the lagoon in 1987 at a cost of $4 million, the Iron
Dragon swoops its riders down dips of 76 feet and 62 feet, along a giant
pretzel-knot loop, and through an eerie mist inches above the lagoon
depths. The 2,800 feet of tubular track is covered in two minutes at
about 40 miles per hour.

The epitome of roller coasters reared its awe-inspiring form over
Lake Erie in May 1989. At an astounding cost of $8 million, the Mag-
num XL-200 is listed in the *Guinness Book of World Records* as the
highest and fastest coaster (at 205 feet and 72 miles per hour), with the
longest vertical drop, which dumps passengers 194 feet at a 60-degree
angle. The extensive track, running 5,106 feet, is completed in a fright-
fully fast two and a half minutes. Excitement is heightened by three
hills, 80-foot-high banked curves, and three tunnels with strobe lighting
and special sound effects. The steel tubular construction appears thin
and fragile, thus serving as an additional scare factor for observers and
brave waiting riders. Built under the direction of Cedar Point's president and chief executive officer, Richard L. Kinzel, the Magnum is the
culmination of the park's coaster history, which began in 1892 when

The Magnum XL-200, the highest and fastest roller coaster to date, Cedar Point park, Sandusky, Ohio, 1989. *Courtesy Cedar Point park.*

revelers first rode the Switchback Railway at the fearsome speed of six miles per hour. The whizzing speed of the Magnum is a mind-boggling transformation from the Switchback, where gravity often did not provide sufficient momentum for the cars to return to the exit platform, necessitating an added pull literally by horsepower or manpower.[29]

Along with its plan to concentrate on installing major thrill rides, Cedar Point's management has maintained an exceptional capital expenditures program to reinvest substantial profits back into the park. Heeding demographic studies, management has recognized the need to appeal to all age groups. The Oceana Marine-Life Center, celebrating its 10th year in 1989, offers a spectacular show with trained dolphins and sea lions. The aquarium provides visitors a close-up look at sharks, penguins, and other exotic sea life. There is a petting zoo, and an African animal show features Bengal tigers, leopards, pigs, and chimps. Primarily for children and teens, the new five-acre water park, Soak City, features 10 inner-tube, speed, and body slides. Meticulous attention continues to be given to flower displays and to maintenance and cleanliness. A large variety of food, available in several distinct restaurants and stands, is of high quality with emphasis on uniqueness and fun. Restaurants provide an alternative quiet and serene atmosphere for those who need a respite from the noise and crowds. Care to preserve Cedar Point's past is evident in restored iron lampposts, now hung with colorful flowerpots, and in prominent display of large iron urns, many featuring marvelous sculpted griffins, which were commissioned for Cedar Point around the turn of the century. There is also deliberate retention of the traditional midway excitement of games of chance. While other parks erect barriers to exclude the real world, Cedar Point makes every effort to bring the spectacular Lake Erie coast into the action. Thus there is a sense of expansion and unbounded freedom rather than confinement and limitations. The Cedar Point experience, a blend of the breathless excitement of thrill rides and pleasing nostalgia or memories of carefree summer days of one's youth, is honest fun without the overwhelming artificiality of some other major parks.

Although it remains independent and does not have corporate coffers for major investment, Cedar Point continues its growth and steadily improves its prominence among American theme parks. Operations through the limited Cedar Fair partnership, with management interests devoted solely to Cedar Point and its smaller sister park, Valleyfair, promises continued success. On tap for the 1990 season are capital improvements totalling $9.5 million, including an enclosed space adventure simulation ride called "Disaster Transport," construction of a 96-suite hotel, and a Lazy River addition to Soak City.[30] The financial and attendance data in table 20 testify to the wisdom of management's strategy in the last two decades and to the park's auspicious future.

☐ Attendance and Revenue

Industrywide growth in attendance and revenues since 1970, as detailed in table 21, indicates the enduring appeal of amusement parks almost in flagrant disregard for economic conditions. By 1988 amusement parks became a $4-billion-a-year industry.

The compilation of the top 20 amusement attractions in the United States, as measured by attendance, actually shows little change from 1979 to 1989, as table 22 reveals. Considering the dominant influence of new rides and major entertainment shows as well as the weather on attendance, most of the major theme parks were able to attract loyal, repeat visitors during the 1980s. One major loser was Great Adventure, in Jackson, New Jersey, which fell from number 4 in 1979 to number 24 in 1988, but recovered somewhat in 1989 to move up to number 15. Its ownership since 1987 by the Six Flags organization, after several disastrous years under Bally Corporation, obviously resulted in a resurgence for the park. The Sea World parks were moving up while the Busch Gardens parks slipped a bit, with the Old Country park, in Williamsburg, Virginia, dropping to number 21 in 1989. Both the Sea

Table 21. Attendance and Revenues of Amusement Parks and Attractions in the United States, 1970–1988, Selected Years (in millions)

Year	Attendance	Revenues
1970	151	$321
1976	173	$832
1980	178	$1,400
1986	215	$2,000
1989	254	$4,000

Sources: *Amusement Business*, 30 December 1989, 80; *Barron's*, 12 July 1971, 11; *Wall Street Journal*, 2 July 1987, 21; Somerset R. Waters, *Travel Industry World Yearbook: The Big Picture, 1987* (New York: Child & Waters, 1987), 16.

Table 22. Top 20 Amusement Attractions by Attendance, 1979 and 1989 (in millions)

1979		1989	
Attraction	Attendance	Attraction	Attendance
1. Walt Disney World Resort	13.2	Walt Disney World Resort	30.0
2. Disneyland Park	11.2	Disneyland Park	14.4
3. Universal Studios Tour	3.5	Universal Studios Hollywood	5.1
4. Six Flags' Great Adventure	3.2	Knott's Berry Farm	5.0
5. Busch Gardens' Dark Continent	2.9	Sea World of Florida	3.96
6. Knott's Berry Farm	2.8	Sea World of California	3.78
7. Marriott's Great America, Gurnee, Ill.	2.8	Busch Gardens' Dark Continent	3.5
8. Sea World, Orlando	2.8	Kings Island	3.17
9. Cedar Point	2.7	Cedar Point	3.15
10. Kings Island	2.5	Six Flags' Magic Mountain	3.1

Rank	Attraction	Attendance		Attraction	Attendance
11.	Sea World, San Diego	2.5		Santa Cruz Beach Boardwalk	2.8
12.	Six Flags over Georgia	2.4		Six Flags over Texas	2.6
13.	Six Flags over Texas	2.3		Canada's Wonderland	2.5*
14.	Busch Gardens' Old Country	2.2		Six Flags' Great America, Gurnee, Ill.	2.4
15.	Marriott's Great America, Santa Clara	2.0		Six Flags' Great Adventure	2.4
16.	Six Flags' Magic Mountain	1.8		Opryland	2.35
17.	Opryland	1.8		Ontario Place, Toronto†	2.3
18.	Kings Dominion	1.7		Six Flags Over Georgia	2.24
19.	Six Flags' Astroworld	1.7		Great America, Santa Clara	2.22
20.				Kings Dominion	2.2

*Amusement Business actually lists attendance at Canada's Wonderland at 2.25 million in 1989; however, its ranking indicates that the figure must be a misprint and should read 2.5 million.

†Ontario Place is not an amusement park but primarily a sports and shopping complex with some amusement attractions.

Sources: U.S. Travel Data Center and Business Research Division, University of Colorado, *Tourism's Top Twenty 1984* (Boulder: Business Research Division, University of Colorado, 1984), 86. This list, which provides attendance figures for both 1979 and 1981, ranks Canada's Wonderland number 18; that park, however, did not exist in 1979; *Amusement Business*, 30 December 1989, 88.

World and the Busch Gardens parks should be watched in coming years following Anheuser-Busch's purchase of the Harcourt Brace Jovanovich Sea World and other attractions in late 1989. Six Flags Magic Mountain was a big mover, jumping from 16th to 10th place. Moving in the opposite direction was the Great America in Gurnee, Ill., which dropped from number 7 in 1979 to number 14 in 1989. Six Flags over Georgia also slipped, from 12th to 18th place on the list. Cedar Point and Knott's Berry Farm are the only two theme parks not operated by large corporate interests that consistently maintain their position in the top 15 amusement attractions.

In late 1986 John R. Graff, executive director of the International Association of Amusement Parks and Attractions, predicted a sunny outlook for the theme park industry. Citing the first study to assess public attitudes toward the parks, which was commissioned by the association and performed by the U.S. Travel Data Center, Graff noted findings that 53 percent of all Americans planned to attend an amusement park during the summer months and that they would go an average of 1.9 times in the season. In addition, over 73 million vacation trips were scheduled to include an amusement or theme park. An estimated 24 percent of the population over 65 years of age would visit a park. To respond to the increase in older visitors, Graff explained that parks were increasing their efforts toward beautification, as well as the provision of diversified entertainment and food services. The rising cost and decreasing availability of insurance coverage Graff considered the only serious problems facing the industry.[31]

Trends in the 1980s indicate that large corporate owner-operators became frustrated by the constant funding demands necessary to achieve immaculate maintenance and new attractions in the parks. Corporations unwilling both to keep vigilant eyes and ears to the desires and preferences of the public and to develop new attractions within the parks every couple of years can only watch their parks decline. Owner-operators must also have managers with the talent to visualize and apply new technologies to the creation of amusement extravaganzas. Americans at the onset of the 1990s are beginning to demonstrate a lack of patience with total artificiality, with programmed activities, and with conspicuous consumption. Spontaneity and the need to assert individuality are showing signs of surfacing in the common cultural psyche, and some theme parks, as presently configured, will be hard-pressed to respond if they maintain the packaging of everything from food to rides to sound.

7

Walt Disney World Resort
Pilgrimage Center and "Back to the Future" Utopia

Wake Up in a Perfect World This Fall!
—1989 advertising slogan for Walt Disney World Resort

IN THE SUMMER OF 1964 AGENTS FOR WALT Disney began quietly to purchase parcels of swamp land and citrus groves in central Florida on the outskirts of the then small city of Orlando. When a few local residents spotted the famous Disney in the vicinity of the vast tracts of orange trees, it was explained that Disney's father and mother were married in Kissimmee and that their son was indulging in a "sentimental pilgrimage."[1] The Disney family roots in central Florida may have influenced Walt to explore the central Florida location for his eastern venture. In a calculated ploy to keep land prices at bargain levels and to secure a vast amount of acreage, Disney's agents bought the parcels in small pieces under a variety of holding companies with names like "Tomahawk" and "Compass East."[2] In fact, speculation centered on the U.S. government as the force behind the massive land acquisition not far from the existing Cape Canaveral complex. By October 1965 Disney's agents had secured 27,443 acres, nearly 43 square miles, at a total cost of just over $5 million or about $200 an acre.

Disney had been frustrated by the lack of space at the comparatively tiny 160-acre Disneyland Park tract, which, although originally ringed by orange groves, soon became surrounded by motels, fast-food enterprises, freeways, and tacky suburban development. To insure against a similar encroachment at the Florida site, Disney planned a massive tract that would serve as a natural buffer against other commercial interests and development. Even in 1990, with three major attractions and several smaller venues, only 5,000 acres are developed.

Citizens of central Florida became alerted to Disney sponsorship of the land purchases in Orange and Osceola counties when Orlando *Sentinal* reporter Emily Bavar, on a promotional trip to Disneyland Park during its 10th anniversary in 1965, asked Walt if he was buying land in Florida for an eastern park. Disney protested too much, citing detailed reasons why central Florida was unsuitable for a theme park, including the rainy climate, the swamplands, the humidity, and transportation inadequacies. Bavar realized that Disney could not be such an expert on the area unless he had intensely studied and surveyed it. Her column identifying the Disney organization as the likely land grabber was soon followed by a front-page article by the *Sentinal*'s publisher, Martin Anderson, stating his conviction that Disney and Mickey Mouse were on their way to central Florida. The secret was revealed, but well after Disney had acquired nearly all the land and made a deal with the state government for absolute control over the vast tract. On 15 November 1965 Florida governor Haydon Burns publicly confirmed plans for the building of Walt Disney World Resort[3] (officially named "Walt Disney World Resort, near Orlando, Florida").

□   Engineering and Environmental Systems

Walt Disney World's rise from the Florida swamps would be an unprecedented engineering feat. The tropical, boggy terrain's water table rests on a stratum of porous limestone rock through which moisture continuously seeps, creating underground caverns. The caverns eventually collapse, resulting in large surface sinkholes. Just to stabilize the building sites, the Disney engineers had to drain off the swamp water, develop a system of canals for continuous drainage, dredge out the unstable muck that seeps into the caverns, pump off all the water and muck to an offsite area, then bring in stable, nonindigenous material to compress into the sinkholes and shape the area to the contours specified by the designers. Walt Disney World's chief sanitation engineer during construction, Arthur Bravo, explains that to achieve a drainage system that would not only provide constant drainage but also ensure flood control, conserve the water table, and protect the projected man-made recreation lakes from runoff from the swamps, 44 miles of canals and channeled streams were constructed. The water level in the lakes and the canals would be controlled by 16 self-regulating dams and seven other weir structures.[4] Because the naturally existing 450-acre Bay Lake, which now forms the entry border to the Magic Kingdom and is ringed by the Contemporary Resort, Polynesian Village, and Grand Floridian Resort, was found to be too polluted, Disney engineers completely drained it, cleared it of weeds and a layer of organic muck, dredged white sand up from under the lake to create beaches, and pumped underground water to refill the lake. The effort was capped off by stocking the lake with 70,000 fingerling bass.[5]

Through an agreement with the state of Florida, Disney was allowed to establish the independent Reedy Creek Improvement District, which encompasses all of the acquired land and is empowered with the authority to develop, own, and operate utility, flood control, and drainage systems and to establish and enforce building codes. Thus the Walt Disney World complex operates much like an independent state—the Vatican City of leisure and entertainment. The Reedy Creek Utilities Company, a Disney subsidiary, owns and operates the water and sewage systems for the parks, hotels, and commercial complexes, the chilled and hot water systems, electrical distribution system, natural gas system, compressed air system, trash collection and processing services, and the complex drainage system. The Reedy Creek Improvement District can also establish its own environmental protection operations including setting air and water pollution standards.

Arthur Bravo has described the utility systems as they existed at the time of the opening of the Magic Kingdom and through the early 1970s. The operating heart of Walt Disney World is the central energy plant, which uses jet turbines fueled by either natural gas or diesel oil to produce electrical power. The system is marvelously efficient, since exhaust gases pass into boilers and absorption chillers, which produce both the hot water and the chilled water for air conditioning needed in the parks and hotels. The energy plant also produces the compressed air used in various systems, including those that manipulate some animated characters.

Wells obtain water from local aquifers and pump it to a storage tank. From there the water is distributed to a pumping station and runs through chlorination treatment. A standby well powered by gas can come online in the event of power failure or other casualty to the main pumping station. Sewage travels by means of gravity lines, force mains, and pump stations to the Disney-owned and -built treatment plant. The plant provides activated sludge treatment, rapid sand filtration, and aeration. The sewage plant must treat more "volatile suspended solids" than those occurring in most domestic sewage because of the high quantities of food waste and grease. Following about 20 days of treatment, the resultant sludge is disposed of in sludge beds or hauled to the experimental tree farm on the Disney property, where the material is "utilized as a humus." Effluent from the treatment plant is partially disposed of on the "living farm," where various ornamental trees are grown and natural filtration is achieved by trees and plants. Remaining effluent is chlorinated and run into a wetlands area.

The solid waste disposal system is perhaps the most technologically intriguing utility system within Walt Disney World. The first application of the Automatic Vacuum Collection (AVAC) system, developed by AB Centralsug, a Swedish company, was installed in a Swedish hospital in 1961. The Disney AVAC system is the largest in the world and the first installed in the United States. AVAC transfers garbage from charging stations down into vertical storage sectors above discharge valves. When activated, the discharge valves drop the waste into vacuum tubes, which whisk the garbage by means of a high-velocity air stream to the central collection compacting plant. The air flow along the tubes reaches a velocity of approximately 60 miles per hour. Once at the compactor, the trash is pressed into parcels, which are then transferred to Disney incinerators. The AVAC system is designed to process three tons of refuse per hour.[6]

By securing an agreement with the state of Florida to develop and control its own utility systems, the Disney organization has established its own 43-square-mile fiefdom where every element is controlled and can be manipulated by corporate leadership. While Disney pollution standards are generally responsive to the protection of the environment, the sheer volume of water needs and waste disposal have an enormous impact on Florida ecosystems.

Disney conceived Walt Disney World to be much more than an East Coast Disneyland. This time he would create a complete vacationland with theme attractions, hotels and resorts, and recreational facilities for boating, tennis, golf, and even bird watching. Lake Buena Vista, a small residential-commercial community with vacation and permanent residences and an industrial sector, was part of the original plan. Walt's most cherished dream, the Experimental Prototype Community of Tomorrow (EPCOT), was actually the visionary core of his eastern project, and it cast a utopian, futuristic prospect over the design of the entire complex. An amusement park would just be one element in this world of illusion and dreams of tomorrow.

Walt Disney planned and supervised preconstruction development of phase 1 of Walt Disney World Resort in intricate detail and prepared general directions for the development of the whole complex. He chose the surrounding shores of Bay Lake, the largest natural body of water, as the site of the Magic Kingdom and the first resort complexes. He directed his closest associates to proceed with the formulation of plans for EPCOT Center, in his conception a showcase City of Tomorrow complete with a permanent resident population, industry, schools, and research facilities. He scoffed at warnings that EPCOT Center could not make money, steadfastly contending that Walt Disney World Resort would pay for his dream metropolis. But on 15 December 1966, Walt Disney died of lung cancer, six months before the first earth-moving equipment arrived at the shores of Bay Lake.

Walt's preoccupation with futuristic technologies at the time of his death has fueled speculation that he arranged to have his body, upon his demise, preserved for possible future resuscitation by being frozen in a cryogenic facility. It was not until several hours after his death that a public announcement was made stating that the body had already been cremated and that there would be no funeral. Some veteran Disney staffers doubted that the ashes of their boss were buried in Forest Lawn in Glendale, California. Instead, they speculated, his body lies in a state of cryogenesis waiting for medical science to catch up with Disney's faith in technology. Longtime associate Ward Kimball has responded to rumors that Walt's body is frozen somewhere by commenting that "Walt was always intensely interested in things scientific, and he, more than any person I knew, just might have been curious enough to agree to such an experiment."[7] There is little doubt that heads would roll at the Disney organization if the founding father ever returned and saw what they did to his EPCOT vision.

☐ The Magic Kingdom: Walt Disney World Resort, Phase 1

The Disney organization, led by Walt's brother Roy, was meticulously faithful to Walt's plans for the creation of the Magic Kingdom and the initial resort areas. At the gala opening of Walt Disney World Resort on 23 October 1971, Arthur Fiedler conducted the World Symphony, composed of 145 musicians from 66 countries, as the whole Disney clan, led by Walt's widow, Lilly, strolled down the entrance to Cinderella's Castle. Representing an initial investment of $400 million, the Magic Kingdom and the accompanying recreational resort facilities lured nearly 11 million people in its first year of operation. Since then Walt Disney World has hosted at least 300 million guests.

When Walt Disney World opened in 1971, then comprising primarily the Magic Kingdom, two resorts, the Contemporary Resort, and the Polynesian Village, as well as the satellite Lake Buena Vista community, prominent progressive architects and planners extolled the complex for its achievements in urban design. Peter Blake called it "the most interesting New Town in the United States." Robert Venturi praised Walt Disney World as "nearer to what people really want than anything architects have ever given them. . . . It's a symbolic American utopia." And Paul Goldberger labeled it "perhaps the most important city planning laboratory in the United States." He considers a trip to Disney World to be an "obligatory pilgrimage for young architects," just as visits to European monuments had been for earlier generations.[8] Its infrastructure, mass-transit systems, People Movers, and pedestrian traffic patterns had been considered unattainable by planners and thus never before seriously considered.

A principal achievement is the construction of the Magic Kingdom, a city in itself, on top of a vast service and utility basement with a network of tunnel-like corridors. Through these corridors, employees traverse to their appropriate sectors, thus ensuring that nonindigenous costumes will never intrude upon the authenticity of a particular locale and that all deliveries can be made without detracting from the enchantment of the Magic Kingdom. Also in the basement area are water, electric, and sewer lines, all exposed and easily accessible for repair or service. Vast stores of costumes, laundries, offices, service areas for employees, and the computers that run the Magic Kingdom are also located in the basement. Disneyland, in comparison, has services and repair shops less efficiently located on the periphery.

Next in praise is the energy-efficient monorail system that loops around Walt Disney World with speed, efficiency, and the quiet afforded by electric power. Although designed by Disney's WED Enterprises and similar to the earlier monorail installed in Disneyland, the sleek Walt Disney World monorail is manufactured by the Martin Marietta Corporation, a Disney neighbor in Orlando. Paul Goldberger contends that while the monorail is surely a "symbol of the future," it has limitations that make it impractical for use in real cities. It has a top speed of 45 miles per hour, limited by the friction created by the beam upon which it rides, and the switching system is extremely complex.[9]

The enormous computer system initially designed by RCA, now joined by Sperry, monitors and operates the entire complex. Not only does it control all rides, audioanimatronic and other mechanical devices throughout the parks, the monorail, all live entertainment shows, and multimedia events, it monitors all environmental control devices (air conditioning, lighting, and so on), utilities, services, and fire-sensing apparatus. Seemingly eons rather than a mere 70 years or so beyond Coney Island, the gears, wheels, and steel have been supplanted by the invisible, secretly silent power of electronics and silicon. The work of the computers is undeniably more magical, but at the same time it is less accessible to the visitor and thus denies a participatory exploration of the workings of a ride or event. While Coney's revelers could often observe or even explore the technologies providing the fun and enchantment, visitors to Walt Disney World are simply awed by the results of computer engineering. While Coney served to engage turn-of-the-century merrymakers with the technologies of the Industrial Revolution, Walt Disney World Resort lets its visitors wonder but not inquire.

The architectural firm of Welton Becket & Associates designed the first two impressive resort hotels at Walt Disney World, the Contemporary Resort and the Polynesian Village. The Contemporary Resort rises 14 stories above Bay Lake, with its rooms snugly fit along the outside of the huge A-frame. On the interior, the rooms open on the spectacular 10-story Grand Canyon Concourse, complete with a station for the monorail trains, which travel directly through the concourse lobby. The Contemporary's major technological contribution is the construction engineering of the prefabricated rooms. Because the Disney organization wanted units larger than a width of 12 feet, which was the size limitation allowable for transport via public roads, a facility was built on the Disney site by U.S. Steel to manufacture the modules. The cost of production of the prefab units soared far beyond expectations. U.S. Steel originally estimated cost at $17,000 per room, but the expense of developing the facility onsite and the construction system raised costs to nearly $100,000 per room. The units when assembled were fully wired, fitted with lighting fixtures, some built-in furniture, carpeting, and very elaborate bathrooms with all plumbing in place. They measure 14½ feet wide, 8 feet tall, and 39 feet long. Although the construction costs were high, U.S. Steel was able to produce a dozen modules a day, thus speeding up the building process. The cost of the Contemporary Resort skyrocketed to nearly $100 million. Architects find the Contemporary to be impressive but evocative of a 1950s comic-book version of futuristic architecture.[10] But it does contain creature comforts worthy of the 1990s, including two swimming pools, lighted tennis courts, electronic games, a movie theater, a health club equipped with sauna and whirlpool, and a rooftop restaurant/entertainment center.

The Polynesian Village is also built of prefabricated rooms produced by the onsite facility. This Hollywood- or at least California-inspired version of the South Seas may be much too glitzy to be at all authentic, but its architecture is of an intimate, relaxing scale and the gardens are splendid. A purely Disney touch is the underwater background music. A nightly luau and South Seas entertainment complete the island paradise à la Disney. Succeeding years have seen the addition of several more hotel resort complexes including the very upscale Grand Floridian Beach Resort, the Disney Inn, Walt Disney World Village, the Caribbean Beach Resort, and Fort Wilderness for campers. In 1990 the massive Dolphin and Swan hotels and conference center project, with nearly 3,000 rooms, was opened.

The Magic Kingdom is much grander in scale than its forerunner, Disneyland. Everything is taller and bigger. The design is essentially similar, with entry through a Victorian town square and Main Street, U.S.A. The familiar lands are repeated—Adventureland, Frontierland, Fantasyland, and Tomorrowland—with the addition of the patriotic Liberty Square as a substitute for Disneyland's New Orleans Square. Recently, Mickey's Birthdayland, a kiddie park, has appeared in celebration of the mouse's 60th birthday. Cinderella's Castle is much more elaborate and dominating than is Sleeping Beauty's relatively modest abode in the original park. The efficient design of a central hub from which sectors radiate outward is retained.

The two Main Streets lend themselves to comparison because of the decidedly different atmosphere created by the increase in scale at the Magic Kingdom. While the buildings at Disneyland were constructed at two-thirds scale to generate a feeling of intimacy, the shops, dwellings, restaurants, city hall, the firehouse, and the train station in the Magic Kingdom are full-scale recreations at ground level. They are higher and more elaborate and lavish than the buildings at Disneyland, resulting in a sense of overbearing closeness that is almost oppressive, especially in the crowded conditions of this area of the park. The sensory overload of the unceasingly elaborate Victorian architectural detail seems to overcome the onlooker. In this case, the reduced scale on successive floors, a technique to create an illusion of greater height, backfires: the buildings seem somewhat threatening, and the narrowness of the sidewalks and the street does not allow the visitor to view entire structures during a walk down Main Street. Small side streets end in buildings rather than trees or greenery, further enforcing a closed-in environment. The architecture itself incorporates many Gothic rather than Victorian shapes.

The Magic Kingdom's Main Street is a musical-comedy stage that places the visitor within a movie set. Like Disneyland's Main Street, it does not attempt to simulate reality. The buildings are visual images of ideal types; they generate the *idea* of a prosperous turn-of-the-century town without conflict, poverty, natural decay, mud, or any problems. It is a mythic conception with only minimal basis in fact. Construction is primarily of fiberglass, quite appropriate for durability in the Florida heat and humidity, but disillusioning to the touch. Main Street is one of the few areas where the attraction is within the visitor's reach, but touching destroys the illusion. The fiberglass is too smooth, rigid, and uniform. Architect-planner Louis Wasserman agrees, noting that Walt Disney World "needs more ground texture, vertical surfaces." It is all "too slick too new!"[11] Fiberglass is technology's improvement over the impermanent staff used to create the heavenly buildings of the World's Columbian Exposition. It adds durability and maintenance ease to staff's facility to be molded into intricate designs.

In his analysis of the two Main Streets, built over fifteen years apart, Richard V. Francaviglia finds that the Magic Kingdom's streetscape "feels exotic, is more surreal, and more eccentric than Main Street in Disneyland." Both the buildings on the street and Cinderella's Castle exhibit a "hyper-accentuation of verticality" as the result of "a greater number of taller turrets, towers and arieles [sic]."[12] All in all, while Disneyland's Main Street is deliberately subdued and therefore relaxing and welcoming, its Florida counterpart is intense, demanding, and almost claustrophobic.

The Magic Kingdom contains thrill rides that were not part of the founder's original vision. Over the years such rides have also found a place in Disneyland. Seemingly as a concession to the popularity of roller coasters in theme parks across the country, the Magic Kingdom boasts the Big Thunder Mountain Railroad in Frontierland and the sublime Space Mountain in Tomorrowland. Space Mountain's race through the blackness of an interplanetary void is for riders a conquering of fear and danger. As riders reach the exit, they are convinced of their own bravery and fortitude. There is a tangible feeling of having risen to meet a challenge.

Perhaps the finest attraction in terms of entertainment and application of technology for amusement is the "Haunted Mansion." As visitors gather in a lobby surrounded with sinister portraits, the floor begins to sink. The dropping floor immediately creates a sense of insecurity and a realization that there is no escape. The slightly unsettled crowd is then led to cabs (black, of course), which transport riders through a series of supernatural sets, in a sequence much like a motion picture. The use of lasers to create free-floating and rapidly mobile spirits is most dramatic and effective, far surpassing audioanimatronic creatures, which are rooted to a spot and limited to repetitive motions.

The rather static nature of audioanimatronic technology is most evident in the "Pirates of the Caribbean" attraction. Boats haul riders through a series of tableaus in which a rowdy gang of pirates endlessly repeats dastardly deeds. The slow, floating pace makes riders aware of the repetitious movements of the robot pirates and animals. A sexist display of buxom women in bondage with a sign reading "Buy a Bride" is more offensive than cute. Finally, the ride reaches a manipulative end, as riders must depart through a commercial clothing and trinket shop.

The other major failure of the Magic Kingdom is the "Hall of Presidents," another audioanimatronic exhibit where overt patriotism is combined with technological wizardry. All U.S. presidents have been re-created as robots that can speak, gesture, stand up, and sit down. Together on a large stage, they speak to an audience assigned to seats distant from the stage in a massive auditorium. Viewers are too far from the recreations to appreciate the technical skill, the attention to detail, and the authenticity evident in the robot creations. Because of the distance and the required passivity of the seated audience, the intricate robots are experienced in the same manner as a movie presentation.

Tomorrowland, which should be the most futuristic sector, is dated, and the dominant bare concrete architecture is visually bland. Apart from the Space Mountain coaster, which is wonderful, the flat, unadorned landscape of Tomorrowland is almost a replica of the 1939 "World of Tomorrow" World's Fair in New York City. The message, too, is precisely the same: progress through technology. Another element in the Magic Kingdom that rings false at the beginning of the 1990s is the extraordinary number of toy guns and other weapons ubiquitously displayed and offered for sale in Frontierland.

The Walt Disney World crowd is predominantly upper middle class, and demographic statistics indicate that a full three-quarters of the adults are professionals, technical personnel, or managers. Only 2 percent are laborers, 3 percent are black, and 2 percent are Hispanic. Walt Disney World is not situated for the poor, as getting there generally requires a prolonged trip by an automobile or airplane. Because 71 percent of guests travel from outside Florida, mostly from the Northeast and Midwest,[13] the resort is completely dependent on jet airlines and the interstate highway system. Cost of admission has risen to $31 a day in 1990, and the discounted three-day ticket has been eliminated and replaced by a four-day ticket costing $100. Unlike Coney Island, where almost every reveler was a laborer, location ensures that the subway crowd has no access to Disney's world.

Many of the visitors to the Magic Kingdom—a remarkably orderly, clean and quiet lot—walk around with glazed eyes, their trancelike state largely induced by sensory overload, the lack of participatory activities (since most attractions engage only the eyes and ears), and the ubiquitous background music piped from unobtrusive speakers. As soon as people enter Main Street, U.S.A., they are encouraged only to shop or simply to stare at consumer goods and elaborate architecture. The succeeding attractions within the park dazzle, but the engagement is momentary, passing as soon as the next wonder competes for attention. Even more tranquilizing are the interminable waits in lines that slowly, endlessly wind through intricate mazes.

Margaret Gullette, in a piece for the *North American Review*, observes that "the technology is awesome, perhaps, but it produces a trivial product, and the awe that it evokes is necessarily insubstantial too." Because spectators are passive and physically disengaged, they greet the technological marvels with an immediate "stupefaction," followed by a "vague discontent."[14] Though Gullette accurately assesses the saturation with wonder that follows an immersion in Walt Disney World, her conclusion that overstimulation trivializes the experience and that reaction to the technologies is immediate but fleeting is probably in error. Visitors demonstrate their craving for the Disney form of amusement with their dollars and their attendance. Furthermore, something in the Disney experience touches our general culture deeply. Disney's worlds reflect such diverse cultural phenomena as corporate managerial structures; the creation of safe, isolated, and technologically dependent residential zones, complete with personal entertainment centers; an emphasis in general and professional education on visual learning and memorization rather than mental strategies demanding individual thought; an unquestioned dependence on and faith in technologies; and a concerted detachment from social problems.

Despite these detractions, from the beginning Walt Disney World has lured tens of millions of visitors each year. Its appeal is a blend of superb organization and absolute cleanliness (on the average a piece of trash in the street sits less than four minutes before removal); attractions that cater to all age groups and employ leading-edge technologies; promotion of family togetherness with ample distractions to avoid the squabbling bound to occur with prolonged contact; pampering in first-class accommodations with spectacular entertainment; the security of a lengthy vacation without the necessity for planning or daily decision making; the assurance that unruly or unsavory members of society will not intrude on the pleasure experience; and perhaps most important of all, reinforcement of corporate American values of technological progress, consumption, and hierarchical managerial structures. These values, evident in the Magic Kingdom, are most emphatically promulgated at EPCOT Center, the second major attraction to rise in the Florida swamps.

☐ EPCOT Center

Opening on 1 October 1982 at a cost of over $900 million, EPCOT Center barely resembles the Experimental Prototype Community of Tomorrow envisioned by Walt Disney. Disney had begun to plan his visionary utopia in 1958 after studying failed utopias and visiting several model cities around the world. While working with WED Enterprises, the creative laboratory for Walt Disney Productions, on several projects for the 1964–65 New York World's Fair, his ideas formed into the shape of a domed city of 20,000 inhabitants. In a television film made in October 1966, just weeks before his death, Walt articulated his conception of a "special kind of new community" dedicated to "finding solutions to the problems of our cities." It would "always be in a state of becoming. It will never cease to be a living blueprint of the future . . . that will take its cue from the new ideas and new technologies that are now emerging from the creative centers of American industry. . . . EPCOT will be a showcase to the world for the ingenuity and imagination of American free enterprise."[15] What emerged 16 years later from WED Enterprises and Walt Disney Productions has no elements of a community—no residential, industrial, or service sectors, no permanent population. Instead, it is, in the words of Martin A. Sklar, in 1981 vice president for creative development at WED Enterprises, "a permanent world's fair of imagination, discovery, education, and exploration that combines the Disney entertainment and communications skills with the knowledge and predictions for the future of authorities from industry, the academic world, and the professions."[16] EPCOT Center has incorporated one major element of Walt's original vision: it is primarily a showcase for American free enterprise and corporate culture. In a presentation to the Urban Land Institute in 1976, then–Disney chairman and chief executive E. Cardon "Card" Walker outlined the essential industrial and corporate essence of EPCOT as a "demonstration and proving ground for prototype concepts," a place to test practical applications of new technologies.[17] So, just 10 years shy of a century after the World's Columbian Exposition, where Walt Disney's father labored in its construction, Walt Disney World unveiled a permanent world's fair designed with essentially the same purpose as its Chicago predecessor, to glorify and advertise American technology and industry.

American corporations were partners in EPCOT Center from the conception of the project. Corporate experts served on an advisory board for EPCOT Center planning beginning in 1975. More significantly, each pavilion is financially sponsored by a major American corporation: "Spaceship Earth," by the Bell System; "Universe of Energy," Exxon;

"Horizons," General Electric; "World of Motion," General Motors; "Journey into Imagination," Kodak; "The Land," Kraft; "The Living Seas," United Technologies; "Wonders of Life," Metropolitan Life; "Communicore," AT&T; "Backstage Magic (EPCOT Computer Central)," Sperry; and "American Adventure," Coca-Cola and American Express. Although the corporations provide the funding, the attractions are completely designed and engineered by WED Enterprises and its manufacturing unit MAPO (named after the movie *Mary Poppins*). Participation in EPCOT Center by the corporations was crucial to its development, providing about $300 million, or more than a third of the total initial EPCOT Center costs. Each corporation paid up to $25 million for the right to affix its name to a pavilion. General Motors chairman Roger B. Smith felt the investment would reap substantial rewards for his company through image enhancement and product promotion. "World of Motion" accentuates and indeed bombards visitors with the message that the private automobile advances individual freedom. The pavilion also exhibits General Motors technical innovations and advances while displaying current automobile models.[18]

Despite yearly attendance figures in excess of 10 million visitors, Walt Disney World apparently needed a boost by 1982. Attendance at the Magic Kingdom peaked at just over 14 million visitors in 1978, followed by a steady four-year decline, which the Disney organization blamed on the economic recession and high gasoline costs.[19] It is likely, however, that the Magic Kingdom had reached the saturation point and that new attractions were needed to lure even more guests and to bring others back for repeat visits. With changing demographics indicating a steadily aging society, with significant decreases in the percentage of the population under 20 years of age, Walt Disney World needed a major attraction designed for mature visitors (see table 32 in chapter 8 for data on the demographic trends evident as the 21st century nears).

The 600-acre EPCOT Center is comprised of two sectors: Future World, with corporate-sponsored attractions providing views of past and future technologies, and World Showcase, a group of exhibits representing foreign countries and the United States. Milton Gerstman, vice president of Tishman Realty & Construction Company, was in charge of building the extravaganza in the midst of the Florida swamps. Tishman Company had plenty of experience with massive construction projects, having overseen the building of the World Trade Center in New York and Detroit's Renaissance Center. As many as 4,500 construction workers had to drain the entire site; fill all the sinkholes with stable material, as at the Magic Kingdom location; excavate and shape a 100-acre lake; remove all pine trees, palmettos, and swamp vegetation; and shape the earth to the contours specified by Disney designers before any building could commence. Workers had to deal with alligators and rattlesnakes, and with protecting the natural habitat of the rare cockaded woodpecker, a small bird that lives in dead tree trunks.[20]

On EPCOT Center's 600 acres (by coincidence, remarkably similar to the World's Columbian Exposition's 686 acres) sits a universal exposition of the products of human activity. Like all of the world's fairs before it, there is a decided emphasis on consumer products produced by industry and technology as well as glimpses of cultural diversity. Just as at the World's Columbian Exposition, there are grand, massive buildings devoted to major industries. The Chicago emphasis on railroads, steam engines, electricity, and agriculture is replaced in Florida by an emphasis on automobiles, computers, petroleum, food processing, communications, and plastics. EPCOT surpasses its predecessors by approaching and representing technology in a social context. Although the various pavilions are organized under the rubric of Future World, each attraction focuses primarily on the past, placing specific technologies within American social history. The unifying aim is to reinvigorate and solidify the public's faith in progress through technology and to sanctify technology as the agent of man's most significant achievements. EPCOT's limitation is that it presents what Michael L. Smith labels "decontextualized history" and "decontextualized technology"—reductions of reality to nostalgia and magic. Both history and technology are removed from the context of "roads not taken, conflicting visions, and failed aspirations,"[21] as well as from the realities of war, environmental pollution, and social problems that have largely resulted from our technological advances and corporate culture. Even the World Showcase is a direct derivative of the exotic villages at the 1893 Columbian Exposition's Midway Plaisance. It too is a reductive condensation of history and culture into easily recognizable architectural forms, landmarks, cuisine, costumes, and consumer goods. The pavilions for Canada, England, France, Japan, Morocco, Italy, Germany, China, Norway, and Mexico present a particularly Americanized view of their cultures, emphasizing food, consumer goods, and travelogues while ignoring noncommercially exploitable aspects of history and culture.

Future World comprises eight corporate-sponsored pavilions and "Communicore," all of which feature technological displays, demonstrations, and entertaining attractions. The ride-through productions in the pavilions transport guests in little cars or boats, not unlike the Perisphere and the General Motors Pavilion at the 1939 "World of Tomorrow" World's Fair in New York City. Each pavilion explains a technology, celebrates its place in American history, and depicts future applications.

Every portrayal is unceasingly soothing and limited to glimpses of the shiny surfaces of final products. There is no attempt to educate visitors about the intricate workings of new technologies nor to portray their awe-inspiring scale and power in our society. To do so would be to intimidate rather than reassure. Back in the beginning of the century, Dr. Martin Couney provided a much more immediate view of technology in his Premature Baby Incubators exhibit at Coney Island's Luna Park. To present at-risk infants, dependent on complex technologies for their survival, would be unthinkable at EPCOT Center. The possibility of death, not to mention the pain and vulnerability of imperfect infants, could never be allowed to intrude on Disney's "perfect," carefree world.

None of the undesirable results of technological progress impinge upon the Disney paradise. There is no pollution or acid rain in the "Universe of Energy"; no famines, dust storms, droughts, or even natural dirt in "The Land"; no gridlock, smog, or highway carnage in the "World of Motion"; no threat of nuclear power, no arms race, no war, no urban ghettos anywhere in Future World. The General Motors "World of Motion" pavilion presents perhaps the most blatantly selective view of the history and prospects for a technology. The history of transportation is focused on the automobile, to the absolute exclusion of options for public mass transportation. Visitors in their little cars are engulfed by disembodied voices on the Personal Audio Listening System (PALS) liltingly and endlessly singing the "World of Motion" theme song, "It's Fun to Be Free." The lesson repeatedly droned into captive ears is the equation of the automobile with personal freedom. The intent of the series of dioramas, chock full of audioanimatronic people and creatures, is "to take a rib-tickling ride through the evolution of transportation." One scene depicts an early traffic jam where the blame is placed on a horse pulling an outmoded cart, which overturns in a busy intersection. The accident holds up three horseless carriages, an automobile, and a bus. General Motors has also offered an "Engine of the Future" show in which cartoon characters promote distinct energy-conscious designs. A robust cowboy pitches for the internal combustion engine, while a sophisticated yuppie woman advocates solar energy, an opinionated slob pushes coal, and a mad scientist with rather menacing Japanese characteristics works on a pollution-free hydrogen-powered engine. After the scientist blows everything up, Cowboy Tex reappears on the screen extolling the "good ol' reliable internal combustion engine" while assuring the audience that General Motors welcomes competition for the benefit of consumers. Finally, near the pavilion exit, in EPCOT's most obvious display of advertisement and commercialism, General Motors offers several of its latest models.

The pavilions offer a series of instantaneous sight and sound bites—brief, immediately recognizable stereotypes removed from their historical causality. New technologies seem to materialize miraculously from a void, without decisions, social effects, or agents of development. Decontextualized technology is most evident in "Horizons," sponsored by General Electric. We are presented with various scenarios of future life, generally in outer-space locales free of earthly constraints. But the situations are mundanely familiar: an appliance runs amok, a population composed almost totally of young people is concerned about dating, and a family discusses Thanksgiving dinner. "Horizons" presents 21st-century views of harvesting food undersea and in the desert and growing crystals for industry in outer space. Again, the message is the same for all scenarios: the future world will be perfect, thanks to total control of every single detail and to new technologies that respond to all needs, from food to entertainment. Among all the wonders of "Horizons," however, there is no wilderness left in Disney's future utopia, and not a single book.

The most spectacular journey into the past happens in Exxon's "Universe of Energy." Following a motion-picture presentation on a huge wrap-around screen that takes viewers around the world in search of alternative energy sources, guests are transported in solar-powered modules back to the age of the dinosaurs to explore the era that generated our fossil fuels. The huge audioanimatronic dinosaurs and other creatures are the apogee of the Disney art of robotics. These breathtaking monsters, electronic evolutions of the enormous mechanized reptiles presented by Sinclair at the 1933 Chicago Century of Progress Exposition, come complete with sounds and even smells from the primeval past. In the finale guests view energy challenges and emerging technologies that will solve the problems of depleted resources. Once again, everyone is assured that technology will "build an energy bridge to the future." There are no coal mines or exploited laborers, no scarred landscapes, no polluted cities, and no oil spills.

"Journey into Imagination" depicts even human creative abilities in terms of technology. Dreamfinder and his playful companion, Figment, journey in a contraption of wheels, gauges, pipes, and gears through a realm of art and innovation with a definite focus on science and invention. It is clear that the highest form of creativity is the development of marketable inventions. In the "Image Works" visitors play with computer graphics, conduct the Electronic Philharmonic, and proceed through a neon maze where swirling patterns of light respond to their voices. Elsewhere in EPCOT Center there are scores of hands-on technologies for visitors to manipulate, particularly in "Communicore," which boasts robot SMRT-1, who talks with guests; the video game "Taxi Driver," which offers lessons on fuel consumption; a computer for designing a roller coaster; telephone communication devices of tomorrow; "Energy Exchange," where guests can explore nuclear technologies without danger and can "generate" energy opinions; and "Electronic Forum," where visitors participate in surveys dealing with current events, life-styles, and entertainment—but no weighty issues demanding thoughtful decisions that might detract from a carefree day.

Turning to World Showcase, the grouping of 11 country exhibits around a large lake, once again the message is sanitized culture. The "American Adventure" exhibit is located exactly in the middle, flanked by Mexico, Norway, China, Italy, Germany, Morocco, Japan, France, the United Kingdom, and Canada. The Disney version of a community of nations includes no political, religious, military, or economic concerns—only picturesque backdrops, colorful exotic costumes, consumer goods, and easily recognizable architecture. The Eiffel Tower, a Mayan pyramid, a beer garden, a *stave kirke*, a torii and pagoda, the doge's palace and campanile, a Chinese temple, a *fez* house, a British pub and Tudor shops, and Canadian totems all beckon the eye and lure visitors to the shops and restaurants that make up the exhibits. Commercial interests are the exhibits' raison d'etre. As in Future World, the substance is missing. In Mexico, the visitor can journey through time from a Mayan ruin to a contemporary resort, but the trip is in a vaccum. There are no indications of the revolution, natural disasters, poverty, or economic stagnation. Corporate underwriting—by Bass Export, Pringle of Scotland, Royal Doulton, Mitsukoshi, American Express, and Coca-Cola—is as evident here as in Future World.

The "American Adventure" attempts to document the entire history of the United States in a 29-minute series of sight and sound bites. The technology is so advanced that the audioanimatronic figures not only move, stand, and sit but also walk up stairs. Hosted by robots Mark Twain and Ben Franklin, the show departs ever so slightly from the Disney sanitized version of history. Only here, in all of Walt Disney World, is there a hint that all was not always perfect in America. Frederick Douglass tells of the evils of slavery just as he did in person at the World's Columbian Exposition nearly a century earlier; graphic Matthew Brady photographs depict the Civil War; Chief Joseph mourns the "final sunset" for his people; immigrants arrive on American shores amid melting-pot platitudes; Susan B. Anthony demands equality; John Muir chronicles the threat of industrial growth to America the Beautiful; both black and white Americans struggle through the Great Depression; Franklin Roosevelt's voice is heard talking about "fear itself" and he announces the Pearl Harbor attack.

Historian Mike Wallace, in his consideration of this depiction of history, finds the "American Adventure" to be a "dramatic departure" for Disney, one probably forced by the social movements of the 1970s, which focused attention on the rights of blacks and women and on antiwar and environmental campaigns. Wallace contends, however, that the production is still "Disney history," with a superimposed theme of "Dreamers and Doers" that allows problems to be presented in an upbeat manner as "opportunities in disguise." Powerful individuals are depicted as agents of change who show us how to transcend social inequalities. "The spokespersons of the discontented knocked and the door was opened."[22]

The presentation does not address the challenges of recent history. Disney imagineers may have decided that contemporary problems would generate controversy and concern inappropriate to the atmosphere of Walt Disney World. Thus, World War II is represented only by Rosie the Riveter, and there is no allusion to Vietnam. Contemporary history becomes blips of popular culture: Marilyn Monroe, Jackie Robinson, Elvis, John Wayne, Martin Luther King, Muhammad Ali, Lucille Ball, John Kennedy, and, of course, Walt Disney. Conspicuous in their absence are race riots, the feminist and ecology movements, Watergate, Korea, Vietnam, and the political assassinations.

Walt Disney World Resort is by far the biggest tourist attraction in the entire world. It draws more than 25 million people, or one-tenth of the population of the United States, each year. Its success must be scrutinized in terms of the satisfaction and enjoyment it gives its guests. For the latter part of the 20th century, Walt Disney World has replaced the religious shrine as a pilgrimage center. Just as a journey to Mecca, Canterbury, Lourdes, or Rome represents a rite of passage that sanctifies a pilgrim as a member of a holy community, a visit to Walt Disney World ratifies the values of corporate culture and allows the 20th-century pilgrim to reaffirm faith in capitalist scriptures of progress through technology, control through managerial hierarchy, and consumerism. Since most visitors belong to the management or technical elite, the Walt Disney World experience is a self-affirming process that, in Mike Wallace's words, provides "reassurance to this class" and presents it "with its own pedigree." The atmosphere of corporate achievement and total control through management is a dream world for white-collar professionals and technocrats. Labor problems and ecological and political considerations are nonexistent. It "ratifies their world" and presents them with comforting stereotypes of corporate achievements.[23]

The form and function of Walt Disney World is a borrowing from the spiritual pilgrimage center. In the postmodern world, play, leisure, the mythic values of the American dream, and the cult of technology have largely replaced the archaic rituals and scriptures of organized religion. Anthropologist Alexander Moore recognizes the traits that identify Walt Disney World as the new Mecca: it is a "bounded place apart from ordinary settlement drawing pilgrims from great distances"; the journey requires a "long separation from their ordinary lives"; the entrance into "sacred precincts" provides a "transition" experience that reaffirms or invigorates commitment to a prescribed set of values; and pilgrims exercise a "fellowship with other pilgrims from widely scattered communities."[24] While illusion, magic, and technology reign in Walt Disney World instead of religious ritual and miracles, a mythic interpretation of American history is a sanctified object of worship. American corporate technology and managerial control are self-avowed saviors of the modern world. In each Walt Disney World attraction, pilgrims embark on a journey where they encounter marvelous icons and symbols that sanctify cultural myths. The themes enshrined as myths are a placid, comfortable, small-town America of the 1890s; the inevitability of progress through technology; the efficacy of the wilderness experience whether it be through tropical jungles, the American West, or outer space; the triumph of technology over death and the natural world; and the "sainthood" of American cultural heroes such as Lincoln, Mark Twain, Franklin, Davy Crockett, and Walt Disney. Margaret J. King agrees in her study of the values conveyed in Disneyland and Walt Disney World. She sees each park as "a temple of consumption made possible by leisure, surplus value, technology and consumerism . . . solidly based on the (American/Protestant) values of production: the work ethic, exploration, faith in progress, industrial expansion, technological inventiveness, pragmatism, efficiency." The parks are "holy cities for the entire U.S., visited by pilgrims, in a constant festival state."[25] Alexander Moore sees the process of engagement with these myths to be a "ritual motion." The orderly progress through long lines, transport in a synchronized vehicle in precisely measured time, perfectly managed movement—all are "the genuflection . . . of members of a mass industrial society."[26] American well-to-do pilgrims may flock to Walt Disney World because a long history of geographic and social mobility leaves them in a crisis of rootlessness. A place of refuge is needed where they are entertainingly reassured that the values of movement up to higher income and elevated social class are sanctioned through ritual, and they are indoctrinated by means of an immersion process in the ideals of corporate culture.

The perfect world of Disney has replaced the biblical Garden of Eden as the American vision of paradise. Even *Time* magazine titled an article on the success of the Disney and other theme parks "If Heaven Ain't a Lot Like Disney." Richard Corliss, the author of the article, proclaimed that all the attractions in EPCOT Center "celebrate the perfectibility of man through democracy and technology."[27] The message of Walt Disney World, as historian of technology Elting Morison tells us, is "not to worry."[28] The limited view through the rosy glass of the Disney cathedral proclaims that our machines have always done well and will soon do better. Ever since the Puritan pilgrims founded America, the nation has been striving to create a perfect world, a "City on a Hill." Our mode of construction of such a splendid realm rapidly moved away from spiritual grace to technological know-how. Thus our Celestial City both in inspiration and fact is Walt Disney World. The subordination of the cultural dream to the reality of an enclosed world of illusion in the swamplands of Florida is indicative of a society that systematically refuses to view itself in the glare of reality and continues to survive only by distorting or repressing its collective memory within the glitz of illusory, decontextualized, selective Mickey Mouse history.

□   The Economics of the Disney Parks

On 1 May 1987 guest number 242,831,300 entered the gates of a Disney park, thus matching total park attendance with the population of the United States. Since the resort's opening in 1971, attendance at Walt Disney World has fluctuated slightly with significant decreases during the economic recession of the early 1980s and a near doubling of guests following the opening of EPCOT Center in late 1982. Attendance, as shown in table 23, remains relatively stable, slightly declining until a new major attraction spurs a notable surge. Disney officials blamed the downturn between 1979 and 1982 at Walt Disney World on the economic recession, reduced gasoline availability and high fuel prices, the Knoxville World's Fair in 1982, and the postponing of visits until the opening of EPCOT Center in late 1982. Even the Disney parks seem to reach a saturation point that requires new attractions to significantly increase or even maintain attendance levels.

Despite the occasional drops in attendance, revenues and operating income for the Disney parks show continuous substantial growth since the advent of Walt Disney World. In fact, revenues have increased

Table 23. Walt Disney World Resort and
Disneyland Park Attendance, 1972–1989 (in
millions)

Year	Walt Disney World Resort	Disneyland Park
1972	10.7	9.6
1974	10.8	9.7
1976	13.1	10.2
1978	14.1	10.7
1980	13.8	11.5
1981	13.2	11.3
1982	12.6	10.4
1983*	22.7	10.0
1984	21.1	9.9
1985	21.7	11.8
1986	24.1	12.5
1987	26.0	13.5
1988	25.1	13.0
1989†	30.0	14.4

*First full year for EPCOT Center
†Disney-MGM Studio theme park opens in spring.

Source: Walt Disney Co. *Annual Reports; Amusement Business*, 24 December 1988, 82; *Amusement Business*, 30 December 1989, 88.

dramatically from approximately $200 million in 1972 to over $2 billion in 1988 (see table 24).

The theme parks are responsible for a major proportion of the revenues and income of the parent company, Walt Disney Company (see table 25). The sudden upsurge in the late 1980s of receipts from filmed entertainment, coinciding with the advent of Touchstone Pictures, has reduced the parks' share of corporate profits and returned motion pictures to a respectable position within Walt Disney Company.

A major factor in the success of the Disney parks is the willingness of corporate leadership to consistently devote generous funding for capi-

Table 24. Revenues and
Operating Income of the Disney
Parks, 1972–1988 (in millions of
dollars)

Year	Revenues	Operating Income
1972	223.4	37.8
1974	287.0	42.5
1976	401.6	70.4
1978	508.4	106.0
1980	643.4	127.5
1982	725.6	132.6
1983	1031.2	197.0
1984	1097.4	185.7
1985	1257.5	255.7
1986	1523.9	˙ 403.7
1987	1834.2	548.9
1988	2042.0	564.8

Source: Walt Disney Co. *Annual Reports.*

tal expenditures within the parks. These expenditures often approach or surpass income figures, as revealed in table 26. Large increases in capital expenditures in 1981 and 1982 reflect the building of EPCOT Center, while in 1988 the construction of the Disney-MGM Studios theme park and Typhoon Lagoon sectors at Walt Disney World required major expenditures.

Despite the robust fiscal health of the Disney organization, and the steady rise in revenues and income, in 1984 Walt Disney Company was the target of a well-publicized takeover bid engineered by corporate raider Saul Steinberg. In March 1984 Steinberg and his Reliance Group began to purchase large blocks of Disney stock at between $61.25 and $67.50 per share. Disney countered by increasing the family's holdings in the company, as well as acquiring the Arvida Corporation, a Florida real estate development company, and Gibson Greetings. These purchases lessened Steinberg's overall holdings in the Disney empire from 12.1 percent to 11.1 percent. Steinberg then went on the offensive, enlisting support from MGM/United Artists owner Kirk Kerkorian. Kerkorian added $75 million to the Steinberg war chest in return for

Table 25. Theme Park Revenues and Income as a Proportion of Walt Disney Company Revenues and Income, 1974–1988, Selected Years

Year	Revenues	Income
1974	66.7%	40.0%
1977	70.7%	54.3%
1980	70.4%	55.1%
1982	70.4%	60.2%
1985	74.0%	74.0%
1988	59.4%	63.8%

Source: Walt Disney Co. *Annual Reports.*

promised rights to the Disney film library. Faced with near certain loss of the corporation, Disney management bought back the Reliance holdings at $70.83 a share with borrowed cash. They also paid Steinberg and Reliance $325.5 million to cease the hostile takeover. Steinberg gave up, but with a clear profit of more than $31 million. The episode cost Walt Disney Company nearly $900 million, and shares of stock lost approximately 29 percent of their former value.[29]

Walt Disney Company has bounced back from this financial setback through an invigorated film entertainment sector, increased emphasis on the consumer products division, and expansion of the Walt Disney World complex. The year 1989 alone saw the opening of the Disney-MGM Studios theme park, Pleasure Island (an evening entertainment sector), Typhoon Lagoon (a water park), and the near completion of a massive hotel/convention center comprising the Swan and Dolphin hotels, with almost 3,000 rooms. These additions to Walt Disney World are considered by most observers to be a blatant attempt to monopolize as much of the Florida tourist trade as possible. Disney is seen to be manipulating visitors to remain in Walt Disney World for their entire vacation trip and never venture out to explore other Orlando attractions.[30] The Orlando business community, as well as many disinterested observers, view Mickey Mouse as a sharp-toothed, gluttonous rat. Studies revealing that most tourists stay in the Orlando area for five days prompted the company to scrap the long-existing three-day discounted ticket for a four-day ticket. The Disney attractions now run the gamut of anything that might also be available outside the Walt

Table 26. Capital Expenditures as
Compared to Income for the
Disney Parks, 1977–1988 (in
millions of dollars)

Year	Capital Expenditures	Income
1977	42.7	92.1
1978	43.7	106.0
1979	54.8	120.6
1980	157.8	127.5
1981	344.4	129.5
1982	645.6	132.6
1983	287.9	197.0
1984	145.3	185.7
1985	155.0	255.7
1986	160.0	403.7
1987	249.1	548.9
1988	559.0	564.8

Source: Walt Disney Co. *Annual Reports.*

Disney World complex. Disney scooped Universal Studios Florida by opening the Disney-MGM Studios theme park ahead of schedule and a year before Universal's June 1990 opening. Moreover, Universal executives claim that Disney stole some of Universal's ideas.[31] Disney's Typhoon Lagoon is an answer to the current popularity of water parks, several of which were already available in the Orlando area.

The $400 million Disney-MGM Studios theme park contains attractions such as "The Great Movie Ride," which transports visitors through famous movie scenes; the "Backstage Studio Tour" through the Golden Girls' house, a New York street, and earthquake and monsoon disasters; the "Epic Stunt Spectacular," including the huge rolling boulder from *Raiders of the Lost Ark*; the "Monster Sound Show," where audience members get a chance to dub sounds; Hollywood Boulevard, a reproduction of filmdom's heyday in the 1930s and 1940s; the Animation Building, where the art of animation is explained and illustrated; and "Superstar Television," which chooses audience members to star in classic TV moments alongside Lucille Ball or Johnny Carson.

In September 1989 Disney officials announced the acquisition of

Henson Associates, thus securing merchandising and publishing rights to Kermit the Frog and Miss Piggy, along with some of the other Muppet characters created by puppeteer Jim Henson. The price of the sale was estimated to be between $100 million and $150 million. The Muppets made their appearance in a ride and movie in the Disney-MGM Studios theme park in 1990.[32] All of the Muppet characters energize and update the stock Disney characters, which are now too predictable, familiar, and stuck in a past era.

8

Overview and Postscript

Disneyland is better.
—overheard by the author in the shadow of the Matterhorn, Zermatt, Switzerland

THE CYCLICAL DEVELOPMENT OF THE AM-
erican amusement park industry from the late 19th century to the present
demonstrates the formative influences of individual entrepreneurial ge-
niuses, as well as the interrelationships between the industry and social,
economic, and cultural factors. George Tilyou, Frederic Thompson and
Elmer "Skip" Dundy, Walter Knott, and Walt Disney created their own
formulas for success. All of these men recognized illusion, technological
wonders, sensory overload, magnitude, and spectacle to be essential elements of a successful entertainment venture. But each man added his
own unique ingredients, which reflected the culture of his time and the
desires of the paying public.

Tilyou provided his Steeplechase Park guests an opportunity to shun
the repressive sexual mores of the Victorian era and titillated his clientele
with "sanitized sex" and somewhat intimate, if haphazard, physical contact, which resulted in a release of muscular and psychological tension. In
Luna Park, Thompson and Dundy created an electric Bagdad with an
architecture of swirling crescents and blazing minarets that combined
chaos with splendor and bizarre fantasy. Their "pyrotechnic insanitarium" was in startling contrast to the drab, dingy tenement dwellings
and mechanized, regimented work of the generally poor, immigrant ur-

ban multitudes. Walter Knott turned his own reverence for the western pioneer experience into a successful, historically based entertainment remarkable for its blend of authenticity, propensity to engage, and infusion of thrills and fun. Knott was a pioneer himself in regard to his commitment to investing most of his profits back into his "berry farm" for upkeep, expansion, constant change, and spectacular attractions.

By the time Walt Disney entered the amusement park business, he recognized the elemental changes in American culture that had occurred in the first half of the century. Because chaos, crime, and squalor had become too overbearing in urban areas, Disney embraced control, exclusivity, minute planning, and fastidious sanitation to actualize a segregated promised land of perfection where technology solves all of civilization's problems and at the same time engineers entertainment extravaganzas. From Coney to Disney, order eliminated chaos, technological wizardry superceded sexual teasing, and relatively well-to-do "guests" replaced poor urban laborers.

As has been demonstrated in this study, the most influential model for amusement parks in this century has been the 1893 World's Columbian Exposition, with its meticulous planning, application of technologies for the purposes of fun and the demonstration of industrial prowess, sectored landscape, presentation of exotic locales as "educational" exhibits, and creation of a utopian Celestial City rising from the wasteland. Other dominant factors, which have dictated the industry's cycle of expansion, decline, and eventual reemergence, have been changes in transportation modes, the rise in personal disposable income, and television.

Trolley parks and seaside amusement resorts evolved as a result of the development of streetcar lines, local mass transit, steamship routes, and, in later years, subway systems. The incredibly rapid appearance of approximately 2,000 parks by 1920 was a direct result of the parks' ability to stimulate patronage of mass transit systems. But after the turn of the century, a new means of transportation was introduced, the automobile. The Model T arrived in 1908. Within two years, over 180,000 private automobiles had been produced; by 1914 there were 2 million cars on the road; and by 1921 the number of automobiles ballooned to 9 million. Suddenly the American people had the means to travel beyond the limits of their local attractions and to choose their vacation destinations. Many of the amusement parks of the era did not have sufficient land to establish parking facilities for the rapidly growing motoring public. Meanwhile, the trolley and mass transit companies that owned the parks were suffering declining revenues or were going out of business. Parks were sold or allowed to become rusting, unpainted eyesores. During the 1930s the Great Depression finished off many of the traditional parks as owners sold or lost their property. In later decades urban development and gang violence would destroy most of the parks that had managed to survive the 1930s.

The number of amusement parks dropped from 2,000 in 1920 to only about 300 in 1935. The industry would not revive until Walt Disney created Disneyland in 1955, a park that was cleverly conceptualized and designed to rely on the automobile as the primary means of access. Disneyland's location beyond the Los Angeles urban area, with no mass transit connections to the city, isolated it from the unruly and poorer elements of the urban population. Thus predominately middle- and upper-class clientele was ensured. The necessity to travel by automobile or airline also encouraged visits by families from throughout the United States who chose Disneyland as a vacation destination and remained for an extended stay. Later theme parks copied Disneyland's features, especially its location beyond the reach of urban transportation systems.

The economic vigor of the amusement park industry grew at a rate paralleling the increase in the amount of disposable income Americans devoted to recreation. From its ebb during the Great Depression in 1935, when annual receipts for the entire amusement park industry were $9 million, the industry zoomed to annual receipts of nearly $106 million by 1963, when the Disney formula had revitalized and invigorated amusement enterprises. It grew to a $1.4 billion industry in 1980 and seemed limitless by 1988 as receipts surpassed $4 billion (see tables 8 and 21). Theme parks and destination paradises of future visions and historical myths responded to American leisure desires with unparalleled success. In 1909 Americans spent about $1 billion for various recreational pursuits and products. That spending rose to $5.5 billion by 1925. Thirty-five years later, in 1960, recreation expenditures had risen only moderately to approximately $18 billion. But in 1980 recreation accounted for expenditures of $115 billion, nearly doubling again to $223 billion in 1987 (see tables 7 and 30).

The 1950s would bring a new technology that would paradoxically both threaten and resurrect amusement parks—television. Television sets, which invaded nearly every home in America in the 1950s, provided entertainment and wonders that could be experienced in the comfort and convenience of the living room. Suddenly, the traditional lures of the local amusement park paled in contrast to the delights emanating from the small screen. While most parks failed to compete, Walt Disney designed Disneyland to mirror the segmented structure of nightly television, with its half-hour and hour shows presenting variety while transporting viewers to illusory worlds distinct in locale and time. He also recognized and capitalized on the advertisement potential of television. Disneyland and the theme parks that followed it embraced the pattern of television entertainment and cleverly augmented it by providing the opportunity for their guests to physically, as well as visually and mentally, immerse themselves in the exotic environments so tantalizing on the television screen. Television raised the entertainment expectations of the American public, and theme parks have responded to the challenge by creating ever more spectacular, technologically sophisticated, and wondrous attractions.

☐ The Contemporary Form of the Industry

Following the theme parks' rapid expansion in the 1970s, the 1980s saw many corporate owners placing the parks back into the control of companies more strictly dedicated to management of amusement enterprises. This trend away from administration and financial oversight of the major parks by conglomerate corporations has stimulated a vitality evident in expenditures for improvements as well as attention to services and visitor satisfaction. The exception is the purchase of the six Harcourt Brace Jovanovich attractions by Anheuser-Busch. For Busch, the theme park sector, including the two Busch Gardens attractions in Tampa, Florida, and Williamsburg, Virginia, along with the newly acquired HBJ parks, is still a small portion of total corporate interests. The 1990s will reveal the extent of Busch's attention to its theme park empire and especially whether the corporation is willing to challenge Disney's domination of central Florida tourism. Busch's intentions appear cloudy in light of its sudden closing of the Boardwalk & Baseball park in January 1990.

A review of revenues for the amusement park industry from 1963 through 1988 is indicative of incredible growth once the Disney park concept literally created a new industry from its moribund traditional predecessor (see table 27). In the last 25 years the amusement park business has grown from just over a $100 million in revenues to a $4 billion industry. Significant surges are evident in most years since the opening of Walt Disney World Resort in late 1971 and EPCOT Center at the end of 1982. The Disney parks in recent years account for over half the revenues of the entire industry. Even considering that revenues of some privately held parks, such as Knott's Berry Farm, may not be reflected in the Bureau of the Census figures, the Disney dominance is still astounding. Revenues have skyrocketed while, paradoxically, the number of amusement park enterprises has diminished. The Bureau of

Table 27. Total Amusement Park Industry Revenues, Disney Parks
(Disneyland Park, Walt Disney World Resort) Revenues, 1963–1988,
Selected Years (in millions of dollars)

Year	Total Industry Revenues	Disney Parks Revenues	Disney Revenues as % of total
1963	106	—	—
1967	174	52.4	30.1
1972	468	223	47.6
1977	1,172	445	38.0
1981	1,791	692	38.6
1982	1,873	726	38.8
1983	2,306	1,031	44.3
1984	2,325	1,097	47.2
1985	2,625	1,256	47.8
1986	3,034	1,524	50. 2
1987	3,483	1,834	52.7
1988	3,912	2,042	52.2

Sources: U.S. Bureau of the Census, *Census of Service Industries, 1972, 1977, 1982, 1985,*
1987, 1989 (Washington, D.C.: Government Printing Office, 1976, 1981, 1985,
1987, 1989, 1990); U.S. Bureau of the Census, *Service Annual Survey, 1983,*
1985, 1988 (Washington, D.C.: Government Printing Office, 1984, 1986, 1989);
U.S. Bureau of the Census, *Census of Business, 1963, 1967* (Washington, D.C.:
Government Printing Office, 1966, 1970); Walt Disney Co. *Annual Reports.*

the Census indicates 997 amusement park establishments in 1963 and
744 in 1987. A resurgence is evident since 1982, however, when the
Census Bureau recorded only 466 amusement park establishments.

During the period from 1963 to 1987 the shape of the amusement
park industry has changed dramatically. Smaller independent parks
have given way to large theme parks controlled by corporations (see
table 28). By 1987, 80.5 percent of the parks were organized as corporations. The high cost of competition and the necessity for extensive and
constant capital expenditures had practically eliminated the individually
owned or family-owned ventures.

While revenues are astronomically high, the nature of the amusement park business dictates that a major proportion of the revenues
must be reinvested for day-to-day operation and for constant maintenance and capital improvements. Labor-intensive park operation is only
one costly factor; another is the need for new attractions nearly every

Table 28. Legal Form of Organization for Amusement Park Enterprises

	1963	1972	1977	1982	1987
Individual Proprietorships	343	106	133	55	92
Partnerships	115	42	52	28	53
Corporations	528	412	477	380	599
Other or Unknown	11	122	1	3	—
Total	997	682	663	466	744

Sources: U.S. Bureau of the Census, *Census of Service Industries, 1972, 1977, 1982, 1987* (Washington, D.C.: Government Printing Office, 1976, 1981, 1985, 1989); U.S. Bureau of the Census, *1963 Census of Business: Selected Services Summary Statistics* (Washington, D.C.: Government Printing Office, 1967).

year. Publications of market analysts indicate an average operating profit through the 1980s of 8 percent to 10 percent each year.[1] The most successful parks realize higher profit margins, however. Operating income for the Disney parks was 16.9 percent to 30 percent during the 1980s. The much smaller Cedar Point in Sandusky, Ohio, ranked as the ninth park in attendance in 1989, achieved operating profits between 20 percent and 30 percent in the last decade. But even in Disney's case, generally 80 percent of the revenues are channeled back into the parks and attractions.[2]

The extraordinary year of 1989 witnessed the opening of several new Disney attractions in Florida, including the Disney-MGM Studios theme park, Typhoon Lagoon, Pleasure Island, and the building of the Dolphin and Swan hotels. Also occurring in 1989 were Anheuser-Busch's $1.1 billion purchase of the HBJ properties, plans for relocation of Denver's century-old Elitch Gardens to a new downtown site, and an explosion of growth and attendance at Disney parks in the United States and abroad.

The major theme parks have undertaken ambitious expansion and improvement efforts in 1990. The Universal Studios Florida park near Orlando opened in June. Disney is continuing development of Euro-Disneyland outside Paris in cooperation with the French government. New roller coasters have appeared in many parks in the summer of 1990; the Vekoma Boomerang at Knott's Berry Farm; the $8 million Viper, a looping steel structure from Arrow Dynamics at Six Flags Magic Mountain; the Iron Wolf, a stand-up looping $5 million thrill ride at Six Flags' Great America, manufactured by Bolliger & Mabillard of Switzerland; a wooden coaster costing $5 million, the Texas Giant, at

Six Flags over Texas; a $4 million standing coaster built by Intamin AG at Six Flags' Great Adventure; the Georgia Cyclone at Six Flags over Georgia; Intamin AG's looping starship Jet Scream at Canada's Wonderland; and "Disaster Transport," Cedar Point's transformation of its Intamin-built Avalanche Run coaster into an enclosed simulation ride. Other major improvement projects are a flume ride, Whitewater Falls, at Great America in Santa Clara; $7.5 million for capital improvements at Hersheypark, including a new coal-mining theme area; a high-tech simulator, "Questor," at Busch Gardens' Old Country; a new hotel as well as a Lazy River addition to Soak City at Cedar Point; and both a "Flight Commander" simulator and a tube ride addition to the water park at Kings Island.[3]

Although many amusement parks by policy do not reveal or report attendance figures even to industry associations, the trade newspaper *Amusement Business* estimates that 254 million guests paid their way through the gates of American amusement parks in 1989. Incredibly, this attendance surpasses the total population of the United States, 245 million people in 1988. Of these, 122.7 million, or approximately half of the total attendance at amusement parks, visited the top 40 theme park attractions.[4] Walt Disney World surpassed an annual attendance of 30 million guests for the first time in 1989. In 1986 the President's Commission on Americans Outdoors reported that 72 percent of American adults visited amusement parks, zoos, or fairs one or more times during 1986. This high percentage represents almost a tripling of participation from the much lower rate of only 24 percent in 1972, before the emergence of most theme parks. The only other active leisure activities with a higher percentage of participation were walking or driving for pleasure, sightseeing, picnicking, and swimming.[5]

The spectacular success of the amusement park industry mirrors the equally massive growth of its big brother, tourism. While amusement parks represent a $4 billion industry, worldwide spending for tourism topped $2 trillion in 1986 (see table 29). *The Big Picture: Travel Industry World Yearbook* claims that tourism is now "the world's largest industry representing twelve percent of the total world economy."[6] The outlook for tourism is considered to be robust at the onset of the 1990s due to the lowest level of inflation in industrial countries in 22 years, relatively cheap prices for energy and raw materials, and the opening of international borders for trade. Perhaps most significant is the dramatic lessening of political tensions and the sudden opening of Eastern bloc countries to democratic forms of government and capitalist enterprises. *The Big Picture* projects a steady annual increase of 4 percent for world tourism through 1996.[7]

Table 29. World and U.S. Tourism Receipts, 1986, and Projections for 1996
(in billions of U.S. dollars)

	1986	1996
World Receipts from Domestic Tourism	1,874	2,721
World Receipts from International Tourism	168	248
Total World Tourism Receipts	2,042	3,022
U.S. Receipts from Domestic Tourism	467	691
U.S. Receipts from Domestic and International Tourism	480	710
World Airline Passenger Revenue	99	161
World Accommodations Revenue	141	209
U.S. Hotel-Motel Revenue	44	65

Source: Somerset R. Waters, *The Big Picture: Travel Industry World Yearbook, 1988* (New York: Child & Waters, 1988), 11.

Another indicator of a favorable economic outlook for the amusement park industry is the steady increase in expenditures for recreation by the American public. While expenditures increased substantially from almost $18 billion in 1960 to over $223 billion by 1987, it is notable that their percentage share of total personal consumption expenditures rose only approximately 2 percent in this period (see table 30). The growth in recreation spending remains steady, however, boding well for most leisure-related industry sectors. The only component of personal consumption expenditures that increased its share of the total expenditures by more than 2 percent during this period was medical care, which rose from 6.2 percent of the total in 1960 to 13.4 percent in 1987.[8]

☐ International Ventures

The saturation of the U.S. market, with established theme parks in the vicinity of most urban areas, has generated a view toward international expansion by some of the major players in the industry. Taft Broadcasting was the first to cross American borders with the development of Canada's Wonderland in 1981. But Disney made the initial giant leap with the construction of Tokyo Disneyland in cooperation with Oriental Land Company, Ltd., itself a joint arrangement between Mitsui Real Estate Development Company and Keizei Electric Railway Company. Opening in 1983, the park is located near Tokyo on a 600-acre tract in Urayasu,

Table 30. U.S. Personal Expenditures for
Recreation and Recreation Expenditures
as a Proportion of Total Personal
Consumption Expenditures (PCE), 1960–
1987, Selected Years (in billions of
current dollars)

Year	Recreation Expenditures	Proportion of PCE (%)
1960	17.9	5.5
1965	25.9	6.0
1970	41.0	6.6
1973	55.2	6.8
1975	66.5	6.8
1978	91.2	6.8
1980	115.0	6.6
1984	168.3	6.9
1985	185.7	7.1
1986	201.7	7.2
1987	223.3	7.4

Source: U.S. Bureau of the Census, *Statistical Abstract of the United States, 1989* (Washington, D.C.: Government Printing Office, 1989), table 693; U.S. Bureau of the Census, *Statistical Abstract of the United States, 1980* (Washington, D.C.: Government Printing Office, 1980), table 733.

with a population base of 30 million people within a one-hour travel time to the park. The agreement between Disney and Oriental Land Company, Ltd., stipulates that construction costs of 150 billion yen and yearly operating costs are furnished by the Japanese company while Disney provides the master plan and operational management expertise.[9] In return, Disney receives a portion of the profits as royalties.

Tokyo Disneyland was an immediate success, achieving sales of $355 million in U.S. dollars during its first year in 1983, of which $20 million went to Walt Disney Company. The atmosphere of the park is a "gleaming microcosm of American culture," but advertising and marketing techniques display a Japanese approach, with media ads rich in imagery and 20 Japanese corporate sponsors within the park.[10] By September 1988 Tokyo Disneyland passed an attendance of 60 million people, equaling half of Japan's population. In 1990 a rail/subway line connecting to downtown Tokyo was scheduled for completion, thereby linking the park with the bullet train system throughout Japan.[11]

Attendance at Tokyo Disneyland, averaging approximately 10 million guests in each of its first five years, shows a pattern of growth, with nearly 12 million guests visiting the park in 1987. *Captain Eo,* the 3-D space adventure movie produced by George Lucas and starring Michael Jackson; Big Thunder Mountain; and "Star Tours" have been transported across the ocean. The continuous appearance of new attractions is a prime ingredient in the park's overwhelming success. More than 70 percent of the guests are repeat visitors.[12] Oriental Land is considering a joint development plan with Disney to build a replica of the Disney-MGM Studios theme park on the Urayasu site. This time, Oriental Land wants an equal sharing of construction and other costs.[13]

The formal advent in 1989 of a five-day workweek in Japan is a boon to the leisure business, and amusement parks are in the forefront of the profit makers. In response to the burgeoning leisure market, many Japanese enterprises are developing amusement devices or attractions and are exhibiting them at international expositions. Senyo Kogyo, Ltd., has developed Cosmoworld, a high-tech playground of computers and other devices, while Togo Japan is exporting stand-up roller coasters to the United States, Canada, and even to the Soviet Union.[14] The Tokyo Bay Maihama Resort Community council, a nine-member organization that includes Oriental Land Company is orchestrating the development of the Urayasu area as a resort complex. Already there are several first-class hotels, including the Dai-ichi Hotel Tokyo Bay, the Sheraton Grande Tokyo Bay, the Tokyo Bay Hilton International, and the Sun Route Plaza Tokyo, all with western (U.S./European) resort atmospheres. There is also the sprawling Tokyo Bay NK Hall, a huge convention center than can accommodate 7,000 people. A yacht harbor and artificially created beaches are soon to come. The aim is to build a prestigious, first-class resort anchored by Tokyo Disneyland with a dominant atmosphere of American culture, where people will stay for a number of days.[15]

Spurred by the success of its Japanese venture, Walt Disney Company decided to develop EuroDisneyland, located in Marne-la-Vallée, 20 miles east of Paris. The complex will comprise a Magic Kingdom theme park and hotels with a total of 5,200 rooms. Under an agreement made with the French government in 1987, the park's opening is scheduled for 1992. The $3 billion park and resort, built on 4,800 acres of former sugar beet farms, is considered the biggest single project ever undertaken by Walt Disney Company. As part of the agreement with the

French government, in November 1989 Disney began to offer stock shares of EuroDisneyland to citizens of the 12 European Community countries. Disney is required to sell 51 percent of the stock to Europeans, and it is listed on the stock exchanges in London, Paris, and Brussels. The ongoing removal of trade barriers and the establishment of consistent commercial codes in the European Community countries is a significant advantage for Disney. In contrast to the ownership arrangement for Tokyo Disneyland, Disney owns 49 percent of EuroDisneyland and will receive the same percentage of the park's income. It is estimated that Disney could realize $1.6 billion annually from the park. Two factors, however, are potential problems for the EuroDisneyland project. The Paris weather is cool and often rainy, less conducive to family outings and outdoor leisure activities in general. With the weather in mind, plans call for more indoor attractions. Also, there is significant competition in the form of three other major theme parks in France that are already open or in the planning stages.[16]

Parc Asterix, which opened in April 1989 in Plailly, 22 miles northeast of Paris, promises to be a vital competitor with EuroDisneyland. The $150 million park is based on the Asterix comic books created by René Goscinny and Albert Uderzo, which have sold over 200 million copies worldwide. Parc Asterix is owned by a group of 20 investors headed by park president Eric Lacoys, director general of Barclays Bank. Rides and attractions are quite similar to American theme parks, with a roller coaster, carousel, flume and rapids water rides, a train, bumper cars, a monster ride called the "Mistral," a dolphin show, a gladiator spectacle with 3-D film, daily parades, three full-service restaurants, and various fast-food stations, including a crepe shop.[17]

Also opening in France in the spring of 1989 is Big Bang Schtroumpf (Smurfs) theme park, just north of Metz. The $110 million park is owned by Paris-based Sorepark S.A., and is designed primarily for children. Planned largely by the architectural firm of Hellman, Hurley, Charvat & Peacock in Orlando, Florida, the park has a wooden roller coaster, a rapid river ride, a carousel, and miniature train and flume rides. Live entertainment and theater shows are the staple of the park, including "Time Tunnel," combining animation, live action, and special effects and starring the Pollution Monster. The Smurfs cavort in five theme areas: the Smurf's Village, City of the Waters, Metal Planet, Wild Continent, and the Entrance Concourse.[18]

In the 1990s Disney will have plenty of company in the development of parks on the international scene, especially in Europe. Both Anheuser-Busch and the Six Flags organization have announced plans for parks in Spain. Busch Entertainment Corporation is planning a $300 million theme park and resort complex on a 2,070-acre site in Catalonia on the Spanish Mediterranean coast. The park's theme is expected to focus on foreign lands, with villages representing a Spanish fishing port, Polynesia, Mexico, China, and the American Old West. The theme park will be accompanied by a golf course, hotel, conference center, tennis and other recreational facilities, and retail areas. The Spanish government approved the project in June 1989. Although Spain is not considered to be an emerging market area for theme parks, Busch considers the Spanish economy to be strong and already has a presence in the Barcelona area, the location of its European headquarters for brewery and food products interests. Opening is targeted for 1992, in time for the 1992 Olympic Games in Barcelona.[19] Six Flags Corporation has signed a 10-year management agreement with Daylong Island Española to act as consultant in design and construction and to manage Montana Magica, a $85 million theme park in the Costa del Sol region of southern Spain. The first international venture for the Six Flags organization, Montana Magica will be part of a resort development with hotels, condominiums, a golf course, tennis courts, an equestrian center, conference center, and commercial shops. The theme park will be similar to the established Six Flags parks, with roller coasters, flume water rides, live entertainment, and lush landscaping.[20]

Large-scale amusement and theme parks are suddenly becoming immensely popular in England. The boom began in 1980 when Alton Towers, a 60-year-old park comprised primarily of historic gardens and a stately manor house on the former estate of the earls of Shrewsbury in North Staffordshire, added a Vekoma roller coaster and other rides. In 1988 the park's attendance reached 2.3 million visitors, drawn by a new monorail and two new coasters, the Alton Beast and the Black Hole. The park is divided into six theme areas: Aqualand, the Gardens, Festival Park, Talbot Street (a Victorian area), Fantasy World, and Kiddies' Kingdom. There are six sit-down restaurants and 120 rides.[21]

The success of Alton Towers in the last decade has led John Broome, chairman of the Alton Group, and investor Paul Bloomfield to form Alton International with the aim of becoming a leading force in the international theme park industry. Alton International now owns Alton Towers, the developing Battersea Power Station amusement/retail complex in central London, and Zygofolis theme park in Nice, France. With assets totaling over £600 million (about $900 million U.S.), the company plans to pursue major acquisitions on the international scene. At home, the Battersea Power Station is a huge mall/amusement park occupying Gilbert Scott's art deco power station building. Large enough to hold St. Paul's Cathedral, it comprises seven floors, each taking as its theme a different continent or historical period, all of which contain rides, attractions, and retail outlets. The refurbishment of this historic structure will cost £200 million. Success will depend on its ability to attract at least 4.5 million visitors a year.[22] Alton International brought in Leisure & Recreation Concepts (LARC) of Dallas, Texas, to totally redesign the Zygofolis park.[23]

LARC is also involved in the design of an amusement park/ marketplace project in Belfast, Northern Ireland, that will focus on the city's maritime and shipbuilding history (the *Titanic* was built there) with a museum, theaters, and simulation attractions, along with rides. The firm is working on plans for a historical attraction at Ireland's Boyne Park of National Heritage that will highlight the Viking history of the area and the Battle of Boyne, fought in 1690, at which the deposed James II was defeated by William III of England.[24]

Two organizations are involved in movie-studio tour ventures in England. The Granada Group, producers of British film and television programs, opened the Granada Studios Tour in Manchester in July 1989. The $15.1 million studio tour has striking similarities to its American counterparts largely because Andrew Grant, formerly of Universal Studios, prepared the feasibility study. The attraction emphasizes behind-the-scenes activities with tours of control rooms, a studio, makeup room, and wardrobe. Sets from Granada Productions include Sherlock Holmes's living room and sets from the long-running British series "Coronation Street." There is also a block-long re-creation of a New York City street.[25] *Amusement Business,* the trade weekly, reports that MCA Enterprises, owner of Universal Studios parks in Hollywood and Orlando, Florida, plans to build a studio tour outside London. MCA is pursuing the project in partnership with the Rank Organization and British Urban Development, a consortium of 11 construction companies. Rank is already a partner in Universal Studios Florida. Plans include not only a studio tour park but also a massive commercial and residential development. Cost is estimated at approximately $3 billion. The land in Rainham Marshes is currently owned by the Ministry of Defence.[26]

Since the opening of Tokyo Disneyland, the development of parks in the Far East is rivaling activity in Western Europe. Kings Entertainment Company, owner of Kings Dominion, Great America Santa Clara, and Carowinds, and operator of Kings Island, is the management consultant for Australia's Wonderland in Sydney. But the down-under park's 1 million attendance in 1988 was not meeting expectations.[27] Lotte World, a themer in Seoul, South Korea, has been so successful since its opening in summer 1989 that plans are moving ahead for a second phase. Battaglia Associates, located in Huntington Beach, California, prepared the master plan for the park and serves as consultant for the project. Lotte World, owned by Korean and Japanese interests, is located within a massive mall, hotel, and sports center complex and is averaging 20,000 to 25,000 attendance on weekends. The centerpiece of the park is a laser game where guests shoot laser cannons at targets projected by lasers on interior walls. The game is so popular that it runs at excess of capacity. Future plans include the addition of an interactive dark ride that will furnish riders with "magic crystals" (lasers) used to determine the course of the car in which they are riding. Thus the ride can be different each time a guest participates. Prices for admission to Lotte World are on a par with theme park fees in the United States, $22.40 for a daily pay-one-price ticket.[28]

Amusement/theme park growth is evident throughout the world. Blackpool Leisure & Amusement Consultantcy is developing Nehruland, a 170-acre complex in Bombay, India. TusenFryd, Norway's first theme park, opened near Oslo in July 1989. Las Cascadas Aquatic Park in Puerto Rico opened in August 1988. Even Turkish investors are being lured to the amusement park business. Netpark, a large public company in Turkey, broke ground in 1988 for an as-yet-unnamed theme park that will comprise three main sectors: Legends and Myths, Magic and Discovery, and History and Adventure. Scheduled to open in 1991, the 300-acre complex will have roller coasters, a water flume ride, other metal rides, dark rides, a cinema, and an open-air theater. Among the planners are Hellman, Hurley, Charvat & Peacock and Sequoia Creative, Sun Valley, California, as chief designer. Economic Research Associates conducted the feasibility study. The developers hope to gross approximately $17 million during the first year of operation.[29]

Perhaps most intriguing in the age of *glasnost* is the growing interest in the Soviet Union for the development of western-style amusement parks. In December 1989 Moscow parks head Arkadi Gavrilenko and Pavel Kiselev, manager of Gorky Park, attended the annual convention of the International Association of Amusement Parks and Attractions, held in Atlanta. The two Soviet delegates indicated that their government is negotiating with Walt Disney Company to build a theme park on an island in Moscow. The island has been officially reserved for an amusement park since the production of a master plan for the city of Moscow in 1971. By late 1989 Disney architects and design teams were visiting the Soviet capital. Also in planning is World of Wonder, a Russian fairy-tale park with theme areas for the 15 republics of the Soviet Union. Construction firms from Italy, Finland, and England are working with the Soviets on the project. The major roadblock for Soviet interests is the lack of convertibility of the Soviet ruble. Until currency can be exchanged in a normal fashion, commercial relations with the Soviet Union will likely remain piecemeal and exceptional. While in Atlanta, Gavrilenko revealed that the Soviets have purchased the design rights to a steel looping coaster from Togo of Japan and are manufacturing the coasters within the Soviet Union. The first one manufactured in the Soviet Union was installed in Izmaylovo, a Moscow park. Gavrilenko also explained that the Soviet government has ordered three defense manufacturers to diversify in order to build amusement rides. At present there are about 300 large amusement parks in the Soviet Union. The best known is Gorky Park in Moscow, which reportedly attracts about 12 million visitors each year. A few of Gorky Park's 21 major attractions were manufactured in the West, but most were built within the Soviet Union at two factories. During their visit to Atlanta, the Russian delegates were reportedly impressed by the "humanistic tendencies" of current trends in the amusement industry, meaning less emphasis on "monsters and horrible creatures" and more "friendly, animated characters." They also noted the trend toward participatory attractions, where the audience or individual guests become an integral part of rides or attractions.[30]

Among the largest amusement/theme parks outside the United States are the attractions listed in table 31, ranked according to estimated attendance figures for 1988.

☐   The Future

At the advent of the 1990s, an important factor remains an area of concern to the American amusement park industry. The demographics of the U.S. population will shift significantly in the next decade and into the 21st century toward an aging population. To maintain its economic vigor, the amusement park industry must cater to an increasingly older clientele. *The Big Picture: Travel Industry World Yearbook* states that in 1988 the average age of an amusement park visitor had already increased to 35 years.[31] Continued growth in attendance and revenues will require changes in attractions to lure older guests. Many parks are already responding by placing greater emphasis on restaurants, landscaping and gardens, and live entertainment. The listing of major improvements for 1990, as outlined earlier in this chapter, however, is indicative of continued current emphasis on new attractions that will appeal to teenagers and young adults, primarily ever more terrorizing roller coasters.

Table 32 indicates the age distribution of the U.S. population from

Table 31. Major International Amusement Parks by Attendance, 1988 (in millions)

Park	Attendance
1. Tokyo Disneyland	12.0
2. Jaya Ancol Dreamland, Jakarta, Indonesia	9.98
3. Blackpool Pleasure Beach, Blackpool, England	6.6
4. Tivoli Gardens, Copenhagen	4.5
5. Riyadh Amusement Park, Riyadh, Saudi Arabia	3.0
6. Toshimaen Amusement Park, Tokyo	3.0
7. Liseberg, Gothenburg, Sweden	2.8
8. Tivoli Park, Rio de Janeiro	2.4
9. Alton Towers, North Staffordshire, England	2.3
10. De Efteling, Kattsheuvel, Netherlands	2.3
11. Phantasialand, Bruhl, West Germany	2.2
12. Bakken, Klampenborg, Denmark	2.0
13. Ocean Park, Hong Kong	1.8
14. Playcenter, São Paulo, Brazil	1.8
15. Reino Aventura, Mexico City	1.5
16. Grona Lund, Stockholm	1.4
17. Walibi, Limal, Belgium	1.4
18. Durban Miniature Railway Park, Natal, South Africa	1.3
19. Sea World, Queensland, Australia	1.2
20. Atallah Happyland, Jeddah, Saudi Arabia	1.0

Source: "A Sampling of International Parks," *Amusement Business,* 24 December 1988, 90.

1960 with projections through 2030. The decline in children under 14 years of age and the projected increase in people aged 65 years and over is especially striking. These projections foresee a significant decrease in the population under 25 years of age, the traditional target group for amusement parks. While in 1980, in the midst of the theme park boom, 41.3 percent of the U.S. population was under 25, by the year 2000 this age group will make up only 33.9 percent of the population, and by 2030 it will decline to 29 percent. In contrast, persons 45 years old and over made up 31.8 percent of the population in 1980, yet by the year 2000 this group will rise to 37.6 percent, and by 2030 it will jump to 48.5 percent, or very

Table 32. Percent Distribution of the U.S. Population, by Age, 1960–2030
(estimated)

Age	1960	1970	1980	1990	2000	2010	2020	2030
< 5	11.3	8.4	7.2	7.4	6.3	6.0	5.8	5.4
5–13	18.2	17.9	13.7	12.9	12.5	11.0	10.8	10.4
14–17	6.2	7.8	7.1	5.3	5.7	5.2	4.8	4.8
18–24	8.9	12.1	13.3	10.4	9.4	9.6	8.5	8.4
25–34	12.7	12.3	16.5	17.5	13.8	13.3	13.3	12.1
35–44	13.4	11.3	11.4	15.1	16.4	13.2	12.8	13.0
45–64	20.0	20.5	19.5	18.7	22.9	27.8	26.4	24.0
> 65	9.2	9.8	11.3	12.6	13.0	13.9	17.7	21.8
> 85	0.5	0.7	1.0	1.3	1.7	2.2	2.3	2.7

Source: U.S. Bureau of the Census, *Current Population Reports*, ser. P-25, no. 1018, *Projections of the Population of the United States, By Age, Sex, and Race, 1988 to 2080*, by Gregory Spencer (Washington, D.C.: Government Printing Office, 1989), table G, p. 8. Middle series projections used for the compilation of this table.

close to half of the populace. The post–World War II baby boom generation will maintain its dominance of American demographics, entering
retirement age in the second decade of the 21st century. Advances in
medical technology and generally more healthy life-styles than in previous generations will probably result in a longer lifespan and more activity
during this group's senior years.

Although roller coasters still prevail, there is ample evidence of a
shift in amusement park attractions toward entertainment appealing to
an older clientele. The end of the 1980s has witnessed the phenomenal
success of movie studio theme parks with the opening of the Disney-
MGM Studios park in 1989 and the debut of Universal Studios Florida in
June 1990. Disney is actively courting the business conference clientele
with its two new massive, upscale conference center hotels, the Dolphin
and the Swan. The "simulation" ride is proving to be at least as popular as
roller coasters. The simulation attractions, which provide a sensory technological thrill, do not impose on participants the physical demands of the
gravity rides. Among the most outstanding simulation "experiences" are
Universal Studio's "Earthquake: The Big One," recreating a severe California quake, and "Star Tours" at Disneyland and Walt Disney World, a
spaceflight simulator developed in collaboration with George Lucas.

Another trend is the placement of amusement parks within shopping malls. The West Edmonton Mall in Alberta, Canada, boasts a 450,000-square-foot amusement area with a roller coaster and even a water park.[32] Ontario Place in Toronto, ranked 17 among amusement/ theme parks in 1989, is a combination sports complex, shopping mall, and amusement center. San Francisco's Pier 39 blends boutique-size shops with restaurants, live performances by actors and musicians plus dolphins and seals, and an amusement area with carousel, games, and bumper cars. Knott's Berry Farm is working with Simon & Associates on the development of the 78-acre Mall of America in Bloomington, Minnesota, which will include Knott's Camp Snoopy, complete with a water flume, Ferris wheel, carousel, roller coaster, and more. Groundbreaking for the complex occurred in the summer of 1989.[33] 1990 marks the opening of Tritor Development's Crystal Palace entertainment center in Toronto. Its components are a hotel, movie theaters, a 60,000-square-foot amusement park, and a community center, all adjacent to the shopping mall.[34] Indianapolis is planning a $96 million amusement center as one sector of a complex that also contains the Indianapolis Zoo, the River Promenade, and the Eiteljorg Museum of the American Indian.[35] The aging population, an increasing trend of eating outside the home, and the declining teenage population all augur well for the concept of blending retail center, theme park, and participatory recreation as the successful amusement format of the 1990s and on into the next century.

Demographer Jeff Ostroff projects leisure activities as one of the "promising niches of need" that businesses should explore in the 1990s. Americans aged 50 and older are considered to represent a "huge market" for restaurants, resorts, and theme parks. Parks are developing marketing strategies that include the organization of singles-oriented events and tours, as well as programs that bring several generations together in group activities. Six Flags' Great America has initiated an advertising campaign to attract grandparents, parents, and grandchildren to visit the park together. Theme parks can especially respond to a growing desire for brief escapes or short "new experiences." By the year 2000 the over-50 age group will be "more educated, more computer literate, and more informed than any previous generation"; thus educational attractions and exciting experiences with new technologies should be especially attractive.[36]

In late 1987 Frank Wells, then chief executive officer of Walt Disney Company, provided a futurist glance at the leisure industry in a presentation to the Travel Industry Association. He emphasized the preeminence of the "entertainment" factor in leisure enterprises. Wells envisioned two vacation formats expected to soar in popularity and demand by the year 2000, namely "soft adventure" and "fantasy vacation" experiences. "Soft adventure" vacations are "safe" versions of challenging or dangerous undertakings like mountain climbing, rafting, big-game hunting, and scuba diving. Such contrived, engineered experiences, where safety is actually assured, indulge "the yen for danger, adventure, new knowledge and out-of-the-ordinary experience in addition to bestowing 'bragging rights.' " "Fantasy vacations" transport the visitor into created environments with heightened exotica and dramatic surroundings where location, landscaping, decoration, and theme intensify traditional vacation activities. Wells sees three primary target groups for these and other leisure enterprises: the elderly, women, and families. Like most of the business world, Walt Disney Company and Wells recognize the demographic trend toward an aging population. Wells notes that the number of people age 65 and over who traveled in 1986 increased by 23 percent over the number in the previous year. By the year 2000 the aged will be "healthier, more mobile, more affluent and better educated than prior generations," and they will have significant disposable income. Women are also a growing market largely because of their rising numbers in the work force since 1970. They too have more disposable income and are traveling more for both business and pleasure. Finally, vacation patterns for the family group will alter in the next decade. Wells predicts shorter, more frequent vacations. One potential factor causing a shift away from the yearly extended vacation is the possibility of year-round school sessions with several short breaks.

Wells also predicts that "second-tier" cities will be discovered by vacationers and amusement entrepreneurs. Cities such as Charlotte, Louisville, Columbus, Kansas City, Cincinnati, and Reno should be able to exploit their economic attractiveness and their uniqueness with the same tremendous success San Antonio has achieved.[37]

The amusement/theme park industry is well structured to respond to and reap profits from these trends for "safe" fantasy or adventure experiences; shorter, more frequent vacations; and the growing numbers of aged citizens, women travelers, and families seeking leisure experiences as a group. Parks must design new attractions to appeal to these clientele while downplaying emphasis on physically demanding thrill rides and other entertainment primarily designed for teenagers. Simulation technologies, as well as the growth of total vacation complexes comprising hotels, restaurants, entertainment, shopping, and amusement parks, are likely to satisfy perfectly the predicted desires of leisure seekers in the coming decade and the new century. The worldwide amusement park industry is poised for a spectacular success boom, provided it maintains responsiveness to changes in the culture within which it exists and demonstrates a commitment to reinvest a very high percentage of profits back into the continuous enhancement of the parks and attractions. At the onset of the 1990s, the world political situation promises greater stability and lessening ideological tensions.

Escape and the need to be entertained will endure as driving cultural forces in the near future, but consumer preferences for satisfaction may curve away from the course charted in the last two decades. Theme park operators should foresee growing public boredom with artificial substitutes for the actual and with reconstructions of the past. People will demand novel applications of technology that create totally new and unexpected experiences beyond the realm of reality. In the 1920s, 1930s, and 1940s we wanted to be titillated; in the 1950s, 1960s, 1970s, and 1980s we needed to be protected, comforted, pampered, and passively entertained; in the 1990s we will demand to be lavishly indulged, actively engaged, and frequently amazed.

APPENDIX A

Some Parks That Established the Traditional, Pre-Disneyland Amusement Park Culture

Cedar Point, Sandusky, Ohio*
Coney Island, Cincinnati
Crystal Beach, Crystal Beach, Ontario (closed in 1989)
Dorney Park, Allentown, Pennsylvania*
Dreamland, Coney Island, New York
Electric Park, Kansas City
Elitch Gardens, Denver*
Euclid Beach, Cleveland
Forest Park Highlands, St. Louis
Glen Echo, Washington, D.C.
Hersheypark, Hershey, Pennsylvania*
Kennywood Park, Pittsburgh*
Luna Park, Coney Island, New York
Olympic Park, Irvington, New Jersey
Pacific Ocean Park, Long Beach, California
Palisades Park, Fort Lee, New Jersey
Playland, Rye, New York*
Playland-at-the-Beach, San Francisco
Pontchartrain Beach, New Orleans
Revere Beach, Boston
Riverview Park, Chicago
Rockaway's Playland, Rockaway Beach, New York
Rocky Glen Park, Scranton, Pennsylvania*
Santa Monica Pleasure Pier, Santa Monica, California
Steeplechase Park, Coney Island, New York
Venice Amusement Park, Venice, California
Willow Grove Park, Philadelphia

*Still in operation in 1990

APPENDIX B
Industry Associations and Publications

☐ Associations

American Coaster Enthusiasts
P.O. Box 8226
Chicago, IL 60680

Historic Amusement Foundation
4410 N. Keystone Avenue
Indianapolis, IN 46205

International Association of Amusement Parks and Attractions
4230 King Street
Alexandria, VA 22302

National Amusement Park Historical Association
P.O. Box 83
Mt. Prospect, IL 60056

National Carousel Association
P.O. Box 307
Frankfort, IN 46041

Outdoor Amusement Business Association
4600 West 77th Street
Minneapolis, MN 55435

☐ Trade Journals and Newsletters

Amusement Business. Weekly
Billboard Publications
Box 24970
Nashville, TN 37202
The principal trade journal for the amusement park industry.

Funworld. Eleven issues/year
International Association of Amusement Parks and Attractions
4230 King Street
Alexandria, VA 22302

National Amusement Park Historical News. Bimonthly
National Amusement Park Historical Association
P.O. Box 83
Mt. Prospect, IL 60056

Roller Coaster! Quarterly
American Coaster Enthusiasts
P.O. Box 8226
Chicago, IL 60680

World's Fair. Quarterly
Corte Madera, CA 94925

CHRONOLOGY

c. 1133	Rahere, a monk, establishes Bartholomew Fair, a 10-day trade fair in the London area.
1661	Vauxhall Gardens established in London.
1742	Ranelagh Gardens opens in London.
1766	Joseph II grants his hunting grounds to the people of Vienna to establish the Prater park.
1804	Russian Mountains, a wheeled roller coaster, built in Paris.
1817	Promenades Aeriennes roller coaster constructed in the Jardin Beaujon.
1855	Last Bartholomew Fair held in London.
1867	Gustav A. Dentzel redesigns his Philadelphia cabinet shop to manufacture carousels.
c. 1870	Frederick Savage, an English mechanic, mounts a steam engine to a wooden carousel.
1884	LaMarcus Thompson builds his Switchback Railway coaster at Coney Island.
1893	World's Columbian Exposition held in Chicago. George Washington Gale Ferris builds and operates the first Ferris wheel at the exposition.
1895	Sea Lion Park, the first enclosed amusement park, opens at Coney Island.
1896	W. B. Basset erects the Riesenrad Ferris wheel in the Prater in Vienna.
1897	Steeplechase Park, built and owned by George Tilyou, opens at Coney Island.

1901	Walter Elias Disney is born 5 December in Chicago.
1903	Philadelphia Toboggan Company is established by Henry Auchy and Chester Albright to manufacture carousels.
1903	Luna Park, built and owned by Frederic Thompson and Elmer "Skip" Dundy, opens 16 May at Coney Island.
1904	Dr. Martin Couney's Premature Baby Incubators "sideshow" first appears in Luna Park at Coney Island.
1904	Dreamland park opens at Coney Island.
1910	Playground Association of America begins to sponsor recreation surveys of individual American cities. Glenn Curtiss breaks the aviation distance record by flying 64 miles from Euclid Beach Park in Cleveland to Cedar Point park in Sandusky, Ohio.
1911	Spectacular fire destroys Dreamland park and most of Coney Island, 27 May.
1920	Subway system is extended to Coney Island.
1923	Walt Disney arrives in Los Angeles.
1924	The Bobs, a roller coaster built by Frederick Church, Harry Traver, and Thomas Prior, opens at Riverview Park in Chicago.
1927	Vernon Keenan and Harry Baker build the Cyclone roller coaster at Coney Island. John Miller builds the Racer coaster at Kennywood Park near Pittsburgh.
1935	The U.S. Bureau of the Census begins to publish data on amusement parks as a distinct business category.
1940	Knott's Berry Farm land in Orange County, California, purchased by Walter Knott.
1955	Disneyland Park opens 17 July in Anaheim, California.
1956	New Jersey Supreme Court declares games of chance illegal.
1961	The first successful non-Disney theme park, Six Flags over Texas, opens, located between Dallas and Fort Worth.

1964	Universal Studios Tour opens in Hollywood, California.
1966	Walt Disney dies, 15 December.
1967	Six Flags over Georgia opens near Atlanta.
1970	Knott's Berry Farm is transformed into a theme park with the addition of thrill rides and distinct sectors.
1971	Walt Disney World Resort opens 23 October near Orlando, Florida.
1972	Kings Island, owned and built by Taft Broadcasting, opens near Cincinnati.
1973	The Great American Scream Machine built at Six Flags over Georgia, the longest wooden coaster to date.
1974	Great Adventure opens in Jackson, New Jersey. Busch Gardens' Dark Continent in Tampa, Florida, becomes a theme park through expansion of the original gardens, addition of thrill rides, and sector development. Busch Gardens' Old Country opens in Williamsburg, Virginia.
1975	Kings Dominion, owned by Taft Broadcasting, opens near Richmond, Virginia.
1976	The world's first triple-looping coaster, the Corkscrew, makes its appearance at Cedar Point. Marriott Corporation opens two identical Great America parks in Gurnee, Illinois, and Santa Clara, California.
1977	Harcourt Brace Jovanovich purchases three Sea World parks.
1982	EPCOT Center opens 1 October in Walt Disney World Resort, near Orlando, Florida.
1983	Tokyo Disneyland opens in Urayasu, Japan.
1984	Both Taft Broadcasting and Marriott Corporation sell all of their theme park interests. Fire at Great Adventure 11 May kills eight people.
1987	Bally Manufacturing Corporation sells its amusement park holdings, including all Six Flags parks, to the newly formed Six Flags, Inc.

1989   The world's highest and fastest roller coaster, the Magnum XL-200, opens at Cedar Point. Disney-MGM Studios theme park opens in Walt Disney World Resort. Harcourt Brace Jovanovich sells four Sea World parks and other amusement holdings to Anheuser-Busch.

1990   Universal Studios Florida theme park opens near Orlando, Florida, in June.

NOTES AND REFERENCES

Chapter 1

1. Figures listed in Edwin Beresford Chancellor, *Pleasure Haunts of London during Four Centuries* (1925; reprint, New York: Benjamin Blom, 1971), 329.

2. Quoted in Samuel McKecknie, *Popular Entertainments through the Ages* (1931; reprint, New York: Benjamin Blom, 1969), 45.

3. Warwick Wroth, *The London Pleasure Gardens of the Eighteenth Century* (1896; reprint, Hamden, Conn.: Archon Books, 1979).

4. Joseph Addison, *The Spectator,* no. 383, 20 May 1712.

5. Quoted in Wroth, *London Pleasure Gardens,* 292.

6. Ibid., 298–99.

7. Histories and descriptions of Vauxhall and Ranelagh Gardens are available in Chancellor, *Pleasure Haunts,* and Wroth, *London Pleasure Gardens.*

8. Felix Salten, *Wurstelprater* (1911; reprint, Vienna: Molden Verlag, 1973). Salten was also the author of the book *Bambi* (1923), on which Walt Disney based his animated feature film.

9. Marcel Brion, *Daily Life in the Vienna of Mozart and Schubert* (London: Weidenfeld & Nicolson, 1961), 123–25.

10. Ibid., 127–29.

11. George M. O'Brien presents an excellent account of the Prater in "The Parks of Vienna," *Journal of Popular Culture* 15 (Summer 1981): 76–86.

12. Frederick Fried, *A Pictorial History of the Carousel* (New York: Barnes, 1964).

13. Patent no. 7419.

14. "How a Carousel Is Made," *New York Times Illustrated Magazine,* 19 March 1899, 13.

15. The major carousel manufacturers in America are docu-

mented in Fried, *Pictorial History*, and in William F. Mangels, *The Outdoor Amusement Industry from Earliest Times to the Present* (New York: Vantage, 1952), 57–67.

16. J. Meredith Neil, "The Roller Coaster: Architectural Symbol and Sign," *Journal of Popular Culture* 15 (Summer 1981): 112.

17. Mangels, *Outdoor Amusement Industry*, 84.

18. Robert Cartmell, *The Incredible Scream Machine: A History of the Roller Coaster* (Fairview Park, Ohio: Amusement Park Books; and Bowling Green, Ohio: Bowling Green State University Press, 1987), 37.

19. Patent no. 198,888.

20. Mangels, *Outdoor Amusement Industry*, 88; Cartmell, *Incredible Scream Machine*, 42–54; and Herma Silverstein, *Scream Machines: Roller Coasters Past, Present, and Future* (New York: Walker, 1986), 18. Thompson's first patent is dated 1885, patent no. 310,966.

21. Quoted in Cartmell, *Incredible Scream Machine*, 49.

22. Silverstein, *Scream Machines*, 39, 43.

23. Neil, "Roller Coaster," 112–13.

Chapter 2

1. Quoted in Ray Ginger, *Altgeld's America: The Lincoln Ideal Versus Changing Realities* (New York: Funk & Wagnalls, 1958), 21.

2. Robert W. Rydell, *All the World's a Fair: Visions of Empire at American International Expositions, 1876–1916* (Chicago: University of Chicago Press, 1984), 71.

3. Montgomery Schuyler, "Last Words about the World's Fair," *Architectural Record* 3 (January–March 1894): 300.

4. Frederick Douglass, Introduction to *The Reason Why the Colored American Is Not in the World's Columbian Exposition*, ed. Ida B. Wells (Chicago: Ida B. Wells, 1893), 4.

5. Cited in Charles Sanford, *The Quest for Paradise: Europe and the American Moral Imagination* (Urbana: University of Illinois Press, 1961), 40.

6. John Winthrop, "A Modell of Christian Charity" (1630), in *The Puritans*, ed. Perry Miller and Thomas H. Johnson (New York: American Book Co., 1938), 119.

7. Edward Johnson, *Wonder-Working Providence of Sions Savior in New England* (1654) and *Good News from New England* (1648), ed. Edward J. Gallagher (Delmar, N.Y.: Scholars' Facsimiles and Reprints, 1974), 3.

8. Ernest Lee Tuveson, *Redeemer Nation: The Idea of America's Millennial Role* (Chicago: University of Chicago Press, 1968), x, 7, 97.

9. David F. Burg, *Chicago's White City of 1893* (Lexington:

University Press of Kentucky, 1976); Reid Badger, *The Great American Fair: The World's Columbian Exposition and American Culture* (Chicago: Nelson Hall, 1979).

10. For organization and construction of the World's Columbian Exposition, see chapters 7 and 8 of Badger, *Great American Fair*, and chapter 3 of Burg, *Chicago's White City*. Saint-Gaudens's statement is quoted in Charles Moore, *Daniel H. Burnham: Architect, Planner of Cities* (Boston: Houghton Mifflin, 1921), 37.

11. Louis Sullivan, *The Autobiography of an Idea* (New York: Dover, 1956), 324–25.

12. Badger, *Great American Fair*, 117–18.

13. Frank D. Millet et al., *Some Artists at the Fair* (New York: Scribner, 1893), 82.

14. Burg, *Chicago's White City*, 95–97, 119–37.

15. F. D. Millet, "The Designers of the Fair," *Harper's New Monthly Magazine* 85 (November 1892): 878.

16. Quoted in Alan Trachtenberg, *The Incorporation of America: Culture and Society in the Gilded Age* (New York: Hill & Wang, 1982), 215.

17. Schuyler, "Last Words," 287.

18. Badger, *Great American Fair*, 128.

19. *The Autobiography of Sol Bloom* (New York: Putnam, 1948), 119.

20. Benjamin C. Truman, *History of the World's Fair* (1893; reprint, New York: Arno Press, 1976), 550.

21. Rydell, *All the World's a Fair*, 40, 64–65.

22. Quoted in Paul Greenhalgh, *Ephemeral Vistas: The Expositions Universelles, Great Exhibitions, and World's Fairs, 1851–1939* (Manchester: Manchester University Press, 1988), 98.

23. Truman, *History*, 550.

24. The total expenditures of the exposition were $25,996,330, while final receipts amounted to $27,820,318, a profit margin of $1,823,988. See Arthur I. Street, "The World's Fair Balance Sheet," *Review of Reviews* 8 (November 1893): 522–23.

25. William Dean Howells, "Letters of an Altrurian Traveller," in *The Altrurian Romances* (Bloomington: Indiana University Press, 1968), 206.

26. Lois Stodieck Jones, *The Ferris Wheel* (Reno, Nev.: Grace Dangberg Foundation, 1984), 18.

27. "The Great Wheel at Chicago," *Scientific American* 69 (1 July 1893).

28. Quoted in Jack Fincher, "George Ferris, Jr., and the Great Wheel of Fortune," *Smithsonian* 14 (July 1983): 118.

29. John J. Flinn, ed., *Official Guide to the World's Colum-bian Exposition* (Chicago: N. Jaul, 1894), 2:386. For accounts of the work of the Department of Publicity and Promotion see Badger, *Great American Fair*, 75–76, and Truman, *History*, 73–75.

30. Peter B. Hales, *Silver Cities: The Photography of Ameri-can Urbanization, 1839–1915* (Philadelphia: Temple University Press, 1984), 153.

31. Badger, *Great American Fair*, 120.

32. Ibid., 90.

33. Ibid., 69.

34. Burg, *Chicago's White City*, 98.

35. J. P. Barrett, *Electricity at the Columbian Exposition* (Chi-cago: R. R. Donnelley and Sons, 1894), xi.

36. See Burg, *Chicago's White City*, 87, and Badger, *Great American Fair*, 91.

37. Badger, *Great American Fair*, 91.

38. *The Education of Henry Adams: An Autobiography* (Bos-ton: Houghton Mifflin, 1918), 343.

39. Trachtenberg, *The Incorporation of America*, 230.

Chapter 3

1. My account of Coney Island is most indebted to the follow-ing: Robert E. Snow and David E. Wright, "Coney Island: A Case Study in Popular Culture and Technical Change," *Journal of Popular Culture* 9 (Spring 1976): 960–75; John F. Kasson, *Amusing the Million: Coney Island at the Turn of the Century* (New York: Hill and Wang, 1978); Oliver Pilat and Jo Ranson, *Sodom by the Sea: An Affectionate History of Coney Island* (Garden City, N.Y.: Doubleday, 1941); Edo McCullough, *Good Old Coney Island* (New York: Scribner, 1957).

2. Quoted in McCullough, *Good Old Coney Island*, 7–8.

3. Ibid., 42.

4. Reginald Wright Kauffman, "Why Is Coney," *Hampton's Magazine* 23 (August 1909): 224.

5. Richard Snow, *Coney Island: A Postcard Journey to the City of Fire* (New York: Brightwaters Press, 1984), 69–70.

6. "To Heaven by Subway," *Fortune* 18 (August 1938): 61–68, 102–6.

7. Ibid., 103; and Pilat and Ranson, *Sodom by the Sea*, 136–38.

8. Snow and Wright, "Coney Island," 969.

9. "To Heaven by Subway," 102.

10. Gary Kyriazi, *The Great American Amusement Parks: A Pictorial History* (Secaucus, N.J.: Citadel Press, 1976), 82.

11. *New York Times,* 17 May 1903, 2; visitor's exclamation quoted in Cartmell, *Incredible Scream Machine,* 66.

12. Kasson, *Amusing the Million,* 63.

13. Frederic Thompson, "Amusing the Million," *Everybody's Magazine* 19 (September 1908): 378; Edwin E. Slosson, "The Amusement Business," *Independent* 57 (21 July 1904), 134.

14. Pilat and Ranson, *Sodom by the Sea,* 148, 150; Snow and Wright, "Coney Island," 968; Frederick [*sic*] A. Thompson, "The Summer Show," *Independent* 62 (20 June 1907): 1463; and *Amusement Business,* 30 December 1989, 88.

15. Mangels, *Outdoor Amusement Industry,* 48.

16. Maxim Gorky, "Boredom," *Independent* 63 (8 August 1907): 309.

17. Pilat and Ranson, *Sodom by the Sea,* 191–99; Mc-Cullough, *Good Old Coney Island,* 276–79; "To Heaven by Subway," 102.

18. Louise Bolard More, *Wage-Earners' Budgets: A Study of Standards and Cost of Living in New York City* (New York: Henry Holt, 1907), 103.

19. U.S. Bureau of the Census, *Historical Statistics of the United States: Colonial Times to 1970* (Washington, D.C.: Government Printing Office, 1975), ser. G582-601.

Chapter 4

1. Kyriazi, *Great American Amusement Parks,* 98; Rollin Lynde Hartt, *The People at Play* (1909; reprint, New York: Arno Press, 1975), 46.

2. Sylvester Baxter, "The Trolley in Rural Parks," *Harpers New Monthly Magazine* 97 (June 1898): 61.

3. Day Allen Willey, "The Trolley Park," *Cosmopolitan* 33 (July 1902): 265–67, 270, 272.

4. Robert M. Coates, "It's the Illusion That Counts," *New Yorker* 30 (8 May 1954): 91–92.

5. See especially Alan A. Siegel, *Smile: A Picture History of Olympic Park, 1887–1965* (Irvington, N.J.: Irvington Historical Society, 1983); Lee Bush et al., *Euclid Beach Park: A Second Look* (Mentor, Ohio: Amusement Park Books, 1979).

6. Hartt, *People At Play,* 60.

7. Foster Rhea Dulles, *America Learns to Play: A History of Popular Recreation, 1607–1940* (New York: Appleton-Century, 1940), 312–13.

8. U.S. Bureau of the Census, *Census of Business, 1935: Places of Amusement* (Washington, D.C.: U.S. Department of Commerce, 1937).

9. Raymond S. Tompkins, "Cathedrals of the Hot Dog," *American Mercury* 20 (May 1930): 52; Dana Gatlin, "Amusing America's Millions," *World's Work* 26 (July 1913), 332.

10. Kasson, *Amusing the Million*, 109.

11. Alan Havig, "Mass Commercial Amusements in Kansas City before World War I," *Missouri Historical Review* 75 (April 1981): 330.

12. Ibid., 331, 341–45.

13. Rowland Haynes, *Recreation Survey of Cincinnati* (Cincinnati: City of Cincinnati, 1913); *Recreation Survey, Detroit, Michigan* (Detroit: Board of Commerce, 1913); *Recreation Survey, Milwaukee*, bulletin no. 17, (Milwaukee: Bureau of Economy and Efficiency, 1911); "Recreation Survey of Kansas City, Mo.," in *Second Annual Report of the Recreation Department of the Board of Public Welfare* (Kansas City: Board of Public Welfare, 1912).

14. Quoted in Havig, 344.

15. Alan A. Siegel, *Smile: A Picture History of Olympic Park 1887–1965* (Irvington, N.J.: Irvington Historical Society, 1983).

16. Ibid., 8–9.

17. Ibid., 25.

18. Ibid., 35.

19. Ibid., 106–10.

20. Ibid., 122.

21. Ibid., 66.

22. Ibid., 139.

23. Cartmell, *Incredible Scream Machine*, 137–38.

24. Chuck Wlodarczyk, *Riverview: Gone But Not Forgotten: A Photo-History, 1904–1967* (Chicago: Riverview Publications, 1977), 74–77.

25. Garry Cooper, "The World That Was at Belmont and Western," *Chicago Tribune Magazine*, 16 May 1976, 24.

26. Cartmell, *Incredible Scream Machine*, 141–42.

27. Wlodarczyk, *Riverview*, 131. Palisades Park, near New York City, was also a victim of voracious developers. Irving Rosenthal sold Palisades in 1972 for $12.5 million to make room for a huge apartment complex (Cartmell, *Incredible Scream Machine*, 176).

28. Charles J. Jacques, Jr., *Kennywood: Roller Coaster Capital of the World* (Vestal, N.Y.: Vestal Press, 1982), 1.

29. Ibid., 2–4.

30. Ibid., 10.

31. It was not until 1971, however, that the Henninger family bought the park outright from the Kenny heirs for $1.3 million (ibid., 168).

32. Ibid., 30.

33. Ibid., 20, 22, 46, 81.

34. Cartmell, *Incredible Scream Machine*, 129.

35. Robert Cartmell, "The Quest for the Ultimate Roller Coaster," *New York Times,* 9 June 1974, section 10, p. 19.

36. Cartmell, *Incredible Scream Machine,* 174.

37. Ibid., 66.

38. Jacques, *Kennywood,* 132–34.

39. Ibid., 188.

40. Two fine sources for the history of Cedar Point are *Cedar Point: The Queen of American Watering Places,* by David W. Francis and Diane DeMali Francis (Canton, Ohio: Daring Books, 1988), and an article written by the park's marketing director at the time, Hugo John Hildebrandt, "Cedar Point: A Park in Progress," *Journal of Popular Culture* 15 (Summer 1981): 87–107.

41. Hildebrandt, "Cedar Point," 87, 90; Francis and Francis, *Cedar Point,* 38.

42. Lee Bush and his associates have produced two volumes on the history of Euclid Beach Park: *Euclid Beach Is Closed for the Season* (Cleveland: Dillon/Liederback, 1977), and *Euclid Beach Park: A Second Look* (Mentor, Ohio: Amusement Park Books, 1979).

43. "Midwest Resort Revives," *Business Week,* 23 September 1961, 106; Francis and Francis, *Cedar Point,* 114.

44. "Midwest Resort Revives," 106.

45. Hildebrandt, "Cedar Point," 100.

46. Ibid.; Francis and Francis, *Cedar Point,* 132.

47. "Midwest Resort Revives," 106; Hildebrandt, "Cedar Point," 103; Francis and Francis, *Cedar Point,* 134, 136.

48. "The Top 40 Amusement/Theme Parks, 1989," *Amusement Business,* 30 December 1989, 88.

49. Candace Carmel, "Competition Too Strong for Crystal Beach Park," *Amusement Business,* 9 September 1989, 1, 23.

50. Marge Thulman Hastreiter, "Fond Memories Remain amid Post Mortems on Crystal Beach," *Buffalo News,* 19 September 1989, B3; Tom Buckham, "Crystal Beach Customers Say Park's Closing Isn't Amusing," *Buffalo News,* 25 August 1989, A1, A5; Anthony Violanti, "Crystal Beach and Its Days of Enchantment," *Buffalo News,* 25 August 1989, C6, C7; Donn Esmond, "At Crystal Beach, It Was a Day for the Selling of Sentiment," *Buffalo News,* 18 October 1989, B7.

51. Esmond, "At Crystal Beach," B7.

Chapter 5

1. Jay Leyda, ed., *Eisenstein On Disney* (London: Methuen, 1988), 2. Walt Disney Company denied my request to reproduce photographs of Disneyland Park, Walt Disney World Resort, and Walt Disney

himself. Teressa Smith, of the Walt Disney Company corporate legal office, states in a letter dated 10 January 1990, "Our refusal to grant the aforesaid permission is not capricious but is based on experience and good reason, and on the necessity of complying with the copyright laws and our company's current obligations." Even personal photographs taken in the parks are barred from reproduction. Walt Disney Company has recently decided that only publications produced by the company itself may contain photographs or illustrations of the parks, Walt Disney, or other corporate employees.

2. Richard Schickel, *The Disney Version: The Life, Times, Art, and Commerce of Walt Disney* (New York: Simon & Schuster, 1968); Leonard Mosley, *Disney's World* (New York: Stein & Day, 1985).

3. See especially Schickel, *Disney Version*, 48–54, and Mosley, *Disney's World*, 27–32.

4. "Father Goose," *Time* 64 (27 December 1954): 44.

5. Mosley, *Disney's World*, 61–62.

6. Mosley, *Disney's World*, 71; Schickel, *Disney Version*, 85.

7. Mosley, *Disney's World*, 89; Schickel, *Disney Version*, 110.

8. Schickel, *Disney Version*, 129.

9. David I. Berland, "Disney and Freud: Walt Meets the Id," *Journal of Popular Culture* 15 (Spring 1982): 96.

10. Quoted in Schickel, *Disney Version*, 275.

11. Randy Bright, *Disneyland, Inside Story* (New York: Abrams, 1987), 49.

12. Quoted in Mosley, *Disney's World*, 230.

13. Schickel, *Disney Version*, 313; Mosley, *Disney's World*, 233.

14. R. Bright, *Disneyland*, 104–7.

15. "The Disneyland Story: A Unique Amusement Park Yields More Pleasure Than Profit," *Barron's* 36 (23 January 1956): 9.

16. Schickel, *Disney Version*, 326.

17. "Top 40, 1989," 88.

18. Quoted in R. Bright, *Disneyland*, 237.

19. Thomas Hine, *Populuxe* (New York: Knopf, 1986), 152.

20. Paul Goldberger, "Mickey Mouse Teaches the Architects," *New York Times Magazine*, 22 October 1972, 95.

21. James H. Bierman, "Disneyland And the 'Los Angelization' Of the Arts," in *American Popular Entertainment: Papers and Proceedings of the Conference on the History of American Popular Entertainment*, ed. Myron Matlaw (Westport, Conn.: Greenwood Press, 1977), 277.

22. Julian Halevy, "Disneyland and Las Vegas," *Nation* 186 (7 June 1958): 511, 513.

23.   John Ciardi, "Manner of Speaking: Foamrubberville," *Saturday Review* 48 (19 June 1965): 20.

24.   Schickel, *Disney Version,* 317, 319, 320, 322, 330–31.

25.   Leyda, *Eisenstein On Disney,* 8.

26.   John Bright, "California Revolution 6: Disney's Fantasy Empire," *Nation* 204 (6 March 1967): 299.

27.   Kevin Wallace, "The Engineering of Ease," *New Yorker* 39 (7 September 1963): 106.

28.   Linda Deckard, "New, $1 Billion Attraction Slated for Southern California," *Amusement Business,* 22 January 1990, 1, 27–28.

Chapter 6

1.   Kyriazi, *Great American Amusement Parks,* 176–79.

2.   Millicent Hall, "Theme Parks: Around the World in 80 Minutes," *Landscape* 21 (Autumn 1976), 6–7; and Kyriazi, *Great American Amusement Parks,* 179–83.

3.   Mark Johnson, "Georgia Joy," *Travel* 129 (April 1968): 37–40; and Pamela A. Keene, "Land of Screams and Dreams," *Sky* (August 1988): 74–80.

4.   James M. Cameron and Ronald Bordessa have produced a detailed study of the land acquisition process, environmental studies, and dealings with local residents that preceded the building of Canada's Wonderland, near Toronto, in *Wonderland through the Looking Glass: Politics, Culture, and Planning in International Recreation* (Maple, Ont.: Belsten, 1981).

5.   Hall, "Theme Parks," 5–6.

6.   *ASTM Standards on Amusement Rides and Devices* (Philadelphia: American Society for Testing and Materials, 1987).

7.   Hal Hellman, "Those Incredible New Amusement Parks: A Taste of Thrills to Come!" *Futurist* 14 (August 1980): 41.

8.   Ibid., 42.

9.   Quoted in Hall, "Theme Parks," 8.

10.   Chuck Y. Gee, Dexter J. L. Choy, and James C. Makens, *The Travel Industry* (Westport, Conn.: AVI Publishing, 1984), 244; Margaret Thoren, "Fun and Profit: Amusement Parks Shrug Off First Bad Season in Years," *Barron's* 60 (3 November 1980), 11.

11.   Taft Broadcasting *Annual Reports* 1982, 1984; Linda Deckard, "KECO Sells 80% of Canada's Wonderland, Buys Out Cal. Park," *Amusement Business,* 5 November 1988, 1, 28.

12.   Anheuser-Busch *Annual Reports* 1974–88.

13.   Marriott Corporation *Annual Report* 1976.

14. "Coasting and Sliding at 12 of America's Amusement Parks," *New York Times*, 13 August 1989, travel section, 19.

15. Elizabeth Walker Mechling and Jay Mechling, "The Sale of Two Cities: A Semiotic Comparison of Disneyland With Marriott's Great America," *Journal of Popular Culture* 15 (Summer 1981): 166–79.

16. Ibid., 174.

17. Bally Manufacturing Corporation *Annual Report* 1983.

18. "Coasting and Sliding," 14.

19. See December issues of *Amusement Business* for annual listings of the top 20 amusement parks, by attendance, in the United States.

20. "Six Flags Corp.," in *Disclosure* online database, 1989.

21. Michael J. McCarthy, "Harcourt to Sell Its Theme Parks and Other Land," *Wall Street Journal*, 21 June 1989, A6; Thomas C. Hayes, "Harcourt Near Sale of Sea World," *New York Times*, 14 August 1989, D1, D6; Tim O'Brien, "Busch Has No Spinoff Plans for Attractions Acquired from HBJ," *Amusement Business*, 14 October 1989, 33, 39; "Busch Closes Boardwalk & Baseball," *Amusement Business*, 22 January 1990, 27, 42.

22. MCA, Inc., *Annual Report* 1980.

23. MCA, Inc., *Annual Report* 1987; Linda Deckard, "MCA Selects London Site for Future Studio Tour," *Amusement Business*, 16 December 1989, 19–20.

24. U.S. Travel Data Center and Business Research Division, University of Colorado, *Tourism's Top Twenty* (Boulder: Business Research Division, University of Colorado, 1984 and 1988 editions), 86 and 74, respectively; and "Top 40, 1989," 88; "Knott's Berry Farm," in *D&B, Dun's Financial Records* online database, 1990.

25. Robert O'Brien, "Walter Knott's Berry Farm and Ghost Town," *American Mercury* 85 (October 1957): 30–31.

26. Ibid., 32. Knott's Berry Farm, because it is a private company, does not make its financial data public, nor did it supply such information to the author.

27. Mary Ann Galante, "Cheap Thrills Not Enough, Theme Parks Say," *Los Angeles Times*, 9 December 1987, part 4, 1–2.

28. Francis and Francis, *Cedar Point*, 154–55.

29. Information on coasters has been provided by the management of Cedar Point.

30. Louise Zepp, "Space Adventure Simulator, Hotel Top Cedar Point's Additions for '90," *Amusement Business*, 28 October 1989, 1, 21.

31. John R. Graff, 1987 Outlook for Theme Parks," in *Travel and Tourism Research Association, 1987 Outlook for Travel & Tourism: Proceedings of the Twelfth Annual Travel Outlook Forum, October 10, 1986* (Washington, D.C.: U.S. Travel Data Center, 1986), 131–33.

Chapter 7

1. Mosley, *Disney's World*, 281.
2. Goldberger, "Mickey Mouse," 96.
3. Mosley, *Disney's World*, 281–82.
4. "Building a Disney Dream," *Industry Week* 205 (26 May 1980): 58–59; Arthur C. Bravo, "Environmental Systems at Walt Disney World," *Journal of the Environmental Engineering Division: Proceedings of the American Society of Civil Engineers* 101, no. EE6 (December 1975): 888–89.
5. Goldberger, "Mickey Mouse," 98.
6. Bravo, "Environmental Systems," 887–95.
7. Mosley, *Disney's World*, 298–99.
8. All quotes cited in Goldberger, "Mickey Mouse," 41, 92.
9. Ibid., 91.
10. Ibid., 97–98; Robert Blake, "The Lessons of the Parks," in *The Art of Walt Disney: From Mickey Mouse to the Magic Kingdoms*, by Christopher Finch (New York: Abrams, 1973), 439–42.
11. Louis Wasserman, *Merchandising Architecture: Architectural Implications and Applications of Amusement Theme Parks* (Sheboygan, Wis.: Louis Wasserman, 1978), n.p.
12. Richard V. Francaviglia, "Main Street, U.S.A.: A Comparison/Contrast of Streetscapes in Disneyland and Walt Disney World," *Journal of Popular Culture* 15 (Summer 1981): 148, 152.
13. Mike Wallace, "Mickey Mouse History: Portraying the Past at Disney World," *Radical History Review* 32 (1985): 53.
14. Margaret Morganroth Gullette, "Sheep May Freely Graze," *North American Review* 267 (September 1982): 5, 6.
15. Quoted in Richard R. Beard, *Walt Disney's EPCOT Center: Creating the New World of Tomorrow* (New York: Abrams, 1982), 13.
16. Ibid., 28.
17. Ibid., 29.
18. Niles Howard, "Can Disney Do It Again?" *Dun's Review* 117 (June 1981): 82.
19. Irwin Ross, "Disney Gambols On Tomorrow," *Fortune* 106 (4 October 1982): 64, 66.
20. "Building a Disney Dream," 55–59.
21. Michael L. Smith, "Back to the Future: EPCOT, Camelot, and the History of Technology," in *New Perspectives On Technology and American Culture*, ed. Bruce Sinclair (Philadelphia: American Philosophical Society, 1986), 72.
22. M. Wallace, "Mickey Mouse History," 51–52.
23. Ibid., 53.

24. Alexander Moore, "Walt Disney World: Bounded Ritual Space and the Playful Pilgrimage Center," *Anthropological Quarterly* 53 (October 1980): 208–10.

25. Margaret J. King, "Disneyland and Walt Disney World: Traditional Values in a Futuristic Form," *Journal of Popular Culture* 15 (Summer 1981): 120–21.

26. Moore, "Walt Disney World," 215.

27. Richard Corliss, "If Heaven Ain't a Lot Like Disney," *Time* 127 (16 June 1986): 80, 83.

28. Elting E. Morison, "What Went Wrong with Disney's World's Fair," *American Heritage* 35 (December 1983): 78.

29. John Taylor, *Storming the Magic Kingdom: Wall Street, the Raiders, and the Battle for Disney* (New York: Knopf, 1987); "Disney Scores Pyrrhic Victory," *Dun's Business Month* 124 (July 1984): 15–16; Lawrence Minard, "Who Will Win the Keys to Disney's Magic Kingdom?" *Forbes* 133 (4 June 1984): 31–35.

30. Stephen Kindel, "Dueling with the Mouse King," *Financial World* 156 (19 May 1987): 40, 42–44.

31. Jeffrey Schmalz, "Movie Theme Park Fight: Nastiness Is Not a Fantasy," *New York Times*, 13 August 1989, 1; Robert Wrubel, "Jaws vs. Mickey Mouse," *Financial World* 158 (16 May 1989): 24.

32. Lisa Zhito, "Disney CEO: Henson Deal Match Made in 'Family Entertainment Heaven,' " *Amusement Business*, 9 September 1989, 20, 21.

Chapter 8

1. Robert Morris Associates, *RMA Annual Statement Studies 1988* (Philadelphia: Robert Morris Assoc., 1988), 314; Dun and Bradstreet, *Industry Norms and Key Business Ratios* (New York: Dun and Bradstreet Credit Services, 1982–88).

2. Walt Disney Company, *Annual Reports* 1980–88; Cedar Fair L.P. *Annual Reports* 1988, 1987.

3. Wyatt, "Park Improvements May Hit Record Proportions in 1990," *Amusement Business*, 30 December 1989, 3, 80–81, 89, 95.

4. Dave Burns, "Majority of Top 40 Attractions Increase Attendance in '89," *Amusement Business*, 30 December 1989, 92.

5. U.S. President's Commission on Americans Outdoors, *Report and Recommendations to the President of the United States* (Washington, D.C.: Government Printing Office, 1986), 26; U.S. Heritage Conservation and Recreation Service, *The Third Nationwide Outdoor Recreation Plan: The Assessment* (Washington, D.C.: Government Printing Office, 1979), 41; U.S. Bureau of the Census, *Current Population Reports*, ser. P-

25, no. 1018, *Projections of the Population of the United States by Age, Sex, and Race: 1988 to 2080*, by Gregory Spencer (Washington, D.C.: Government Printing Office, 1989), 7.

6. Somerset R. Waters, *The Big Picture: Travel Industry World Yearbook* (New York: Child & Waters, 1988), 4.

7. Ibid., 11.

8. U.S. Bureau of the Census, *Statistical Abstract of the United States, 1989* (Washington, D.C.: Government Printing Office, 1989), table 693; *Statistical Abstract of the United States, 1980* (Washington, D.C.: Government Printing Office, 1980), table 733.

9. Jon Woronoff, "Everyone Wins in Theme Park Swings and Roundabouts," *Asian Business* 20 (March 1984): 52–53.

10. Terry Trucco, "How Disneyland Beat All the Odds in Japan," *Advertising Age* 55 (6 September 1984): 14, 16.

11. Walt Disney Company, *Annual Report* 1988.

12. Kenichi Komahashi, "The Disneyland Effect: California Dreaming in Urayasu," *Tokyo Business Today*, October 1988, 46.

13. Ibid., 48.

14. Toshiyuki Matsuura, "Amusement Park Business Zooms, Zips, and Soars," *Business Japan* 34 (July 1989): 113–18.

15. Komahashi, "Disneyland Effect," 46–47.

16. Warren Strugatch, "51% of EuroDisneyland Stock to Be Sold in Europe," *Amusement Business*, 11 November 1989, 35–36; Robert Wrubel, "Le Defi Mickey Mouse," *Financial World* 158 (17 October 1989): 18, 21.

17. Lisa Zhito, "Opening Weeks Encouraging at Parc Asterix," *Amusement Business*, 10 June 1989, 1, 18.

18. Linda Deckard, "May 9 Opener Set for France's Smurfs Themer," *Amusement Business*, 18 March 1989, 17.

19. Lisa Zhito, "Busch Proposing $300 Mil Themer Project in Spain," *Amusement Business*, 20 May 1989, 19; Lisa Zhito, "Spanish Government Okays Busch's Themer/Resort Plans," *Amusement Business*, 15 July 1989, 19.

20. "Six Flags Corp. Signs Pact With $85 Mil Spanish Park," *Amusement Business*, 17 December 1988, 17.

21. Tim O'Brien, "U.K.'s Alton Towers Celebrates Two Birthdays with $2.3 Mil Gate," *Amusement Business*, 12 November 1988, 41, 43, 68.

22. Alan Bailey, "The Pitfalls of the Pleasure Dome," *Director* 42 (April 1989), 33–34.

23. Lisa Zhito, "Alton Intl. Plans Global Expansion; France's Zygofolis First Acquisition," *Amusement Business*, 29 July 1989, 27, 29.

24. "Projects in England and Ireland on Drawing Boards for LARC," *Amusement Business*, 24 June 1989, 34.

25. Mary Ann Simpkins, "Manchester's Granada Studios Tour, First Attraction of Its Kind in Europe," *Amusement Business*, 7 January 1989, 18–19.

26. Linda Deckard, "MCA Selects London Site for Future Studio Tour," *Amusement Business*, 16 December 1989, 19–20.

27. Tim O'Brien, "KECO Now Concentrating on Formulating Longterm Plans," *Amusement Business*, 18 February 1989, 1, 20.

28. Linda Deckard, "Phase Two Work Accelerated at Korea's Lotte World Themer," *Amusement Business*, 18 November 1989, 25.

29. Lisa Zhito, "1988 a Year of Growth, Change for Amusement Park Industry," *Amusement Business*, 7 January 1989, 19; Linda Deckard, "$60 Million Turkish Themer Projects 1,250,000 Attendance for First Year," *Amusement Business*, 17 December 1988, 18.

30. Linda Deckard, "Soviets Plan Expansion of Amusement Industry by Producing Some Rides & Trading for Others," *Amusement Business*, 2 December 1989, 23–24; "Soviets Entering Parks Business, Report Swedish Industry Officials," *American Business*, 15 October 1988, 30.

31. Waters, *Big Picture*, 15.

32. "Parks That Provide Playtime for Parents, Too," *New York Times*, 3 July 1988, F13; Candice Carmel, "Session Examines Placing of Entertainment Centers in Malls," *Amusement Business*, 23 December 1989, 18, 26; Candice Carmel, "Entertainment Centers in Shopping Malls Seen as Growing Trend," *Amusement Business*, 9 December 1989, 21, 30.

33. Linda Deckard, "Van Gorder has 5-year Plan for Knott's Berry Farm," *Amusement Business*, 24 December 1988, 79; Louise Zapp, "Knott's 'Camp Snoopy' Themer Centerpiece of Mall of America," *Amusement Business*, 1 July 1989, 16, 25.

34. Lisa Zhito, "Crystal Palace Family Entertainment Center to Be First Such Complex in Atlantic Canada," *Amusement Business*, 20 May 1989, 18.

35. Louise Zepp, "Indianapolis Planning $96 Million Family Amusement Ctr. Project," *Amusement Business*, 12 November 1988, 34.

36. Jeff Ostroff, "An Aging Market: How Businesses Can Prosper," *American Demographics* 11 (May 1989): 26, 28, 33, 58.

37. Frank G. Wells, "Travel and Tourism 1983 to the Year 2003," *Vital Speeches of the Day* 54 (1 January 1988): 168–73.

SELECTED BIBLIOGRAPHY

Bibliographies

Dunning, Glenna. *The American Amusement Park: An Annotated Bibliography.* Architecture Series Bibliography A1318. Monticello, Ill.: Vance Bibliographies, 1985.

Leebron, Elizabeth, and Lynn Gartley. *Walt Disney: A Guide to References and Resources.* Boston: G. K. Hall, 1979.

Starbuck, James C. *Theme Parks: A Partially Annotated Bibliography of Articles about Modern Amusement Parks.* Exchange Bibliography 953. Monticello, Ill.: Council of Planning Librarians, 1976.

White, Anthony G. *Amusement Parks: A Selected Bibliography.* Architecture Series Bibliography A1052. Monticello, Ill.: Vance Bibliographies, 1983.

Wilmeth, Don B. *American and English Popular Entertainment: A Guide to Information Sources.* Detroit: Gale Research, 1980.

———. *Variety Entertainment and Outdoor Amusements: A Reference Guide.* Westport, Conn.: Greenwood Press, 1982.

Books

ASTM Committee F-24 on Amusement Rides and Devices. *ASTM Standards on Amusement Rides and Devices.* 2d ed. Philadelphia: American Society for Testing and Materials, 1987.

Badger, Reid, *The Great American Fair: The World's Columbian Exposition and American Culture.* Chicago: Nelson Hall, 1979.

Barrett, J. P. *Electricity at the Columbian Exposition.* Chicago: R. R. Donnelley and Sons, 1894.

Beard, Richard R. *Walt Disney's EPCOT Center: Creating the New World of Tomorrow.* New York: Abrams, 1982.

Bogdan, Robert. *Freak Show: Presenting Human Oddities for Amusement and Profit.* Chicago: University of Chicago Press, 1988.

Braithwaite, David. *Fairground Architecture: The World of Amusement Parks, Carnivals, and Fairs.* New York: Praeger, 1968.

Bright, Randy. *Disneyland, Inside Story.* New York: Abrams, 1987.

Burg, David F. *Chicago's White City of 1893.* Lexington: University Press of Kentucky, 1976.

Burnham, Daniel Hudson, and Francis Davis Millet. *The Book of the Builders.* Chicago: Columbian Memorial Publication Society, 1894.

Bush, Lee, et al. *Euclid Beach Is Closed for the Season.* Cleveland: Dillon/ Liederback, 1977.

———. *Euclid Beach Park: A Second Look.* Mentor, Ohio: Amusement Park Books, 1979.

Cameron, James M., and Ronald Bordessa. *Wonderland through the Looking Glass: Politics, Culture, and Planning in International Recreation.* Maple, Ontario: Belsten, 1981.

Carlson, Raymond, and Eleanor Popelka. *1988 Directory of Theme and Amusement Parks.* Babylon, N.Y.: Pilot Books, 1988.

Cartmell, Robert. *The Incredible Scream Machine: A History of the Roller Coaster.* Bowling Green, Ohio: Bowling Green State University Popular Press; Fairview Park, Ohio: Amusement Park Books, 1987.

Chancellor, Edwin Beresford. *The Pleasure Haunts of London during Four Centuries.* 1925. Reprint. New York: Benjamin Blom, 1971.

Davis, Michael Marks, Jr. *The Exploitation of Pleasure: A Study of Commercial Recreations in New York City.* New York: Department of Child Hygiene of the Russell Sage Foundation, 1911.

Dulles, Foster Rhea. *America Learns to Play: A History of Popular Recreation, 1607–1940.* New York: Appleton-Century, 1940.

Edwards, Richard Henry. *Popular Amusements.* 1915. Reprint. New York: Arno Press, 1976. Social and moral investigation that includes commercial amusement parks.

Finch, Christopher. *The Art of Walt Disney: From Mickey Mouse to the Magic Kingdoms.* New York: Abrams, 1975.

Findling, John E., ed., and Kimberly D. Pelle, asst. ed. *Historical Dictionary of World's Fairs and Expositions, 1851–1988.* New York: Greenwood Press, 1990.

Flinn, John J., ed. *Official Guide to the World's Columbian Exposition.* 2 vols. Chicago: N. Jaul, 1894.

Francis, David W., and Diane DeMali Francis. *Cedar Point: The Queen of American Watering Places.* Canton, Ohio: Daring Books, 1988.

Fried, Frederick. *A Pictorial History of the Carousel.* New York: Barnes, 1964.

Funparks Directory, 1989 International Guide to Tourist Attractions, Themed Parks, and Fun Parks. Nashville, Tenn.: Amusement Business, 1989.

Griffin, Al. *Step Right Up Folks!* Chicago: Henry Regnery, 1974. Survey of American amusement parks.

Greenhalgh, Paul. *Ephemeral Vistas: The Expositions Universelles, Great Exhibitions, and World's Fairs, 1851–1939.* Manchester, England: Manchester University Press, 1988.

Gupta, Shiv K. *An Economic and Cultural Impact Study of the Amusement Park and Attraction Industry.* Philadelphia: Wharton Applied Research Center, University of Pennsylvania, 1977.

Hales, Peter B. *Silver Cities: The Photography of American Urbanization, 1839–1915.* Philadelphia: Temple University Press, 1984. Includes Charles Dudley Arnold's photography of the World's Columbian Exposition.

Hartt, Rollin Lynde. *The People at Play: Excursions in the Humor and Philosophy of Popular Amusements.* Boston: Houghton Mifflin, 1909.

Haynes, Rowland. *A Community Recreation Program.* Cleveland: Cleveland Foundation Committee, 1920.

———. *Recreation Survey, Detroit Michigan.* Detroit: Board of Commerce, Committee on Recreation System, 1913.

———. *Recreation Survey, Milwaukee.* Bulletin No. 71. Milwaukee: Bureau of Economy and Efficiency, 1911.

———. *Recreation Survey of Cincinnati.* Cincinnati: City of Cincinnati, 1913.

Haynes, Rowland, and F. F. McClure. "Recreation Survey of Kansas City, Mo." In *Second Annual Report of the Recreation Department of the Board of Public Welfare.* Kansas City: Board of Public Welfare, 1912.

Ilyinsky, Paul, and Dick Perry. *Goodbye, Coney Island, Goodbye.* Englewood Cliffs, N.J.: Prentice-Hall, 1972. Coney Island park in Cincinnati.

Ives, Halsey C. *The Dream City: A Portfolio of Photographic Views of the World's Columbian Exposition.* St. Louis: N. D. Thompson, 1893.

Jacques, Charles, J., Jr. *Kennywood: Roller Coaster Capital of the World.* Vestal, N.Y.: Vestal Press, 1982.

Kasson, John F. *Amusing the Million: Coney Island at the Turn of the Century.* New York: Hill & Wang, 1978.

Kyriazi, Gary. *The Great American Amusement Parks: A Pictorial History.* Secaucus, N.J.: Citadel, 1976.

Leyda, Jay, ed. *Eisenstein on Disney.* London: Methuen, 1988.

Lundberg, Donald E. *The Tourist Business.* 5th ed. New York: Van Nostrand Reinhold, 1985.

McCullough, Edo. *Good Old Coney Island.* New York: Scribner, 1957.

————. *World's Fair Midways: An Affectionate Account of American Amusement Areas from the Crystal Palace to the Crystal Ball.* New York: Exposition Press, 1966. Reprint. New York: Arno Press, 1976.

McKechnie, Samuel. *Popular Entertainments through the Ages.* London: Samson Low, Marston, 1931. Reprint. New York: Benjamin Blom, 1969.

McKennon, Joe. *A Pictorial History of the American Carnival.* Sarasota, Fla.: Carnival Publishers, 1972.

Mangels, William F. *The Outdoor Amusement Industry from Earliest Times to the Present.* New York: Vantage, 1952.

More, Louise Bolard. *Wage-Earners' Budgets: A Study of Standards and Cost of Living in New York City.* New York: Holt, 1907.

Mosley, Leonard. *Disney's World: A Biography.* New York: Stein & Day, 1985.

National Recreation Association. *The Leisure Hours of 5,000 People: A Report of a Study of Leisure Time Activities and Desires.* New York: National Recreation Association, 1934.

North, Francis R. *Indianapolis Recreation Survey.* Indianapolis: Indianapolis Chamber of Commerce, 1914.

————. *Recreation Survey of the City of Providence, R.I.* Providence: Providence Playground Association, 1912.

Pilat, Oliver, and Jo Ranson. *Sodom by the Sea: An Affectionate History of Coney Island.* Garden City, N.Y.: Doubleday, 1941.

Rydell, Robert W. *All the World's a Fair: Visions of Empire at American International Expositions, 1876–1916.* Chicago: University of Chicago Press, 1984.

Sanford, Charles. *The Quest for Paradise: Europe and the American Moral Imagination.* Urbana: University of Illinois Press, 1961.

Schickel, Richard. *The Disney Version: The Life, Times, Art, and Commerce of Walt Disney.* New York: Simon & Schuster, 1968.

Schlinger, Bob. *The Unofficial Guide to Disneyland.* Rev. ed. Englewood Cliffs, N.J.: Prentice-Hall, 1985.

Schulz, Max F. *Paradise Preserved: Recreations of Eden in Eighteenth- and Nineteenth-Century England.* Cambridge: Cambridge University Press, 1985.

Siegel, Alan A. *Smile: A Picture History of Olympic Park, 1887–1965.* Irvington, N.J.: Irvington Historical Society, 1983.

Silverstein, Herma. *Scream Machines: Roller Coasters Past, Present, and Future.* New York: Walker, 1986.

Snow, Richard. *Coney Island: A Postcard Journey to the City of Fire.* New York: Brightwaters Press, 1984.

Taylor, John. *Storming the Magic Kingdom: Wall Street, the Raiders, and the Battle for Disney.* New York: Knopf, 1987.

Thomas, Bob. *Walt Disney: An American Original.* New York: Simon & Schuster, 1976.

Trachtenberg, Alan. *The Incorporation of America: Culture and Society in the Gilded Age.* New York: Hill & Wang, 1982. Contains an excellent discussion of the World's Columbian Exposition.

Truman, Benjamin C. *History of the World's Fair: Being a Complete and Authentic Description of the Columbian Exposition from Its Inception.* Philadelphia: H. W. Kelley, 1893. Reprint. New York: Arno Press, 1976.

U.S. Bureau of the Census. *Census of Service Industries, 1972, 1977, 1982, 1987.* Washington, D.C.: Government Printing Office, 1976, 1981, 1985, 1989.

———. *Projections of the Population of the United States by Age, Sex, and Race: 1988 to 2080.* By Gregory Spencer. Current Population Reports, series P-25, no. 1018. Washington, D.C.: Government Printing Office, 1989.

———. *Service Annual Survey.* Washington, D.C.: Government Printing Office, 1984–89 (published annually).

U.S. Travel Data Center and Business Research Division, University of Colorado. *Tourism's Top Twenty.* Boulder: Business Research Division, University of Colorado, 1984.

Wasserman, Louis. *Merchandising Architecture: Architectural Implications and Applications of Amusement Theme Parks.* Sheboygan, Wis.: Privately printed, 1978.

Waters, Somerset R. *The Big Picture: Travel Industry World Yearbook 1988.* New York: Child & Waters, 1988.

Weir, Lebert Howard. *Recreation Survey of Buffalo.* Buffalo, N.Y.: City Planning Association, 1925.

Wlodarczyk, Chuck. *Riverview: Gone but Not Forgotten. A Photo History, 1904–1967.* Chicago: Riverview Publications, 1977.

Wroth, Warwick. *The London Pleasure Gardens of the Eighteenth Century.* London: Macmillan, 1896. Reprint. Hamden, Conn.: Archon, 1979.

Articles

"The American Amusement Park." In-depth section. Edited by Margaret J. King. *Journal of Popular Culture* 15 (Summer 1981): 56–179.

"Amusement Parks Unveil Their Winter's Work." *Business Week*, 15 May 1954, 182–86.

Bailey, Alan. "The Pitfalls of the Pleasure Dome." *Director* 42 (April 1989): 33–34. The amusement park business.

Baxter, Sylvester. "The Trolley in Rural Parks." *Harper's Monthly* 97 (June 1898): 60–69.

Berland, David I. "Disney and Freud: Walt Meets the Id." *Journal of Popular Culture* 15 (Spring 1982): 93–104.

Bierman, James H. "Disneyland and the 'Los Angelization' of the Arts." In *American Popular Entertainment*, edited by Myron Matlaw, 273–83. Westport, Conn.: Greenwood Press, 1979.

Blake, Robert. "The Lessons of the Parks." Reprinted in *The Art of Walt Disney: From Mickey Mouse to the Magic Kingdoms*, edited by Christopher Finch, 423–49. New York: Abrams, 1975.

Bradbury, Ray. "The Machine that Tooled Happyland." *Holiday* 38 (October 1965): 100–102. Bradbury's visit to Disneyland.

Bravo, Arthur. "Environmental Systems at Walt Disney World." *Journal of the Environmental Engineering Division, Proceedings of the American Society of Civil Engineers*, 101, no. EE6 (December 1975): 887–95.

Bristol, Michael. "Acting Out Utopia, the Politics of Carnival." *Performance* 1 (May–June 1973): 13–28. Considers medieval carnivals, Mardi Gras, amusement parks.

Brody, Michael. "Wonderful World of Disney: Its Psychological Appeal." *American Imago* 33 (Winter 1976): 350–60.

"Building a Disney Dream" *Industry Week* 205 (26 May 1980): 55–59. EPCOT Center.

Cartmell, Robert. "Roller Coaster: King of the Park." *Smithsonian* 8 (August 1977): 44–49.

Cawalti, John G. "America on Display: The World's Fairs of 1876, 1893, 1933." In *The Age of Industrialism in America*, edited by Frederic Cople Jaher, 317–63. New York: Free Press, 1968.

Ciardi, John. "Manner of Speaking: Foamrubberville." *Saturday Review* 48 (19 June 1965): 20. Reaction to Disneyland.

Coates, Robert M. "Reporter at Large: It's the Illusion That Counts." *New Yorker* 30 (8 May 1954): 91–109. Palisades Park.

"Coney Island: Its Architecture Is the Stuff That People's Dreams Are Made Of." *Architectural Forum* 87 (August 1947): 82–87.

Conniff, Richard. "Coasters Used to Be Scary, Now They're Downright Weird." *Smithsonian* 20 (August 1989); 82–93.

Corliss, Richard. "If Heaven Ain't a Lot Like Disney." *Time* 127 (16 June 1986): 80–81, 83–84.

Cox, Richard. "Coney Island, Urban Symbol in American Art." *New York Historical Society Quarterly* 60 (January–April 1976): 35–52.

Crichton, Kyle. "All on One Ticket: Story of the Atlantic City Piers." *Collier's* 102 (30 July 1938): 20–21, 37.

Cuber, John F. "Patrons of Amusement Parks: Case Studies." *Sociology and Social Research* 24 (September–October 1939): 63–68.

DeRoos, Robert. "The Magic Worlds of Walt Disney." *National Geographic* 124 (August 1963): 159–207.

Doenecke, Justus D. "Myths, Machines, and Markets: The Columbian Exposition of 1893." *Journal of Popular Culture* 6 (Winter 1972): 535–49.

"Father Goose." *Time* 64 (27 December 1954): 42–46. Walt Disney.

Fincher, Jack. "George Ferris, Jr., and the Great Wheel of Fortune." *Smithsonian* 14 (July 1983): 109–18.

"Fortunes Found in Fantasy." *Industry Week* 171 (8 November 1971): 30–31, 36–37.

Francaviglia, Richard V. "Main Street U.S.A.: A Comparison/Contrast of Streetscapes in Disneyland and Walt Disney World." *Journal of Popular Culture* 15 (Summer 1981): 141–56.

Francis, David W. "Steamship Service to Cedar Point, 1870–1952." *Inland Seas* 33 (Summer 1977): 106–12; 33 (Fall 1977): 184–91.

"From Cyclones to Houses of Mystery: How the Mechanical Wonders in Modern Outdoor Amusement Parks Are Invented and Constructed." *Popular Mechanics* 42 (November 1924): 756–64.

Gatlin, Dana. "Amusing America's Millions." *World's Work* 26 (July 1913): 325–40.

Gillman, Lucy P. "Coney Island." *New York History* 36 (July 1955): 255–90.

Goldberger, Paul. "Mickey Mouse Teaches the Architects." *New York Times Magazine*, 22 October 1972, 40–41, 92–98.

Graff, John R. "1987 Outlook for Theme Parks." In Travel and Tourism Research Association, *1987 Outlook for Travel and Tourism: Proceedings of the Twelfth Annual Travel Outlook Forum, October 10, 1986*, 131–33. Washington, D.C.: U.S. Travel Data Center, 1986.

"The Great Wheel at Chicago." *Scientific American* 69 (1 July 1893): 8–9.

Gorky, Maxim. "Boredom." *Independent* 63 (8 August 1907): 309–17. Response to experiencing Coney Island.

Gullette, Margaret Morganroth. "Sheep May Freely Graze." *North American Review* 267 (September 1982): 4–8. The discontent of visitors to Walt Disney World Resort.

Halevy, Julian. "Disneyland and Las Vegas." *Nation* 186 (7 June 1958): 510–13.

Hall, Millicent. "Theme Parks: Around the World in 80 Minutes." *Landscape* 21 (Autumn 1976): 3–8.

Harris, Elmer Blaney. "The Day of Rest at Coney Island." *Everybody's Magazine* 19 (July 1908): 24–34.

Harris, Michael. "It's the Berries." *Finance Magazine* 94 (June 1976): 38–41. Knott's Berry Farm.

Hartt, Rollin Lynde. "The Amusement Park." *Atlantic Monthly* 99 (May 1907): 667–77.

Havig, Alan. "Mass Commercial Amusements in Kansas City before World War I." *Missouri Historical Review* 75 (April 1981): 316–45.

Heller, Alfred. "Stalled in EPCOT's World of Motion." *World's Fair* 3 (Winter 1983): 13–16.

Hellman, Hal. "Those Incredible New Amusement Parks: A Taste of Thrills to Come." *Futurist* 14 (August 1980): 38–43.

Hildebrandt, Hugo John. "Cedar Point: A Park in Progress." *Journal of Popular Culture* 15 (Summer 1981): 87–107.

Hirschl, Jessie Heckman. "The Great White City." *American Heritage* 11 (October 1960): 8–21, 75.

"How a Carousel Is Made." *New York Times Illustrated Magazine,* 19 March 1899, 13.

Howard, Niles. "Can Disney Do It Again?" *Dun's Review* 117 (June 1981): 80–82.

Johnson, David M. "Disney World as Structure and Symbol: Re-Creation of the American Experience." *Journal of Popular Culture* 15 (Summer 1981): 157–65.

Johnson, Lara L. "Cheap Thrills and the New Urban Order: Forest Park Highlands." *Gateway Heritage* 8 (Winter 1987–88): 22–31.

Johnson, Mark. "Georgia Joy." *Travel* 129 (April 1968): 37–40. Six Flags over Georgia.

Kindel, Stephen. "Dueling with the Mouse King." *Financial World* 156 (19 May 1987): 40–44.

King, Margaret J. "Disneyland and Walt Disney World: Traditional Values in Futuristic Form." *Journal of Popular Culture* 15 (Summer 1981): 116–40.

———. "The New American Muse: Notes on the Amusement/Theme Park." *Journal of Popular Culture* 15 (Summer 1981): 56–62.

Koepp, Stephen. "Do You Believe in Magic?" *Time* 131 (25 April 1988): 66–73. Walt Disney Company.

Komahashi, Kenichi. "The Disneyland Effect: California Dreaming in Urayasu." *Tokyo Business Today,* October 1988, 46–48.

Kouwenhoven, John A. "The Eiffel Tower and the Ferris Wheel." *Arts Magazine* 54 (February 1980): 170–73.

Le Gallienne, Richard. "Human Need of Coney Island." *Cosmopolitan* 39 (July 1905): 239–46.

Leigh, John Garrett. "Amusements: The Economic Value of the Leisure of the People." *Economic Review* 22 (July 1912): 249–63.

Levy, Robert. "Theme Parks: The Profits in Pleasure." *Dun's Review* 109 (April 1977): 88, 91, 114.

"Lifting the Methodist Amusement Ban." *Literary Digest* 81 (3 May 1924): 33–34.

Lyon, Peter. "The Master Showman of Coney Island." *American Heritage* 9 (June 1958): 14–21, 92–95. George Cornelius Tilyou.

McDonald, John. "Now the Bankers Come to Disney." *Fortune* 73 (May 1966): 139–41, 218, 223–24, 226, 228.

McReynolds, William. "Disney Plays the Glad Game." *Journal of Popular Culture* 7 (Spring 1974): 787–96.

"The Mechanical Joys of Coney Island." *Scientific American* 19 (15 August 1908): 101, 108–10.

Mechling, Elizabeth Walker, and Jay Mechling. "The Sale of Two Cities: A Semiotic Comparison of Disneyland with Marriott's Great America." *Journal of Popular Culture* 15 (Summer 1981): 166–79.

Menen, Aubrey. "Dazzled in Disneyland." *Holiday* 34 (July 1963): 68–70, 72–75, 106.

Meredith, Dennis. "Revolution on the Midway: An Exotic World Unfolds." *Science Digest* 86 (August 1979): 58–63.

"Midwest Resort Revives: Ohio's Cedar Point." *Business Week*, 23 September 1961, 104–6.

Miller, Daniel T. "The Columbian Exposition of 1893 and the American National Character." *Journal of American Culture* 10 (Summer 1987): 17–22.

Minard, Lawrence. "Who Will Win the Keys to Disney's Magic Kingdom?" *Forbes* 133 (4 June 1984): 31–35.

Moellenhoff, Fritz. "Remarks on the Popularity of Mickey Mouse." *American Imago* 1, no. 3 (1940): 19–32.

Moore, Alexander. "Walt Disney World: Bounded Ritual Space and the Playful Pilgrimage Center." *Anthropological Quarterly* 53 (October 1980): 207–18.

Morison, Elting E. "What Went Wrong with Disney's World's Fair." *American Heritage* 35 (December 1983): 71–78.

Neil, J. Meredith. "The Roller Coaster: Architectural Symbol and Sign." *Journal of Popular Culture* 15 (Summer 1981): 108–15.

Nelson, Steve. "Walt Disney's EPCOT and the World's Fair Performance Tradition." *Drama Review* 30 (Winter 1986): 106–46.

Neufeld, Maurice F. "The White City: The Beginnings of a Planned Civilization in America." *Journal of the Illinois State Historical Society* 27 (April 1934): 71–93.

Nye, Russel B. "Eight Ways of Looking at an Amusement Park." *Journal of Popular Culture* 15 (Summer 1981): 63–75.

O'Brien, George M. "The Parks of Vienna." *Journal of Popular Culture* 15 (Summer 1981): 76–86.

O'Brien, Robert. "Walter Knott's Berry Farm and Ghost Town." *American Mercury* 85 (October 1957): 29–33.

Ostroff, Jeff. "An Aging Market: How Businesses Can Prosper." *American Demographics* 11 (May 1989): 26–28, 33, 58.

Pacey, Margaret D. "For Fun and Profit: Amusement Parks Are a Hit at the Box Office and in the Boardroom." *Barron's* 51 (12 July 1971): 11, 20–21.

Ross, Irwin. "Disney Gambles on Tomorrow." *Fortune* 106 (4 October 1982): 62–68. EPCOT Center.

Rubin, Barbara. "Aesthetic Ideology and Urban Design." *Annals of the Association of American Geographers* 69 (1979): 339–61. The World's Columbian Exposition.

Rudnitsky, Howard. "Mickey Is Eating My Lunch." *Forbes* 144 (18 September 1989): 86–92.

Schmalz, Jeffrey. "Movie Theme Park Fight: Nastiness Is Not a Fantasy." *New York Times*, 13 August 1989, 1, 22.

Schuyler, Montgomery. "Last Words about the World's Fair." *Architectural Record* 3 (January–March 1894): 292–301.

Shedlock, Robert E. "Developing Successful Theme Recreation Centers." *Real Estate Review* 12 (Winter 1983): 86–90.

Slosson, Edwin E. "The Amusement Business." *Independent* 57 (21 July 1904): 134–39.

Smith, Marguerite T. "Mystery Trains." *Money* 18 (August 1989): 54–61. Roller coasters.

Smith, Michael L. "Back to the Future: EPCOT, Camelot, and the History of Technology." In *New Perspectives on Technology and American Culture*, edited by Bruce Sinclair, 69–79. Philadelphia: American Philosophical Society, 1986.

Snow, Robert E., and David E. Wright. "Coney Island: A Case Study of Popular Culture and Technical Change." *Journal of Popular Culture* 9 (Spring 1976): 960–75.

Street, Arthur I. "The World's Fair Balance Sheet." *Review of Reviews* 8 (November 1893): 522–23.

Taylor, Frank J. "Garden of Fun." *Saturday Evening Post* 227 (11 June 1955): 24–25, 136, 138–40. Elitch Gardens in Denver.

"Theme Parks." Special Issue. *Theatre Crafts* 11 (September 1977): 27–103.

"Theme Parks, the American Dream, and the Great Escape." *Economist* 298 (11 January 1986): 83–87.

Thompson, Frederic. "Amusing the Million." *Everybody's Magazine* 19 (September 1908): 378+.

———. "The Summer Show." *Independent* 62 (20 June 1907): 1460–63.

Thoren, Margaret. "Fun and Profit: Amusement Parks Shrug Off First Bad Season in Years." *Barron's* 60 (3 November 1980): 11, 67–69, 71.

Tilyou, Edward F. "Why the Schoolma'am Walked into the Sea." *American Magazine* 94 (July 1922): 18–21, 86, 91–92, 94.

"To Heaven by Subway." *Fortune Magazine* 18 (August 1938): 60–68, 102–4, 106. Superb article on Coney Island with excellent illustrations.

Tompkins, Raymond S. "Cathedrals of the Hot Dog." *American Mercury* 20 (May 1930): 51–59.

Trucco, Terry. "How Disneyland Beat All the Odds in Japan." *Advertising Age* 55 (6 September 1984): 14–16.

Wallace, Kevin. "Onward and Upward with the Arts: The Engineering of Ease." *New Yorker* 39 (7 September 1963): 104–29. Disneyland Park.

Wallace, Mike. "Mickey Mouse History: Portraying the Past at Disney World." *Radical History Review* 32 (1985): 33–57.

"Walt Disney World EPCOT Center: The Construction Adventure." *Engineering News Record* 209 (25 November 1982): 33–63.

Weinberger, Julius. "Economic Aspects of Recreation." *Harvard Business Review* 15 (Summer 1937): 448–63.

Wells, Frank G. "Travel and Tourism 1983 to the Year 2003." *Vital Speeches of the Day* 54 (1 January 1988): 168–73.

Willey, Day Allen. "The Trolley Park." *Cosmopolitan* 33 (July 1902): 265–72.

"A Wonderful World: Growing Impact of the Disney Art." *Newsweek* 45 (18 April 1955): 60–69.

Wrubel, Robert. "Jaws vs. Mickey Mouse." *Financial World* 158 (16 May 1989): 24–25.

Zolotow, Maurice, and Harold S. Kahm. "Ride 'em and Weep." *Saturday Evening Post* 217 (9 June 1945): 16–17, 42, 44.

INDEX

accidents, 13, 73, 106, 111
Adams, Henry, 40
Addison, Joseph, 4
Adler, Dankmar, 22
Administration Building. *See* World's Columbian Exposition
admission fees and tickets, 2, 4, 6, 7, 14, 32, 43, 44, 46, 48, 51, 58, 65, 69, 70, 86, 96, 106, 107, 127, 146, 159, 175. *See also* pay-one-price admission ticket
advertising, 36, 76, 82, 105, 106, 111, 119, 170
Adventureland. *See* Disneyland Park; Magic Kingdom
Aero-Coaster (roller coaster), 17
Agriculture Building. *See* World's Columbian Exposition
Albright, Chester E., 11
alcoholic beverages, 21, 39, 55, 59, 62, 68, 69
Alcoke, Charles, 14
Allen, John, 17
Alton International, 173–74
Alton Towers, 173, 177
American Adventure. *See* EPCOT Center
American Broadcasting Company, 94–95, 96–97
American Coaster Enthusiasts, 84, 184
American dream, 21, 87, 101, 155
American Express, 149, 153
American Motors Corporation, 94

American Museum of Public Recreation, 12
Amusement Business, 184
Anderson, Marion Knott, 127
Anderson, Martin, 138
Anheuser-Busch Corporation, 115–18, 123, 128, 136, 165, 167, 172–73
Anthony, Susan B., 153
architecture, 4–5, 6, 12–13, 18, 19, 21–27, 47–48, 78, 97–98, 109, 142, 143–45, 146, 150, 153, 162
Armitage-Herschell Company. *See* Herschell-Spillman Company
Arnold, Charles Dudley, 24 (ill.), 26 (ill.), 36–37
Arrow Development Company, 77
Arrow Dynamics, 167
Arts Building. *See* World's Columbian Exposition
Asbury Park, 12
Astroworld. *See* Six Flags Astroworld
AT&T, 149
attendance, 31, 45, 49, 56, 58, 65, 68, 69, 83, 95, 96, 97, 104, 112, 115, 116, 117, 121, 124, 125, 130, 133–35, 136, 141, 146, 147, 149, 154, 156, 157, 168, 171, 173, 174, 175, 176, 177
attire, 16 (ill.), 26 (ill.), 33 (ill.), 37, 60, 69, 70, 75, 77, 101
Atwood, Charles B., 22

Auchy, Henry B., 11
audioanimatronics, 99–100, 142,
    145–46, 151, 152, 153
Aunt Jemima, 20
Australia, 174
Australia's Wonderland, 174
Automatic Vacuum Collection (AVAC)
    system, 140
automobile, 17, 62, 63, 64, 66, 70,
    71, 76, 77, 79, 82, 94, 108, 109,
    111, 146, 149, 150, 151, 163,
    164
Avalanche Run (roller coaster), 129,
    168

Backstage Magic. *See* EPCOT Center
Baker, Harry, 17, 75
Baker, W. Randolph, 123
Bally Manufacturing Corporation,
    120–22, 133
band concerts. *See* music
Barrel of Love (ride), 44
Barrett, John P., 38
Bartholomew Fair, 1–3
Basset, W. B., 8
Battersea Power Station, 173–74
Bavar, Emily, 138
Beck, F., 9
Becker, John A., 68
Becker's Grove. *See* Olympic Park
Bellamy, Edward, 27
Belle Isle Park, 71
Bell System, 148
Beman, S. S., 22
Berlin Exposition (1896), 50–51
Bethlehem Iron Company, 31
Big Bad Wolf (roller coaster), 17, 116
Big Bang Schtroumpf (park), 172
Big Thunder Mountain Railroad (roller
    coaster), 145, 171
Biondolillo, Joseph, 84
Bleroit, Louis, 78
Bloom, Sol, 29
Bloomfield, Paul, 173–74
Boardwalk & Baseball (park), 118,
    122–23, 165
Bobs, the (roller coaster), 17, 72–73
Boeckling, George A., 78–80, 128

Bonifascio, Rudy, 84
Bollinger & Mabillard, 167
Boomerang (roller coaster), 127, 167
Boswell, James, 4
Boysen, Rudolph, 126
Boyton, Paul, 43, 47
Brady, Matthew, 153
Brighton Beach Hotel, 42
Broome, John, 173–74
Buehler, Frank, 68
Burney, Fanny, 4
Burnham, Daniel H., 21, 22, 31, 35
Burns, Haydon, 138
Busch, Adolphus, 115
Busch, August, Jr., 115, 128
Busch Gardens, The Dark Continent,
    29, 105, 115–17, 133, 134–35,
    136
Busch Gardens, The Old Country, 18,
    29, 83, 116–17, 133, 134–35,
    136, 168
Buser, Louis, 78

Canada's Wonderland, 84, 86, 113–15,
    134–35, 168, 169, 198n4
Canarsie Indians, 42
capital expenditures, 17, 32, 45, 47,
    49, 52, 58, 69, 75, 77, 80, 82,
    83, 84, 96, 101–102, 105, 106,
    107, 109, 112, 114, 115, 117,
    118, 119, 120, 121, 122, 123,
    127, 128–30, 132, 136, 141,
    143, 148, 149, 157–58, 160,
    163, 166, 167–68, 170, 171,
    174, 181
capitalism, 20, 21, 24, 27, 148–49,
    154–56
Captain Bonavita, 53
Captain Eo, 171
carousel, 7, 9–12, 59, 69, 71, 72, 74,
    84, 118, 172, 179
Carowinds (park), 113–14, 115
Caruso, Enrico, 80
Cascadas Aquatic Park, Las, 175
Cedar Fair, L. P., 128, 132
Cedar Point (park), frontispiece (ill.),
    18, 59 (ill.), 67, 78–83, 79 (ill.),
    80 (ill.), 81 (ill.), 120, 127–32,

129 (ill.), 131 (ill.), 134–35, 136, 167, 168, 183
Cedar Point Cyclone (roller coaster), 80
Century of Progress Exposition, Chicago (1933), 152
Cernigliaro, Salvatore, 10
Cheltenham Beach (park), 59
Chestnut Hill (park), 12
Chicago Company. *See* World's Columbian Exposition
Chief Joseph, 153
Church, Frederick, 17, 72
Chutes, the (park), 59
City Beautiful Movement, 20, 35
"City on a Hill" or promised land, 20–21, 24, 40, 101, 156, 163
city planning, 19, 35–39, 97, 142
Civil Rights Movement, 70–71
Cobb, Henry Ives, 22
Coca-Cola Company, 149, 153
Codman, Henry Sargent, 22
Columbia Broadcasting System (CBS), 94, 106
Columbus, Christopher, 19, 20
Comet (roller coaster), 83–84, 85, 86 (ill.)
Communicore. *See* EPCOT Center
computer technology, 18, 35, 99, 110, 112, 142–43, 150
concessions, 2, 5, 7–8, 28–29, 38, 39, 146
Coney Island, 10, 14, 16, 17, 19, 41–56, 59, 65, 69, 78, 99, 108, 143, 151, 163. *See also* Luna Park; Steeplechase Park; Dreamland
Coney Island, Cincinnati (park), 59, 113, 183
Coney Island Road & Bridge Company, 42
consumption, 1–2, 27, 98, 119, 136, 146, 147, 150, 151, 153, 155
Contemporary Resort. *See* Walt Disney World Resort
control, 97, 110, 154
Corkscrew (roller coaster);
Cedar Point, frontispiece (ill.), 128, 129 (ill.)
Knott's Berry Farm, 127

corporate takeover, 123, 128, 158–59
correre dela quintana. *See* tilting at the quintain
Couney, Martin Arthur, 50–52, 151
Court of Honor. *See* World's Columbian Exposition
Creation, the (ride), 52
crime and criminals, 1–3, 5, 8, 15, 21, 42–43, 44, 48–49, 71, 73, 76–77, 78, 109, 163, 164
cryogenics, 141
Crystal Beach Park, 83–86, 85 (ill.), 86 (ill.), 183
Crystal Palace (entertainment complex), 179
Culver, Andrew, 42
Curtiss, Glenn, 78–79 (ill.)
Cyclone (roller coaster), 17
Cypress Gardens, 118, 122–23

dance marathon, 69–70
dancing, 52, 65–66, 68, 79, 84. *See also* dance marathon
danger, 15, 17, 32, 60, 63, 99, 118–19, 130, 145, 180
Dare, Charles W. F., 11
Darien Lake Park, 84
Dayton Fun House and Riding Device Manufacturing Company, 17
democracy, 7, 8, 23, 36–37, 63, 98
demographics, 53–55, 67, 102–104, 109, 111, 117–18, 132, 146, 149, 176–78, 179, 180
Dentzel, Gustav A., 10–11, 74
Dentzel, William, 11, 74
Disaster Transport (roller coaster), 168
Disney, Elias, 88–89
Disney, Lillian Bounds, 91, 141
Disney, Roy, 88–90, 91, 93, 141
Disney, Walter Elias, 7, 12, 15, 19, 29, 36, 46, 66, 71, 87–101, 126, 137–38, 140–41, 148, 154, 155, 162–63, 164–65
Disneyland Park, 15, 28, 41, 49, 67, 77, 82, 87, 88, 93–104, 105, 106, 107, 108, 124, 125, 127, 134–35, 137–38, 140, 142, 144–45, 155, 162, 164–66, 178

Adventureland, 95–99
Fantasyland, 95, 99
Frontierland, 95, 99
Main Street, U.S.A., 88, 95, 97–98, 99
Tomorrowland, 95, 99, 104
Disney-MGM Studios Theme Park, 125, 158, 159–61, 167, 171, 178
Dolphin and Swan hotel complex. *See* Walt Disney World Resort
Dorais, Gus, 79
Dorney Park, 183
Douglass, Frederick, 20, 153
Dreamland, 52–53, 183
Duke Ellington Band, 86
Dundy, Elmer "Skip," 45, 46–52, 78, 162–63

Earthquake: The Big One (ride), 49, 124, 178
Edison, Thomas Alva, 38
education, 19, 28–29, 52, 106, 110, 148, 151, 163, 179
Eisner, Michael, 104
El Dorado carousel, 10
electricity, 15, 22, 26, 37–38, 41, 47–48, 50, 52, 57, 60, 68–69, 74, 150. *See also* illumination
Electricity Building. *See* World's Columbian Exposition
Electric Park, 65, 89, 183
Elitch Gardens, 12, 167, 183
Elysium, 4, 19, 27, 39–40, 65, 156
Engle system, 39
EPCOT Center, 19, 29, 117, 140–41, 148–54, 165–66
   American Adventure, 149, 153–54
   Backstage Magic, 149
   Communicore, 149, 150, 152–53
   Horizons, 149, 152
   Journey into Imagination, 149, 152
   Land, the, 149, 151
   Living Seas, the, 149
   Spaceship Earth, 148
   Universe of Energy, 148, 151, 152
   Wonders of Life, 149
   World of Motion, 149, 151

escape, 45, 46, 101
ethnic groups, 7, 20, 29–30, 39, 65, 66, 71, 73, 81, 83, 98, 100–101, 146, 153
Euclid Beach Park, 12, 59, 78, 81, 183
EuroDisneyland, 167, 171–72
expenditures. *See* personal consumption expenditures
Exxon Corporation, 148, 152

family, 8, 12, 49, 53, 59–60, 68, 77, 82, 97, 108, 109, 164
Fantasy Island (park), 84
Fantasyland. *See* Disneyland Park; Magic Kingdom
Ferris, George Washington Gale, 31–34
Ferris wheel, 2, 7, 8–9, 19, 29, 31–35, 32 (ill.), 33 (ill.), 35 (ill.), 43, 59, 74, 120, 179
fiberglass, 145
Fiedler, Arthur, 141
Fielding, Henry, 4
Fireball (roller coaster), 73
fires, 39, 43, 46, 52, 53, 69, 111, 120–21
fireworks, 6, 8, 59, 69
Fisheries Building. *See* World's Columbian Exposition
flume ride, 59 (ill.), 77, 107, 108, 112, 116, 118, 120, 127, 168, 172, 173, 175, 179. *See also* shoot-the-chutes
food, 38, 39, 51, 68, 119, 120, 126–27, 132, 136, 150, 172, 179
Forest Park, 65, 89
Forest Park Highlands (park), 59, 69, 183
France, 171–72
Franklin, Benjamin, 153, 155
freaks and human abnormalities, 2, 29, 50–52, 53, 70, 79, 83
Freedomland (park), 106
French, Daniel Chester: *The Republic*, 24 (ill.), 25
frontier, 18, 21, 24, 25
Frontierland. *See* Disneyland Park; Magic Kingdom

Funworld, 185
future, 18, 21, 40, 87, 140–41, 143, 148, 150, 152, 179–81

games of chance, 59, 69, 70, 79, 132
Gavrilenko, Arkadi, 175–76
Gemini (roller coaster), 128–29
General Electric Company, 38, 149, 152
General Motors Corporation, 149, 151
Georgia Cyclone (roller coaster), 168
Gerstman, Milton, 149
Gerstner, Franz von, 8
Giant Coaster (roller coaster), 84
Gibson, W. Hamilton, 24
Glen Echo Park, 73, 183
Gorky, Maxim, 50, 100
Gorky Park, 175–76
Granada Studios Tour, 174
Grand Floridian Beach Resort. *See* Walt Disney World Resort
Great Adventure (park), 111, 120–21, 133, 134–35, 168
Great America parks, 29, 118–20, 121, 134–35, 136, 167, 168, 179
Great American Scream Machine (roller coaster), 108, 120
Great Britain, 173–74
Great Depression, 11, 12, 17, 46, 55, 66, 69, 76, 80, 126, 153–54, 163–64
Greenfield Village. *See* Henry Ford Museum and Greenfield Village
Guenther, Henry A., 69, 71
Guttaquoh, 42

Haase, Hugo, 10
Hall, Ed, 84
Hall, G. C., 84
Hall of Presidents. *See* Magic Kingdom
Handel, George Frideric, 6
Handy, Moses P., 36
Hanna Barbera cartoon characters, 113
Harcourt Brace Jovanovich, 118, 122–23, 136, 165, 167
Harris, J. T., 30
Haunted Mansion (ride), 145

Hayden, Sophia G., 22
Haynes, Rowland, 66
Hell's Gate (ride), 53
Henninger, Frederick W., 74–75, 76, 77
Henry Ford Museum and Greenfield Village, 11, 93
Henson, Jim, 161
Herschell, Allen, 11
Herschell Carrousel Factory Museum, 11
Herschell-Spillman Company, 11
Hersheypark, 108, 183
Hinckle, Phillip, 14
Historic Amusement Foundation, 184
history, 87, 98, 106, 107–108, 110, 126–27, 150, 151, 152, 153–54
Hogarth, William, 4, 13
  Southwark Fair, 3 (ill.)
Home Brewing Company, 69
Horizons. *See* EPCOT Center
Horticulture Building. *See* World's Columbian Exposition
Hotel Breakers, 78, 79 (ill.), 80, 81, 82
hotels, 42, 78, 79 (ill.), 80, 81, 82, 139, 140, 144, 159, 167, 168, 171, 173, 178, 179
hours of work, 55–56, 60–61, 171
Howells, William Dean, 31
Human Pool Table (ride), 45
Human Roulette Wheel (ride), 45
Hunt, Richard M., 22

Illions, Marcus Charles, 12
illumination, 2, 4–5, 6, 15, 38, 47–48, 58, 68, 74, 78
illusion, 19, 21, 28, 40, 41, 45, 48, 50, 95, 99, 110, 140, 155, 156, 162
"imagineers," 94
immigrants, 41, 42, 53, 63, 68, 78, 98, 153, 162–63
India, 175
industrialization, 41, 48, 53–55, 56, 60, 65, 153, 163
Industrial Revolution, 4, 15, 34–35, 143

Ingersoll, Fred, 74
"Insanitarium," 45
insurance, 136
interstate highway system, 108, 109,
    146
Intamin AG, 77, 108, 129, 168
International Association of Amuse-
    ment Parks and Attractions, 75,
    136, 175, 184
Iron Dragon (roller coaster), 129–30
Iron Wolf (roller coaster), 167
Iwerks, Ub, 90, 91

Jack Rabbit (roller coaster), 75
Japan, 169–71
Jenney and Mundie (architectural
    firm), 22
Jenny's Whim (park), 6–7
Jet Scream (roller coaster), 168
Johnson, Fred R., 65–66, 89
Johnson, Samuel, 4
Jones, William, 6
Jonson, Ben: *Bartholomew Fair,* 2
Joseph II, 7
Journey into Imagination. *See* EPCOT
    Center

Kaiser Aluminum, 94
Kansas City, 65, 66, 88, 89
Kansas City Film Ad Company, 90
Keenan, Vernon, 17
Kennedy, John F., 97
Kennywood Park, 59, 67, 73–78,
    183
Kerkorian, Kirk, 158–59
Kingdom of the Dinosaurs (ride), 127
Kings Dominion, 113–15, 134–35
Kings Entertainment Company
    (KECO), 115, 120, 174
Kings Island (park), 17, 113–14, 115,
    134–35, 168
Kinzel, Richard L., 130
Kiselev, Pavel, 175–76
Knott, Walter, 125–27, 162–63
Knott family, 125–27
Knott's Berry Farm, 49, 125–27,
    134–35, 136, 165, 167, 179
Knudsen, Richard, 14, 15 (ill.)

Kodak, 94, 149
Kraft Foods, 149
Kurasawa, Akira, 125
Kurz, Christian, 68–69

Land, the. *See* EPCOT Center
Laser Loop (roller coaster), 77
laser technology, 145, 175
Lausche, Frank, 81
Leap Frog Scenic Railway (roller
    coaster), 79, 81 (ill.), 130
Legros, Emile, 81–83, 128
Leisure & Recreation Concepts (LARC),
    174
Liberty carousel, 71
Liberty Square. *See* Magic Kingdom
lighting. *See* illumination
Little Egypt, 30–31
Living Seas, the. *See* EPCOT Center
Loch Ness Monster (roller coaster), 18,
    116
Log Jammer (ride), 77
Lotte World (park), 174–75
Louis XIV, 9
Louisiana Purchase Exposition, St.
    Louis (1904), 34, 115
Luna Park, 12, 46–52, 47 (ill.), 108,
    151, 162, 183

McCay, Winsor, 90
McClure, Fred, 65–66, 89
Machinery Building. *See* World's Co-
    lumbian Exposition
McKane, John Y., 42–43
McKim, Mead & White (architectural
    firm), 22
MacMonnies, Frederick, 25
McSwigan, Andrew Stephen, 75, 76,
    77
Magic Kingdom, 139, 141–47, 149,
    171
    Adventureland, 144
    Fantasyland, 144
    Frontierland, 144, 146
    Hall of Presidents, 146
    Liberty Square, 144
    Main Street, U.S.A., 144–45
    Mickey's Birthdayland, 144

Tomorrowland, 144, 146
 See also Walt Disney World Resort
Magic Mountain (Calif.). *See* Six Flags
 Magic Mountain
Magic Mountain (Denver), 105
Magnum XL200 (roller coaster), 18,
 120, 130, 131 (ill.)
Main Street, U.S.A. *See* Disneyland
 Park; Magic Kingdom
Mall of America (entertainment com-
 plex), 179
Mangels, William F., 12, 13
Manhattan Beach (park), 59
Manhattan Beach Hotel, 42
Manufactures and Liberal Arts Build-
 ing. *See* World's Columbian Expo-
 sition
Marceline, Mo., 88–89
Marco Engineering, 82
Marineland, 84
Marriott Corporation, 118–19, 120,
 121, 128
Martin Marietta Corporation, 142
Matterhorn (roller coaster), 15
Mauch Chunk, Pa., 14
Maxwell, Robert, 123
MCA, Inc., 123–25, 128, 174
mechanical figures, 7. *See also* au-
 dioanimatronics
Meghan, A. F., 74–75
Melba, Nellie, 80
Melies, Georges, 90
Mellon, Andrew, 74
merry-go-round. *See* carousel
Metropolitan Life Insurance Company,
 149
Mickey Mouse, 91–92, 138, 144,
 156, 159
Mickey's Birthdayland. *See* Magic King-
 dom
midway, 19, 28–31, 48, 68, 72, 78,
 113, 132. *See also* Midway
 Plaisance
Midway Plaisance, 28–31, 37, 39, 150
Miller, Glenn, 80
Miller, John A., 17, 72, 75
Millet, Frank, 27
Mind Bender (roller coaster), 108

Mines and Mining Building. *See*
 World's Columbian Exposition
Monongahela Street Railway, 73–74
monorail, 142, 143, 173
Monsanto, 94
Montana Magica (park), 173
morality, 49, 65–66, 75
motion pictures, 62–63, 64, 66, 123–
 24, 157, 160, 174
moveable sidewalk, 37
Mozart, Wolfgang Amadeus, 6, 7
Mueller, Daniel C., 71
Muir, John, 153
Munger, Robert L., Jr., 83, 128
Muppets puppet characters, 104, 161
music, 4, 6, 7, 59, 60, 62–63, 64, 68,
 74, 79, 80, 84, 144, 147

National Amusement Park Association.
 See International Association of
 Amusement Parks and Attractions
National Amusement Park Historical
 Association, 184
*National Amusement Park Historical
 News*, 185
National Association for the Advance-
 ment of Colored People, 83
National Carousel Association, 184
Nehruland (park), 175
Newark Law and Order League, 68
New York World's Fair (1964–65), 148
Norway, 175

Ocean Park, 12
Olmsted, Frederick Law, 21, 22
Olympic Park, 67, 68–71, 183
Ontario Place (entertainment complex),
 134–35, 179
Opryland (park), 83, 134–35
Oriental Hotel, 42
Oriental Land Company, Ltd., 169–71
Outdoor Amusement Business Associa-
 tion, 184

Pacific Ocean Park, 106, 183
Palisades Park, 12, 59, 183, 195n27
Pan-American Exposition (1901), 45

Parc Asterix, 172
Paris Exposition (1889), 28, 38, 39
Paris World's Fair (1878), 22
park revenues, 49, 65, 67, 69, 70, 76,
    79, 83, 95, 101–102, 112–13,
    114, 117, 119, 121, 122, 123,
    124, 125, 128, 130, 132–33,
    156–58, 159, 164, 165–66, 167,
    170, 175
Parker, Charles Wallace, 12
patents, 10, 12, 13, 14, 15, 17
pay-one-price admission ticket, 44, 96,
    107, 175
Peabody & Stearns (architectural firm),
    22
Pearce, Fred, 72
Pepsi-Cola (Pepsico Inc.), 94
Personal Audio Listening System
    (PALS), 151
personal consumption expenditures,
    55, 61–63, 82, 104, 164, 169,
    170
personal income and earnings 55, 60–
    61, 102, 104, 163, 180
Peter Pan, 94
Philadelphia Centennial Exposition
    (1876), 39
Philadelphia Toboggan Company, 11–
    12, 71, 72
Pier 39 (entertainment complex), 179
pilgrimage center, 97, 137, 154–56
pilgrims, 20–21, 40, 97, 154–56
Pippin (roller coaster), 75
Pirates of the Caribbean (ride), 145–46
Pittsburgh Railways Company, 74
plastics, 18, 35, 87, 99, 112, 150
Playland Amusement Park, 17, 183
Playland-at-the-Beach, 183
pleasure garden, 3–7
Pleasure Island (park), 105–106
Polynesian Village. *See* Walt Disney
    World Resort
Pontchartrain Beach (park), 183
Post, George B., 22
Potter, E. C., 25
Prater, the (park), 7–9
prejudice, 20, 29, 65, 66, 71, 83, 98–
    99

Premature Baby Incubators, 50–52,
    151
Prior, Thomas, 72
progress, 8, 9, 20–21, 24, 27, 30, 32,
    36, 39, 97, 101, 146, 147, 150,
    151, 154–56
Prohibition, 62, 66, 69, 80
Promenades Aeriennes (roller coaster),
    13
Prospect Park & Coney Island Railroad,
    42
psychology, 45–46, 87, 92, 100
Puerto Rico, 175
Puritans, 20–21
Putnam, F. W., 29
Python (roller coaster), 116

Racer (roller coaster), 17, 75
Rahere, 1
railroad, 8, 23, 37, 42, 58, 66, 76, 79,
    83, 88, 89, 150, 171
railroad, elevated, 37. *See also* mono-
    rail
Ranelagh Gardens, 4, 6
RCA Corporation, 142
recreation expenditures. *See* personal
    consumption expenditures
Reedy Creek Improvement District,
    139
religion, 20–21, 27, 52, 65, 97, 98,
    101, 154–56
Republic, the (statue). *See* French, Dan-
    iel Chester
revenues. *See* park revenues
Revere Beach (park), 59, 183
Reynolds, William H., 52
Riesenrad (Ferris wheel), 8
Riggs, Robert, 45
Ringling Circus Museum, 12
Riverview Park, 12, 17, 67, 71–73,
    77, 183
Rockne, Knute, 79
Rockaway's Playland, 183
Rocky Glen Park, 183
roller coaster, frontispiece (ill.), 12–18,
    15 (ill.), 16 (ill.), 32, 59, 60, 71–
    73, 74, 75–76, 79, 81 (ill.), 83,
    107, 108, 118, 120, 127, 128–

30, 132, 145, 153, 167–68, 171, 172, 173, 175, 176, 178, 179
Roller Coaster!, 185
Roose, George A., 81–83, 128, 129
Roosevelt, Franklin Delano, 154
Root, John W., 21
Russian Mountains (ride), 13

safety, 14, 15, 17, 32–34, 63, 73, 111, 118–19, 180
Saint-Gaudens, Augustus, 22, 25
Salten, Felix, 7, 190n8
sanitation and sewage systems, 38–39, 69, 82, 94, 96, 101, 139–40
Santa Cruz Beach Boardwalk, 134–35
Santa Monica Pleasure Pier, 183
Savage, Frederick, 10
Schmidt, George, 72
Schmidt, Herman, 68–69
Schmidt, Wilhelm, 72
Schuyler, Montgomery, 19–20, 28
Scorpion (roller coaster), 116
Scripture, Eliphalet S., 10
Sea Lion Park, 43, 47
Sea World parks, 118, 122–23, 125, 133, 134–35, 136
sewage systems. *See* sanitation and sewage systems
sexuality, 89–90, 92, 99
sexual titillation, 43, 44, 45, 46, 48, 65, 162
shoot-the-chutes, 49, 52, 108. *See also* flume ride
shopping mall-entertainment centers, 178–79
simulation rides and exhibitions, 6, 45–46, 48, 49, 52, 124, 132, 160, 168, 178
Six Flags, Inc., 29, 107–109, 120–21, 122, 133, 134–35, 136, 167–68, 172, 179
Six Flags Astroworld, 121, 134–35
Six Flags Magic Mountain, 83, 127, 134–35, 136, 167
Six Flags over Georgia, 12, 72, 83, 107–108, 134–35, 136, 168
Six Flags over Mid-America, 107

Six Flags over Texas, 107, 134–35, 167–68
Skelton, Red, 70
Smithfield Common, 1
Snow White and the Seven Dwarfs, 92–93
Sousa, John Philip, 60
South Korea, 174–75
Space Mountain (roller coaster), 15, 145
Spaceship Earth. *See* EPCOT Center
Spain, 172–73
speed, 13, 15, 17, 18, 60, 63, 72
Sperry Unisys, 142, 149
Spillman, Edward, 11
staff, 27, 48, 145
Stanford Research Institute, 94
Star Tours (ride), 49, 171, 178
Star Trek Adventure (ride), 49, 124
Steam engine, 10, 14, 150
steamship, 37, 42, 79, 163
steel, 15, 18, 26, 27, 31, 35, 60, 74, 108, 128, 130, 143
Steeplechase (ride), 44–45, 46
Steeplechase Park, 10, 43–46, 44 (ill.), 52, 162, 183
Steinberg, Saul, 158
Stevens, George Alexander, 2
Stieglitz, Alfred, 37
streetcar. *See* trolley
Stuwer, Johann, 8
subway, 56, 163
Sullivan, Louis, 22–23
Summit Beach (park), 12
Swift, Jonathan, 4
Switchback Railway (roller coaster), 14, 43

Taft Broadcasting, 113–15, 128, 169
takeover. *See* corporate takeover
technology, 4, 6–7, 8, 9–18, 21, 27, 31, 36, 39–40, 43, 46, 50, 51–52, 63, 83, 87, 91, 92, 93, 99, 101, 109, 136, 143, 145, 146, 147, 148, 150, 151, 152, 154–56, 162, 163, 179, 181. *See also* computer technology and laser technology

television, 66, 70, 76, 81, 94–95, 96–
97, 106, 109–10, 111, 113,
123–24, 163, 164–65
Texas Giant (roller coaster), 167
theme parks, 17, 19, 21, 28, 29, 67,
83, 84, 97, 105–36, 164, 165,
166, 167–76, 181
Thompson, Frederic, 45, 46–52, 78,
162–63
Thompson, LaMarcus Adna, 14–15,
16 (ill.), 43
Thunderbolt (roller coaster), 75–76
Tickler (ride), 50
Tiffany, Louis Comfort, 78
tilting at the quintain, 9
Tilyou, Edward, 46
Tilyou, George Cornelius, 43–46, 78,
162
Tishman Realty & Construction Com-
pany, 149–50
Tivoli Gardens, 93, 177
toilet facilities. *See* sanitation and sew-
age systems
Tokyo Disneyland, 169–71, 177
Tomorrowland. *See* Disneyland Park;
Magic Kingdom
Tonawanda machine, 11
Topsy (elephant), 49–50
tourism, 168–69
Transportation Building. *See* World's
Columbian Exposition
transportation systems, 37–38, 60,
100, 107, 142, 151, 163
Trans World Airlines, 94
Traver, Harry, 17, 72, 80
Trip to the Moon (ride), 45–46, 49
trolley and trolley park, 42, 57–60,
68, 72, 73–74, 75, 76, 163
Turkey, 175
Turner, Frederick Jackson, 25
Turnpike (ride), 77
TusenFryd (park), 175
Twain, Mark, 153, 155
Twenty Thousand Leagues under the
Sea (ride), 48
Tyers, Jonathan, 4, 6
Typhoon Lagoon. *See* Walt Disney
World Resort

Union of Soviet Socialist Republics,
175–76
U. S. Steel Corporation, 143
United Technologies, 149
Universal Studios Florida, 123–24,
125, 160, 167, 178
Universal Studios Hollywood, 49,
123–24, 127, 134–35, 174
Universe of Energy. *See* EPCOT Center
utopia, 15, 20, 21, 28, 30, 39–40,
87, 101, 137, 140–41, 142, 148,
152, 163. *See also* Elysium; "City
on a Hill"

Van Brunt & Howe (architectural firm),
22
Van Depoele, Charles J., 57
Van Gorder, Terry, 127
Vauxhall Gardens, 4–6
Vekoma International, 127, 167, 173
Venice Amusement Park, 183
Vettel, Andrew, 75–76
village and locale reproduction, 29, 48,
110, 113, 116, 117–18, 122,
150, 153, 173
Viper (roller coaster), 167
Vollmer, Jane, 86

Walker, E. Cardon, 148
Walpole, Horace, 4
Walt Disney Company, 122, 157–61,
165–66, 167, 169–72, 175,
179–80, 196–97n1
Walt Disney Productions, 95, 96, 101–
102
Walt Disney Studio, 91, 93
Walt Disney World Resort, 12, 15, 28,
39, 49, 71, 88, 97, 101, 112,
124, 125, 134–35, 137–61,
165–66, 168, 178
Contemporary Resort, 139, 142,
143
Dolphin and Swan hotel complex,
144, 159, 167, 178
Grand Floridian Beach Resort, 139,
144
Polynesian Village, 139, 142, 143–
44

Typhoon Lagoon, 159, 167
See also Disney-MGM Studios
Theme Park; EPCOT Center;
Magic Kingdom
water fountains, 38–39, 95, 96, 120
Watschenmann (game), 7
WED Enterprises, 93–94, 142, 148,
149
Welles, Orson: *The Third Man*, 8
West Edmonton Mall (entertainment
complex), 179
Westinghouse Company, 38
Whalom (park), 58
Whirlpool (ride), 45
"White City." *See* World's Columbian
Exposition
Whitman, Walt, 42
Willow Grove (park), 12, 59, 60, 183
Winkler, Margaret, 91
Winthrop, John, 20
Women's Building. *See* World's Colum-
bian Exposition
Wonders of Life. *See* EPCOT Center
World of Motion. *See* EPCOT Center
World of Tomorrow World's Fair, New
York (1939), 140, 146
World of Wonder (park), 175
World's Columbian Exposition, 19–40,
24 (ill.), 26 (ill.), 32 (ill.), 33 (ill.),
43, 48, 68, 88, 98, 145, 148,
150, 153, 163, 192n24

Administration Building, 22, 25
Agriculture Building, 22, 25
Arts Building, 22, 26
Chicago Company, 22
Court of Honor, 21, 22, 23, 24 (ill.),
28, 39
Electricity Building, 22, 26
Fisheries Building, 22, 26
Horticulture Building, 22, 26
Machinery Building, 22, 25, 38
Manufactures and Liberal Arts Build-
ing, 22, 25, 26 (ill.)
Mines and Mining Building, 22, 25–
26
Republic, the. See French, Daniel
Chester: *The Republic*
Transportation Building, 22, 23, 26
Women's Building, 22
See also Ferris wheel; Midway
Plaisance
World's Fair, 185
World War I, 46, 60, 66, 90
World War II, 9, 17, 46, 70, 80, 93,
102, 154, 178
Wright Brothers, 78
Wurstelprater, 7
Wynne, Angus, 107

Z Force (roller coaster), 108
Zistel, Louis, 78
Zygofolis (park), 173–74

The author enjoying the Keansburg, New Jersey, kiddie rides, 1948.

THE AUTHOR

JUDITH A. ADAMS IS THE DIRECTOR OF LOCK-
wood Memorial Library, State University of New York at Buffalo. She was
born and raised in Keansburg, New Jersey, near the Jersey shore's major
summer amusement areas. She holds a B.A. in English from Wilkes College,
an M.L.S. from Syracuse University, and an M.A. in English from Lehigh
University. Her publications include coauthorship of *Technology and Values
in American Civilization* (1980), *Jules Verne: A Primary and Secondary
Bibliography* (1980), and the annual "Current Bibliography in the History of
Technology," which appears in the journal *Technology and Culture*. She has
also published numerous articles in the fields of library/information science
as well as interdisciplinary studies merging technology and the humanities.
She has previously held professional positions at the Library of Congress and
in the libraries at Lehigh University, Georgetown University, Oklahoma
State University, and Auburn University.